ENTREPRENEURSHIP
and the
PRIVATIZING of GOVERNMENT

ENTREPRENEURSHIP
and the
PRIVATIZING of GOVERNMENT

Edited by CALVIN A. KENT

1987

Q
QUORUM BOOKS
New York • Westport, Connecticut • London

Library of Congress Cataloging-in-Publication Data

Entrepreneurship and the privatizing of government.

Includes bibliographies and index.
1. Privatization. I. Kent, Calvin A.
HD3850.E57 1987   338.9   86-25555
ISBN 0-89930-196-7 (lib. bdg. : alk. paper)

Library of Congress Catalog Card Number: 86-25555
ISBN: 0-89930-196-7

First published in 1987 by Quorum Books

Greenwood Press, Inc.
88 Post Road West, Westport, Connecticut 06881

Printed in the United States of America

The paper used in this book complies with the
Permanent Paper Standard issued by the National
Information Standards Organization (Z39.48-1984).

10 9 8 7 6 5 4 3 2 1

This book is dedicated to
N. S. K.
for continued support in all endeavors

CONTENTS

PREFACE

Perhaps the two "hottest" topics in the fields of government and economics are privatization and entrepreneurship. Both have been viewed as ways of shrinking the public sector and providing the necessary stimulus to keep the American economy on a path of steady and sustained growth in the decades to come. The interrelations between the two has often been assumed but rarely studied. The chapters in this volume are designed to remedy that deficiency.

The chapters combine both the theory and the practice of privatization. They indicate that privatization is not just good government policy in terms of reducing the tax burden on individuals while maintaining or even expanding the quality of government services; it is good economics, because privatization opens new opportunities for entrepreneurial innovation. All economies, whether in the United States, other developed nations, or the less developed world, would benefit from privatization of governmental functions. The entrepreneurial instinct is likewise universal. The private sector can respond and is responding given the opportunity to provide services previously purveyed by the state. Perhaps the best hope for sustained growth in the developed world and for breaking the cycle of poverty in the less developed world lies in unleashing the entrepreneurial talents of the people. Privatization is a major step in that process.

I extend my thanks to all who have made this book possible. This includes not only the authors but the Association of Private Enterprise Education, sponsor of the annual conferences where drafts of several of these chapters were presented. Earlier versions of some were printed in the APEE's *Journal of Private Enterprise*. Thanks also go to the Heartland

Institute in Chicago, one of the major organizations working for more privatization. Some of the material in chapters 1 and 10 of this volume were previously published by the Heartland Institute. We gratefully acknowledge both APEE and Heartland's willingness to grant permission to reproduce.

Special thanks go to Pat Wilborn, Secretary to the Center for Private Enterprise at Baylor University, who is responsible for coordinating the final manuscript. Those assisting with the typing included Kim Tatum, Diane Milam, Jennifer Beehner, and Kayla Howard. Nita Sue Kent edited the chapters; her efforts have resulted in a much more readable final product. Sandra Wooten served as research assistant. Special thanks also go to Martha Horn Schroeder, Program Coordinator at the Center for Private Enterprise, for her help. All authors assume responsibility for the content of their manuscripts and the views expressed are their own.

ENTREPRENEURSHIP
and the
PRIVATIZING of GOVERNMENT

I. THE THEORY OF PRIVATIZATION

1

PRIVATIZATION OF PUBLIC FUNCTIONS: PROMISES AND PROBLEMS

Calvin A. Kent

During the 1970s the majority of American states adopted restrictions on the ability of state and local governments to spend. These restrictions usually took the form of ceilings on local property taxes or restrictions on the percentage of state income that could be taxed.[1] The Gramm-Rudman-Hollings Amendment, passed by Congress in 1985, will similarly restrict federal spending in hopes of achieving a balanced budget by 1991.

Voters are dictating lower taxes, but they are not reducing their demands for government services. In fact, the political coalition of service providers, service recipients, and government appropriation committees appears stronger than ever. The problem facing state and local governments is compounded by the inability of most of these bodies to run deficits. The friction between competing demands for lower taxes and for expanded services has led many cities and states to turn to innovative methods of financing and providing traditional services. One of these methods has come to be called "privatization."

The purposes of this book are to explain what privatization is and how it works, and to study in-depth examples of privatization proposed as well as already in operation. The chapters review proposals and privatization programs at local, state, and federal levels, as well as those in developed and developing nations. Because privatization is a complex subject, this book can offer only an introduction to the major issues. Notes appearing at the end of each chapter provide leads for those seeking more detailed information.

WHAT IS PRIVATIZATION?

It is often assumed that privatization consists solely in the selling of state-owned enterprises to private investors. This is only one form, however; to view the process solely in this context is inaccurate. Privatization refers to the transfer of functions previously performed exclusively by government, usually at zero or below full-cost prices, to the private sector at prices that clear the market and reflect the full costs of production.

Kolderie identifies at least two different ideas that are encompassed by the term *privatization*.[2] He indicates that governments perform two separate functions, either of which—or both—could be privatized. The first function, *provision*, is the policy decision actually to provide a good or service. The second, *production*, is the administrative action to produce that good or service. A government may decide a service is to be provided but allow the private sector to product it. On the other hand, the private sector may decide to provide a service but call upon the government to produce it. Kolderie uses the example of a security service and delineates four cases.

Case 1.   Both functions are public. The city assigns its police officers to nighttime foot patrol in the business district to reduce burglaries. Neither function is private.

Case 2.   Production is private, provision is public. The city decides to provide security when high school hockey teams play at the city arena and contracts with Pinkertons to provide the guards.

Case 3.   Provision is private, production is public. Government sells a service to private buyers. The hockey team wants security at the sports center and contracts with the city police to provide it.

Case 4.   Both functions are private. A department store decides that it wants uniformed security and employs its own guards. Government performs neither function.

Kolderie's taxonomy is useful as it demonstrates that the government may privatize either the provision or the production of a service, or it may privatize both. The taxonomy also explains the wide variety of types and forms of privatization that have been adopted in this nation and worldwide.

It should not be assumed that privatization will always involve substituting private profit-making firms for government bureaus as service providers. The private sector also encompasses volunteers, self-help groups, and nonprofit agencies. The type of private organization that will best provide a particular service depends on many factors, including the type of service, demand for the service, incomes of those who will receive the service, resources and leadership of existing for-profit and nonprofit organizations, and the regulatory environment.

THE POLITICS OF PRIVATIZATION

Privatization is not a new idea, but until recently it was not very popular in the United States and Western Europe. Privatization in the United States has accelerated at the state and local levels primarily because of "taxpayer revolts" during the late 1960s and early 1970s. In a recent report the International City Management Association listed over sixty local government functions that were being successfully privatized in whole or in part by American cities.[3] These ranged from public works, transportation, and safety to health, human services, parks and recreation, and administration support functions. What such a list demonstrates is that almost everything that local governments do is being turned over to the private sector somewhere.

There is no shortage of documentation that privatization works, providing service quality at least as high as previously at substantially lower cost to taxpayers.[4] In summarizing these studies of local government privatization, Hanke concludes:

Whether the public services be water supply, waste water treatment, fire protection, police protection, refuse collection, ship repair, air transport, urban bus transport, electric supply or ambulance service we obtain the same result: for the same quantity and quality of service, the cost of public supply is approximately twice that of private supply.[5]

Local government officials seeking detailed information on how other cities have completed privatization can take advantage of the Privatization Database of the Local Government Center of Santa Barbara, California, which is a registry of state and local governments that have privatized or provided alternate delivery systems for over seventy public services.

The evidence that privatization at the local level works and is both less costly and equally acceptable to the public is overwhelming. The greatest successes have been in municipal trash collection, street construction, street cleaning, mass transit, recreation, and administrative services including bookkeeping, inspection, data processing, and planning. Although less extensively privatized, police and fire protection, wastewater treatment, health services, and upkeep of equipment and vehicles are functions in which impressive cost savings have been achieved with no decrease in service quality.

At the state level, privatization has been proceeding less rapidly but now is gaining additional impetus. If the proposal to reduce federal tax rates while broadening the base by eliminating the deductibility of state and local sales taxes succeeds,[6] then additional pressure may be placed on state legislators to find more cost-effective ways to meet citizen demands for services.

Savas reports that privatization of road maintenance and construction is preferred two to one by state officials because the public crews cannot perform at the same costs as can the private.[7] As was the case with city halls, administrative expenses can best be controlled through private arrangements. Privatization has already taken hold in the area of corrections. Although private prisons, halfway houses, and immigration detention centers now hold only a small percentage of the nation's prisoners, the potential is great.[8]

Until recently the federal government has been the most reluctant level to privatize. Although it has relatively few enterprises to sell in comparison to European nations, the Reagan administration, in its proposed budget for fiscal year 1987, has suggested that the government divest itself of some of its property.[9] This move is done more on philosophical than economic grounds as the sales would raise only about $8.5 billion, or 1%, of the government's anticipated revenues for that year. All of the proposed privatization efforts are proving to be highly controversial.

Sale of Power Administrations

The Reagan administration proposes to sell five regional power administrations, which account for approximately 6% of the electric power produced in the United States. The government's largest power producer, the Tennessee Valley Authority (TVA), is exempted. Included on the bill of sale is the Bonneville Power Administration, which serves four northwestern states. The federal government would continue to own the dams for flood control purposes but would sell the power-generating and distribution facilities. Opposition to the proposal was not long in coming. Political representatives fearing that electric rates could more than double have joined in opposition on grounds that the sale would destroy jobs, particularly in the aluminum industry, weakening the already sagging economy of the area. As a counterproposal it has been suggested that the four northwestern states (Washington, Oregon, Idaho, and Montana) might want to purchase Bonneville and assume its debts.

Sale of Airports

Almost as controversial is the proposal that the government divest itself of both Washington National Airport and Dulles International Airport. Because there are no major airports in the United States that are in private hands, this is perhaps the most radical of the administration's proposals. Voters in Maryland would like to keep both airports under-developed to promote Baltimore's own facility.

Sale of Public Housing

The proposal that stands the best chance of being enacted recommends that the government stop building houses and apartments for the poor and expand the use of vouchers for renting private property. The government already has 800,000 families on the voucher program and wishes to add 50,000 a year. Some have opposed the suggestion on the grounds that private landlords would be unlikely to rent to the poor even if they had vouchers sufficient to pay the rent. The House has already favorably considered a program whereby low-income tenants may buy their dwelling units from the federal government at approximately one-quarter of their market value. Both proposals are based on the same idea: that better housing for the poor can be obtained through the market with reduced government expenditures as a bonus.

Sale of Loans

Perhaps the least appealing of the Reagan administration's proposals is to sell some $2 billion worth of loans made by federal agencies, including loans to small businesses, rural housing, and students. This proposal actually would not reduce the deficit but would *increase* it, as these loans currently are earning $1.1 billion a year. The administration's justification is that the government should remove itself from financial markets.

Sale of Naval Petroleum Reserves

Until the recent collapse of oil prices there was considerable interest among private oil companies in acquiring the federally owned naval petroleum reserves at Elk Hills, California, and Teapot Dome, Wyoming. This may be a poor time to sell these fields, but the rationalization is taken from the pages of the business finance texts, which say, "When any organization is faced with an enormous debt it is prudent to sell assets."

Sale of Railroads

The final proposal is for the government to divest itself of the two railroads it now owns, Conrail and Amtrak. The sale of Conrail to Nor-

folk and Southern Railroad was approved by the Transportation Department and Senate, but the railroad withdrew its offer because of
objections raised in the House. Conrail came into being a decade ago
when the federal government purchased the Penn Central and five other
northeastern railroads that were either bankrupt or about to become so.
Conrail ran deficits of $1.5 billion for its first five years but now is
profitable.

The House Commerce Committee voted to sell Conrail through a
public offering with a minimum price of $1.7 billion for the government's
85% share.[10] The full House and Senate would have to concur. Considering that Conrail has been profitable for the last five years, the economic
incentive for divestiture is clearly less than in the case of Amtrak.

Despite the administration's desire to sell Amtrak, it is unlikely that
the entire system will be sold because Amtrak earns only about 53% of
its expenses. The administration's proposal is to halt all subsidies by
1987, let the system go bankrupt, and allow private investors and perhaps state and local governments to salvage whatever is left. Considering
Amtrak's huge deficit and rather limited benefits, mainly to middle- and
upper-income riders, this approach appears solid but still is likely to
face stiff political opposition.

The Reagan administration has also suggested an impressive list of
"turnbacks"—functions and revenue sources now performed or used at
the federal level that could pass to the state and local levels.[11] If the
revenue sources are not adequate to fund these programs, the fiscal heat
on state and local governments could intensify.

Although contracting for federal services has doubled under Reagan,
the Grace Commission has determined that the three-year savings from
privatization could total $37 billion over the next three years.[12] The
Congressional Budget Office estimated that private sector contracting
could shift 81% of the governments nonmilitary jobs, with an additional
savings of $1 billion a year.[13] Butler has contended that the great failure
of supply-side economics has been the assumption that government
could cut spending to live within its income. He views privatization as
the most feasible methods to achieve a balanced budget.[14]

One of the more controversial attempts at privatization at the federal
level concerns public lands and is discussed in chapter 4. One of the
early goals of the Interior Department was to transfer both grazing and
timberlands now under federal control to private hands.[15] This suggestion was immediately attacked as being dangerous to our national well-
being—environmental rape, it was argued, would be the inevitable consequence. Hanke has suggested that the current system of public ownership and bureaucratic regulation serves neither the government's nor
the environmentalist's best interests.[16] Five specific reasons undergird
his contention.

1. The productivity of public lands would improve.
2. Consumers would be better served, as land would be utilized to its highest use.
3. Additional federal revenues would be generated.
4. The state and local tax base would expand as these properties passed to private hands.
5. Land use decisions would become less politicized.

Even though the proposed privatization would have affected only a small percentage of federal lands, progress has slowed because of political opposition.

An additional area of potential privatization for the federal government that would affect the state and local units is in the area of wastewater management. The Reagan administration has reduced the amount of funding for grants in this area. This is not because the administration favors dirty streams and rising levels of toxic wastes; studies show that construction and operating efficiencies of private providers result in costs 20% to 50% below public production.[17]

Additional current privatization issues at the federal level discussed in this book include postal services, air traffic control, weather forecasting, prisons, and urban transit.[18] In all these cases the issue is the same. Can the public interest be served at lower cost? A growing number of experts are saying yes.

Privatization is not limited to the United States. Under the Thatcher administration, Great Britain has pioneered by transferring hundreds of functions from the public to the private sector and selling nationalized industries to private investors.[19] As chapter 11 relates, governments in a dozen developed countries have increasingly turned to the private sector for services. Some of the more successful programs include transit, public housing, fire protection, solid waste collection, hospitals, health care, wastewater treatment, cultural programs, building maintenance, recreation, and administrative services.[20]

Although the rhetoric has been more impressive than the results, chapter 13 shows that less developed countries are seeking to shrink their public sectors and reduce the burden on taxpayers by resuscitating the entrepreneurial spirit inherent in the private sector. Early in 1984 a new government in Turkey pledged to restore competition and increase the competitiveness of its products in world markets by privatization. The Turkish parliament responded by authorizing the sale of almost 250 government enterprises. In Mexico the government promised a partial dismantling of government enterprise. Bangladesh sold over one hundred nationalized companies; Pakistan denationalized over two thousand. Jamaica, Uganda, Brazil, Peru, Argentina, Thailand, and Malaysia have also put state-owned industry on the market.[21]

THE RATIONALE FOR PRIVATIZATION

Privatization is premised on four eminently sound ideas.

1. Those who want goods provided by the government should pay the full cost of having public goods and services provided for them.
2. Production in the private sector that results from competition is likely to be more efficient and thereby less costly than government provision.
3. The consumer is likely to be most satisfied when given a variety of alternative providers of services from which to choose.
4. Unlocking the innovative genius of the entrepreneur will provide new service delivery systems and technologies.

Each of these deserves closer examination.

Full Cost Pricing

At first glance, the reader may be suspicious of this rationale. One of the ways that government bureaucracies have cultivated support for public provision is by undercharging for what they provide. People like low rates for water and sewage management. They resist increased rates for garbage collection and tend to advocate the seemingly "free" governmental services for which they are not directly charged. For that reason bureaucratic pricing tends to be below the cost of production of these services. A full discussion and application of user fees as applied to Canadian water systems is contained in chapter 12.

 In addition to this political reason, however, as chapter 3 reports, there are more subtle economic reasons as to why government services are underpriced. First, current government accounting systems do not adequately assign the cost of capital to government enterprises. A private firm that must either borrow or equity finance its operation includes both interest and depreciation as part of the cost that it must recover with the fees that it charges. These capital costs are rarely allocated to projects in the public sector.[22]

Second, the pricing of public services is further complicated because general overhead costs are rarely allocated to specific governmental functions. Although the techniques already exist for doing this, the widespread practice is for governments to charge administrative and other overhead expenses to general expenses without assigning the cost to specific departments or agencies.

There exists still a third economic reason for underpricing. The bureaucrat has no idea about market demand for what is being provided. There is no price signal. Consumers have no alternative but to use the monopoly service being provided. There is no competitive price to be used as a benchmark. The easiest way for the bureaucrat to compensate for this lack of information about consumer demand is to charge a low fee while subsidizing the service from the general revenues. The low fee ensures high usage, which is then presented as evidence of high demand.

If economics teaches anything, it is that prices should be set equal to costs.[23] If they are not, resources are diverted from more highly valued options to those that give lesser satisfaction. Under bureaucratic provision individuals pay for the service whether they value it little or use it extensively. The free swimming pool may be used in lieu of the babysitter. When general taxes are used to subsidize specific functions, a transfer is made from one group (taxpayers) to another (service recipients). Individual preferences are distorted and the demand for the items appears high when in fact it is merely being subsidized.

Competition

The virtues of competition as a regulatory mechanism assuring the highest quality, lowest prices, and introduction of new technology have been touted since the dawn of economics. Smith referred to competition as the "invisible hand" that caused producers, while they pursued their own self-interests, to maximize the well-being of all.[24]

The critics of privatization contend that because private firms must make a profit as well as pay local, state, and federal taxes, they cannot possibly provide the service at as a low a cost as a government department. These critics lost sight of a crucial point that invalidates their contention. The private entrepreneur is goaded by the desire for profit to find the best ways to satisfy the variety of consumer demands the marketplace presents. In addition, he knows that by introducing a less costly method he can gain a competitive advantage over his rivals in the marketplace.

The bureaucrat not facing competition is motivated primarily by the desire to expand. In the public sector prestige and power are both related to the size of the agency's budget and the number of employees, not to how well the consumer has been satisfied or to how low costs have been driven. The very nature of bureaucratic provision militates against efficiency.

Consumer Satisfaction

In the marketplace the consumer is king. If dissatisfied with either price or quality, the consumer can turn to another provider. In a town where garbage is picked up only twice a week at the curb, consumers who would like to have more frequent cartage and to have it removed from their garages are denied the opportunity. Consumers' preferences and tastes vary widely. The market is structured to accommodate them. The political process is not.

ENTREPRENEURSHIP

There is ample evidence that the privatization of local government functions in Europe, the United States, and less developed nations has unleashed a torrent of innovative creativity on the part of private entrepreneurs.[26] The case studies presented in chapter 10 show how entrepreneurs have developed new technologies and service delivery systems for functions such as sanitation, mail service, air traffic control, emergency medical services, fire protection, prison systems, schools, mass transit, and park maintenance, just to name a few.[27]

Under government monopoly the entrepreneur is denied the opportunity to find ways of better meeting consumer demand at lower cost. It is a quaint paradox that monopoly in the private sector is thoroughly condemned as being high-priced, noninnovative, and unresponsive to consumer needs, yet the same type of negative behavior is tolerated when conducted by a governmental monopoly.

FORMS OF PRIVATIZATION

Although privatization can and does take many forms, the best form of privatization is not to allow the government to produce goods and services to begin with. As is detailed in chapter 2, government provision of goods and services should be limited to those instances in which goods or services are clearly of what economists would call a public or collective nature.[28] These collective or social goods will be consumed jointly by all individuals in equal amounts. Examples are national defense, a levee built for flood protection, or a lighthouse. Those who do not pay for these public or collective goods cannot be excluded from receiving the benefits except at extremely high costs. If my home is defended, my neighbor's will be also whether or not he pays. The levee keeps the flood waters from both our doors regardless of our tax payment. The lighthouse shines for nonpayer and payer alike.

The only other instance in which public provision of goods and services appears justified is when strong external benefits accrue to some groups of people providing goods and services.[29] The classic example is education: both the consumer (student) and society at large benefit from a better-educated populace. Immunization and other public health services may also be covered using this justification. Even in these two instances, however, one of the variants of privatization discussed later may be a more appropriate method of the state supporting the consumption than is socialized production. The use of vouchers can enable those whom the political system feels should consume without paying full cost.

There are four different strategies for privatizing services:

1. Sale of a government enterprise to a private organization
2. Contracting with a private organization to provide a service
3. Charging user fees to recover the cost of a publicly provided service
4. Providing vouchers to low-income persons so they can afford to purchase goods or services from private providers

Sale of Government Enterprises

The first form of privatization is outright sale of all or part of the enterprise to private investors.[30] This has been successfully accomplished in Great Britain, which has sold British National Oil, Cable and Wireless, British Aerospace, Associated British Ports, Jaguar, National Freight Consortium, and Amersham, the electronics corporation. A recent press report related,

Since 1979, a total of 12 major companies plus a number of smaller companies have been sold. Around 400,000 jobs have been transferred to the private sector; about a third of a million employees have acquired shares in the companies for which they work; and state sell-offs have raised over £6 bn for the Exchequer.[31]

If it is not possible to sell all of the enterprise, then the government may wish to sell the controlling interest. With 51% of the shares in the hands of private investors, government control and influence no longer dominate. This alternative also permits the private sector to gain control with a smaller initial investment.

It is assumed that there will be buyers for firms to be privatized. This will be the case only if the firm is either profitable or potentially profitable. In the case of potential profit, a government enterprise currently experiencing losses due to bad management or overstaffing could be turned around under private operation.

If the entire firm cannot be sold, it is possible that parts of the firm could be spun off into private enterprises. Again the British experience is instructive. Discovering that British Railways could not be sold because of its unprofitability, the government was able to divest itself of the British Rail Hotels and the cross channel ferries, which were profit makers.

Finally, an enterprise can be sold to the workers. British Freight, a losing operation under government ownership, became profitable within one year after it was conveyed to the workers.

Contracting

A second form of privatization consists of contracting with the private sector to provide public services.[32] The experience in the United States, Britain, Europe, and Japan with the contracting of municipal refuse and garbage services has been nothing short of spectacular. Cost savings of 40% to 60% are common when local governments have selected this alternative.

Contracting has worked well with other municipal services, such as wastewater and sewage treatment, in which the costs of contracting these functions have been half of what they were when the municipality or local council provided them. The cost of municipal hospitals has been significantly reduced by contracting out services such as ambulance, maintenance, laboratories, and food services.

Municipal recreation facilities such as golf courses, swimming pools, and stadiums (see chapter 7) are desirable possibilities for privatization through contract operation. Although the facilities still remain under municipal ownership, the actual service provision is in the hands of a private contractor.

A word of caution is in order.[33] Advocates of contracting with the private sector often tend to oversell. If contracting involves nothing more than the exchange of a private monopoly for a governmental one, than little has been achieved. Secure with its exclusive franchise and its government-mandated rates, the private monopolist's performance will vary little from that of the public counterpart. For that reason contracting requires government regulation to ensure that franchise provisions are met. Fortunately a significant body of literature has developed that can assist in this process.[34]

When at all possible, the exclusive contract should be avoided. One of the virtues of privatization is that it allows for competition by opening the door for entrepreneurs. There is ample evidence that just as a variety of grocery stores array themselves before consumers, so should a variety of service providers for municipal services be allowed.

The old assumption that a single private purveyor would be more efficient than many in providing services to an entire city has now been debunked by empirical investigations.[35] If exclusive franchises are granted, they should be for short periods with an open bidding system for future contracts being ensured. Thus competition over time becomes the regulating force.

The experience of the United States in defense contracting dramatically demonstrates the problems of privatization using this method. The Department of Defense makes only a tiny percentage of its own equipment. It issues almost 15 million separate acquisition contracts per year. In their detailed analysis the President's Blue Ribbon Commission on Defense Management recognized that the current contracting system is defective:

All of our analyses lead us unequivocally to the conclusion that the defense acquisition system has basic problems that must be corrected. These problems are deeply entrenched and have developed over several decades from an increasingly bureaucratic and overregulated process. As a result, all too many of our weapons systems cost too much, take too long to develop and by the time they are fielded, incorporate obsolete technology.[36]

Despite this stinging condemnation the Task Force found that these problems were common of all large bureaucracies, whether public or private. The report also found that when DoD acquisitions used special streamlined procedures, such as those employed for the Polaris, Minuteman, and Cruise missiles, then costs could be reduced significantly.

In comparing DoD development programs with successful programs from the private sector that compare favorably in complexity and size to a major weapons system development, such as the IBM 360 computer, Boeing 767 transport, the AT&T telephone switch, and the Hughes communication satellite, the Tast Force found that each of these private programs took only about half as long to develop and cost proportionately less. The principal problem in private contracting was bureaucratic meddling in the privatization process.

Streamliing of acquisition procedures, by expanded use of the commercial products, the rejection of sole-source contracting, and increased use of competition, in addition to the upgrading of acquisition personnel, were recommended by the Task Force as ways of making defense privatization effective.

Private Payment

A third alternative route to privatization is private payment for public services. Under this alternative, although the government still provides the service, the public pays the full cost of the service through user fees. There are over a hundred different municipal functions that should be paid for in this fashion.[37] It is customary for government to provide services at less than their full cost even to those who can pay. This results in overuse of the facility and general misallocation of public resources.

There is no reason why the costs of putting in streets, water lines, and sewers should not be borne full upon those who develop the property. The cost of airports and harbors should be borne by fees assessed against those who use them. Cities should charge for special services, such as additional police patrols, building inspection, and other regulatory functions. Recreation facilities should be placed on a "pay as you go" basis.

Private payment for public services, even when user fees covering the full cost of the service are employed, is a poor alternative to full privatization. If costs can be allocated to users with nonpayers excluded, then the private sector should be given the opportunity to provide the service. User fees accurately assign costs and benefits, but they do not ensure efficiency, as would moving the activity to the private sector.

Competition

Another alternative for privatization is to allow private competition with public enterprise. Under this option the state maintains its own public operation but permits private companies to produce the good or provide the service. In this way the private and the public sector keep each other honest and consumers are allowed the opportunity to choose which product or service provider best maximizes their satisfaction. Certainly one of the more novel and promising approaches to contracting is to allow government agencies to bid along with private firms. This approach has been successfully tried in sanitation and vehicle maintenance and repair.

The first step toward privatization of social security in the United States seems to have been taken following this alternative (see chapter 6). Congress established the Individual Retirement Account; the IRA can be viewed as a private alternative to an expanded social security system. As another example, most foreign nations operate state television networks. Some, but not all, allow for competing commercial channels. As critical as one might be of U.S. networks, fewer compliments can be paid to operation of these state monopolies when they face no competition.

Public Funding of Private Services

A final privatization alternative is the public funding of private services. Under this option the consumer purchases the good or service from private businesses but is reimbursed all or part of the cost by a payment from the state. This has been done, albeit ineptly, in the United States in the case of medical services.[38] Under both Medicaid for low-income individuals and Medicare for those covered by social security, the individual is free to select his or her own doctor or hospital with total or partial reimbursement coming from public funds.

This system is in stark contrast to that in European nations[39] where the individual must use the socialized medical system and often has little choice as to the type of treatment or provider. The result has been a movement in Europe toward a "parallel" system of private medical services competing with the public, although the public sector rarely funds the private. The contracting of certain portions of medical services within the socialized system such as maintenance, ambulance, and laboratories has proved to be cost-effective.

This privatization option has also been proposed for education and takes the name of the voucher system. Over half of the states now provide some form of tuition assistance or tax credits to parents of students who are attending private colleges. Advocates of the voucher system in education would not only maximize freedom of choice but would also create the kind of competition that would upgrade public schools.[40] Recent decisions of the Supreme Court regarding public payments to private church-related schools may cloud the future for the voucher system, however.

The use of public payment for private services defeats a major objection to privatization: fairness. Under privatization the poor may not be able to pay for the service if it is provided by private firms that would charge the full price of the service. The voucher system meets this objection. In addition it recognizes that often "free" public services are used only because they are free. Certainly choice is maximized when consumers can select their own service provider.

Given that state and local taxes are generally regressive, bearing more heavily upon low-income than high-income individuals,[41] it may be more equitable to establish users' fees and supply vouchers to those with low incomes than to provide the service on a "free" or reduced cost basis to all individuals regardless of their ability to pay. If the government feels that a service or good is so essential or desirable that people should not be excluded from consuming because they lack funds, then the use of vouchers is an excellent alternative.

PROBLEMS WITH PRIVATIZATION

The case for privatization is not all one-sided. There are problems with privatization that are political as well as economic.[42]

Loss of Jobs

Concern over the loss of jobs has led to strong opposition from organized labor.[43] Often public enterprises are overstaffed. When these public enterprises constitute major employers, privatization would lead to a significant reduction in the number of public-sector jobs. For nations grappling with the problem of unemployment, this reduction of jobs may be politically risky.

There are several ways to handle employee concerns about job security.[44] Several governments have required private contractors to hire existing city employees or at least extend to them a preferential option for jobs. The loss of jobs may place obligations upon the government to retrain and relocate workers whose jobs have disappeared because of privatization.

An even more innovative approach would be to assist public employees in becoming the entrepreneurs who provide the private service. This approach would involve elimination of any barriers to entry of employee-operated firms that might be present and provision of legal, technical, and perhaps financial assistance to firms organized by previous employees, and it would also facilitate the transition.

Britain provided an even more radical approach to reducing employee resistance when it gave the National Freight Corporation to its own employees. The trend for employees to take over failing firms in the United States is accelerating. There is no reason to assume that this trend could bypass the public sector.

Increased Prices

An additional objection is that privatization may mean increased prices, particularly if the governmental function has been provided at zero or low cost. There is a strong tendency on the part of public consumers to resist price increases for subsidized activities. Unless privatization is accompanied by some form of voucher system, it may be viewed as unfair. Butler has commented that contracting as a form of privatization does not necessarily guarantee lower costs. In fact, just the opposite may result.[45] His reasoning is that contracting strengthens the private coalition, which can then agitate for expanded spending on a particular function. Without privatization only the government bureaucracy lobbies, perhaps with some help from special interest groups that benefit from the program. When contracting is added, the "iron triangle" is established and the contractor and the interest group can both engage in political agitation, either for increased expenditures on the function or for higher prices.

Contracting, particularly with a sole source on a long-term basis, may neither contract the size of government nor reduce its costs even though it is likely to improve its efficiency. Contracting may be the most prevalent form of privatization, but it is certainly the most dangerous. The oft-repeated warning in this book is that contracting without adequate competition is foolhardy at best.

Adequate Capital

An additional problem is whether there will be adequate private capital to finance the privatization. Britain and the United States have both achieved a great deal of privatization, but these are the world's financial capitals drawing on the savings and export earnings not only of their own citizens but of the world. Whether or not this option is available in other countries with less developed credit markets remains to be seen as more of these nations move down the road of privatization.

Loss of Control

Those who have opposed privatization often contend that once a function is privatized there is no longer responsible political control of that function. This point reflects an inability on the part of some to distinguish adequately between public provision and public production. If the government chooses to continue to be the provider but not the producer, then it in no way relinquishes its responsibilities to produce the desired output in an acceptable fashion. If a government is looking for ways to avoid its responsibilities for service quality through privatization, it is searching for what neither can nor should be.

CONCLUSION

The promise and problems of privatization can be summarized as follows:

1. By allowing for the forces of competition to work in a market system, the costs of providing the government service may be significantly lowered, thereby freeing public resources for other activities or permitting the reduction of taxes.

2. By providing a variety of alternative suppliers instead of one, consumers are more likely to be satisfied because their choices are maximized. This argument is particularly appealing to those who place a high value on individual liberty and freedom of choice.

3. By opening up the provision of government services to competition, new opportunities are created for private business initiators—the entrepreneurs. When the government provides a service as a monopoly, this is one area of the nation's economic life in which private entrepreneurial effort will be absent.

4. By the employment of users' fees, all costs are assigned to those who actually enjoy the benefits of government services or consume government goods. Those who do not need or want the good or service are not asked to contribute to its provision.

5. By privatizing and using vouchers a more efficient way to provide government services to low-income people is enacted. Low-income consumers are better served by giving them the same freedom in consumption that higher-income individuals enjoy.

6. By far the most compelling reason for privatization is that it solves the dilemma faced by virtually all governments: how to provide more and better
services without raising taxes.

These privatization alternatives provide an opportunity for national,
state, and local governments to have the best of both worlds.

NOTES

1. R. Poole, Jr., *Cutting Back City Hall* (New York: Universe Books, 1980),
p. 18.
2. T. Kolderie, "The Two Different Concepts of Privatization," *Public Administration Review* (July/August 1986): 285–290.
3. C. F. Valente and L. D. Manchester, *Rethinking Local Services: Examining
Alternative Delivery Approaches* (Chicago: Management Information Service Special Report, International City Management Association, 1984), p. xv.
4. Poole, *Cutting Back City Hall*; E. S. Savas, *Privatizing the Public Sector—How
to Shrink Government* (Chatham, N.J.: Chatham House, 1982); D. Fisk et al., *Private
Provision of Services—An Overview* (Washington, D.C.: The Urban Institute, 1978);
H. Hatry, *A Review of Private Approaches for Delivery of Public Services* (Washington,
D.C.: The Urban Institute, 1983).
5. S. Hanke, "The User Fee Illusion," *Reason* (August 1983): 33.
6. A. Murray, "Unparelled Tax Bill Will Affect Everyone," *Wall Street Journal*,
18 Aug. 1986, pp. 1, 7.
7. E. S. Savas, "Tax Plan's Boost to Privatizing Services," *Wall Street Journal*,
10 July 1985, p. 17.
8. K. Farrell, "Public Services in Private Hands," *Venture* (July 1984): 35.
9. The White House, *Budget of the United States for Fiscal Year 1987*, 5 Feb.
1986. For discussion, see L. Smith, "Reagan's Budget: Selling Off the Government," *Fortune*, 3 Mar. 1986, pp. 70–74.
10. A. Karr, "Plan for Conrail Sale Approved by House Panel," *Wall Street
Journal*, 18 Sep. 1986, p. 53.
11. Advisory Commission on Intergovernmental Relations, "Devolving Federal Program Responsibilities and Revenue Services to State and Local Governments," March 1986.
12. Office of the President, *President's Private Sector Survey on Cost Control*,
1983. For a discussion of the federal government's difficulties in implementing
its own privatization mandates, see R. Fitzgerald and G. Lipson, *Pork Barrel*
(Washington, D.C.: Cato Institute, 1984), pp. 98–105.
13. Congressional Budget Office, 1982.
14. S. M. Butler, *Privatizing Federal Spending: A Strategy to Eliminate the Deficit*
(New York: Universe Books, 1985).
15. Office of the President, *Budget Message for Fiscal Year 1983*, January 1982.
16. S. Hanke, "On Privatizing the Public Domain," in P. N. Truluck, ed.,
Private Rights in Public Lands (Washington, D.C.: The Heritage Foundation, 1983).
See also "An Exchange on Privatization," *Journal of Contemporary Studies* (Spring
1984), for a full discussion.

17. S. Hanke, "A Case for Privatization," *Baltimore Sun*, 10 May 1985.

18. Butler, *Privatizing Federal Spending*.

19. R. N. Holwill, *Mandate for Leadership Report: Agenda '83*, (Washington, D.C.: The Heritage Foundation, 1983); Butler, *Privatizing Federal Spending*; P. Madsen, *Dismantling the State: The Theory and Practice of Privatization* (Dallas: National Center for Policy Analysis, 1985).

20. P. E. Fixler, Jr., "Germany's Privatization Rush," *Fiscal Watchdog* (September 1984); J. T. Marlin, "Privatization of Local Government Activities: Lessons from Japan" (Santa Barbara, Calif.: Local Government Center, 1984).

21. These examples are taken from A. Kaletsky, "Everywhere the State Is in Retreat," *Financial Times* (August 1985).

22. R. A. Waters, "Privatization: A Viable Policy Option" (Babcock Graduate School of Management, Wake Forest University, 1985).

23. P. A. Samuelson and W. D. Nordhouse, *Economics*, 12th ed. (New York: McGraw-Hill, 1985), pp. 59–76, 409–432.

24. A. Smith, R. H. Campbell, and W. B. Todd, eds., *An Inquiry into the Causes of the Wealth of Nations* (London: Liberty Classics, 1976), p. 456.

25. W. Niskanen, *Bureaucracy and Representative Government* (Chicago: Aldine-Atherton, 1971); C. M. Lindsay, "A Theory of Government Enterprise," *Journal of Political Economy* (October 1976).

26. Farrell, "Public Services in Private Hands," in J. LeGrand and R. Robinson, eds., *Privatization and the Welfare State* (London: Allen & Unwin, 1984).

27. R. Q. Armington and W. D. Ellis, *This Way Up: The Local Official's Handbook for Privatization and Contracting Out* (Chicago: Regnery Gateway, 1984). See also Poole, *Cutting Back City Hall*, Savas; *Privatizing the Public Sector*; Fisk, *Private Provision of Public Services*.

28. R. Musgrave and P. Musgrave, *Public Finance in Theory and Practice* (New York: McGraw-Hill, 1984), pp. 47–67.

29. T. Tietenberg, *Environmental and Natural Resource Economics* (Glenview, Ill.: Scott, Foresman, 1985), pp. 38–54.

30. These alternatives are explained in M. Pirie, *Dismantling the State* (Dallas: National Center for Policy Analysis, 1985).

31. S. Cameron, "U.K. Privatization: What Managers Really Think," *Financial Times* 20 July 1985.

32. For bibliographical references on contracting, see M. E. Huls, "Contracting Out—Alternatives in Municipal Service Delivery," Public Administrative Bibliography (Monticello, Ill.: Vance Bibliographies, August 1985), p. 1744. The case studies and data provided in this section came from Savas, *Privatizing the Public Sector*, and Poole, *Cutting Back City Hall*.

33. The advantage and drawbacks of contracting are discussed in D. Fink et al., *Private Provision of Public Services: An Overview* (Washington, D.C.: The Urban Institute, 1978).

34. See citations in Huls, "Contracting Out—Alternatives in Municipal Service Delivery"; also see Armington and Ellis, *This Way Up*; Hatry, *A Review of Private Approaches for Delivery of Public Services*; E. C. Hayes, *Service Contracting—Student Manual and Service Book* (San Diego: Metro Associates, 1984); and J. T. Martin, *Contracting Municipal Services—A Guide for Purchase from the Private Sector* (New York: John Wiley & Sons, 1984).

35. D. King, *Fiscal Tiers: The Economics of Multi-Level Government* (London: Allen & Unwin, 1984), pp. 50–85; W. Hirsch, *The Economics of State and Local Government* (New York: McGraw-Hill, 1970), pp. 185–194; Musgrave and Musgrave, *Public Finance in Theory and Practice*, pp. 502–515.

36. "A Formula for Action," A Report to the President on Defense Acquisition, The President's Blue Ribbon Commission on Defense Management, April 1986, p. 5.

37. M. Z. Kafoglis, "Local Service Charges: Theory and Practice," in H. L. Johnson, ed., *State & Local Tax Problems* (Knoxville: University of Tennessee Press, 1969), pp. 164–186. An excellent discussion is found in the selections in S. J. Mushkin, ed., *Public Prices for Public Products* (Washington, D.C.: The Urban Institute, 1972).

38. For a discussion of privatizing medical services, see J. A. Meyer, ed., *Market Reforms in Health Care* (Washington, D.C.: American Enterprise Institute, 1983).

39. A. Maynard and A. Williams, "Privatization and the National Health Service," in Le Grand and Robinson, *Privatization and the Welfare State*, pp. 95–110.

40. M. Friedman and R. Friedman, *Free to Choose* (New York: Harcourt Brace Jovanovich, 1980), pp. 150–188; and D. S. Seeley, *Education Through Partnership* (Washington, D.C.: American Enterprise Institute, 1985), pp. 83–92.

41. J. A. Peckman and B. A. Okner, *Who Bears the Tax Burden* (Washington, D.C.: The Brookings Institution, 1974).

42. These are discussed in R. Poole, Jr., "Objections to Privatization," *Policy Review* (Spring 1983) 105–121. See also Fisk, *Private Provision of Public Service*.

43. American Federation of State, County and Municipal Employees, AFL-CIO, *Passing the Buck* (Washington, D.C., 1984).

44. P. E. Fixler, Jr., "Reducing Employee Opposition to Privatization," *Fiscal Watchdog* (August 1985).

45. S. Butler, *Privatizing Federal Spending*, p. 56.

2

BUREAUCRACY, PRIVATIZATION, AND THE SUPPLY OF PUBLIC GOODS

Lawrence W. Lovik

Economics has the analytical tools and methodology necessary to analyze bureaus in the same fashion that other decision-making units are evaluated. There is a large body of literature that treats private decision-making units as operating in their own self-interest but, at the same time, views virtually all governmental activities as "axiomatic proof of an objective social need for such activity."[1] It is often postulated that bureaus, as governmental agents, operate in the public interest. The implicit assumption is that bureau chiefs and other high-level civil servants are not motivated by self-interest concerns as are their counterparts in the marketplace. To the contrary, both public agencies and private firms are managed by people who have individual as well as collective objectives. Public administrators, like management in private firms, when viewed in the light of positive economic analysis, are "rational, utility-maximizing individuals reacting to the constraints and incentives present in the bureaucratic institutions in which they operate."[2] Utilizing such an approach permits us to predict human action and to consider alternative criteria to affect behavior in ways that may yield more effective and efficient results.

In contradistinction to those who zealously endorse more public-sector influence in resource utilization, there are those who question the legitimacy of certain governmental activities. In doing so this latter group blames the inability of bureaus to solve problems efficiently on inept bureaucrats. Although this may be correct in some cases, these critics presume that public administrators are seeking to accomplish the objectives set forth in the preambles to legislation authorizing the existence of bureaus.[3] Bureau chiefs may, in pursuit of their own self-interest, seek to achieve their particular individual or organizational goals rather than those ideal objectives contained in legislative preambles. In this scenario, removing so-called inefficient public-sector personnel and replacing them with those who have a track record of productivity in the private sector may not alleviate the problem. In such a case the fundamental issue is the nature of incentives in the public sector vis-à-vis the private sector.

Public choice theory offers illumination on what government actually does as contrasted to what government ideally should do. Rejected is the notion that individuals act out of greedy self-interest in the market; rather, they act out of altruistic public interest in political activity. The public choice paradigm postulates that the main distinction between economic and political behavior is not one resulting from differences in human motives but in the institutions governing human interaction in these two areas.

The premise of this chapter is that in a democratic society characterized by substantial free market activity, most goods and services are likely to be private; nevertheless some will be public. The assumption of public provision of some goods does not necessarily imply that public production is required; for example, fire protection, garbage collection, voucher systems for education, or school bus service for public schools could be provided by public service contracts with private firms. Thus through the process of privatization the production of certain goods and services can be transferred from the public to the private sector.

The theory of public choice approaches the issue of collective action from the perspective of positive rather than normative analysis. Recognizing that the market is not a perfect system, nevertheless competitive markets do generally yield results that tend to be both technically and socially efficient while enhancing individual liberty. The question, then, quite naturally arises as to whether the "invisible hand" is simulated in the public sphere when people act out of self-interest.

Specific questions addressed in this chapter include the following: (1) Are public agencies needed to supply public services, or can private enterprise provide such services? (2) Does the choice to supply public services through private firms rather than public bureaus have implications concerning both the quality of the services as well as the efficiency by which they are provided? Challenged is the view that governmental assumption of decisions from private-sector decision-making units is prima facie evidence that such public action is necessary to remedy deficiencies in the manner by which resources are allocated and distributed.

INSTITUTIONAL CHARACTERISTICS OF PRIVATE CHOICE

A market economy allocates resources from less valued to more valued uses. This requires the existence of property rights that allow both exclusive ownership of valued resources and the transfer of such owner-ship. Acting within such an environment, the business entrepreneur seeks to engage in advantageous exchanges. The entrepreneur is mo-tivated by being a residual claimant with a property right to receive a portion of the expected gain—a profit—from the exchange.

Economic efficiency, an activity undertaken when expected benefits exceed expected costs, is attained through the efficacy of the market. Efficiencies of the pricing system include communicating information, coordinating activity, and motivating decision makers. Competitive mar-kets result in social cooperation. Efficient decisions and resource allo-cation occur to the extent that property rights are clearly defined and competitive markets exist. When these conditions prevail, the benefits of Adam Smith's metaphor are realized. The "invisible hand" simulta-neously prompts and constrains the behavior of the would-be profiteer. In marketing a product, the entrepreneur seeks to solve the dual problem of maximizing profits and minimizing costs.

The entrepreneur is subjected to the tests of the market. Within this context individuals, be they producers or consumers, are not compelled to engage in trade. If they do it is because both expect to gain. On the average this constitutes a positive sum game.

PRIVATE GOODS, PUBLIC GOODS, AND QUASI-PUBLIC GOODS

In the absence of nonexclusive ownership the social cooperation of competitive markets may not occur. Without exclusive and transferable ownership, public provision of goods may be superior.

Goods that are nonexclusive and nonrival in consumption, such as national defense, are defined as *public goods*.[4] However, many goods provided collectively have characteristics that are both public and pri-vate. Examples of these hybrids include mortgage loans, education, and food stamps. Wagner has noted, "Collective goods give rise to difficulties in economic coordination and calculation only when exclusivity of own-ership is exceedingly costly to implement."[5]

In evaluating public-sector policies that are intended to correct market deficiencies, it seems essential to recognize that both market and public-sector decisions are a result of human action. It is axiomatic in public choice theory that self-interest is an important motivator in the public sphere as well as in the marketplace. Economic choices, whether private or public, are usually made in accordance with the individual's own particular values. Self-interest may include unselfish acts and goals that are intended to benefit others.

Public-sector action is merely an extension of individual behavior. It is not enough to consider only the potentiality of market failure that might yield undesirable and inefficient outcomes. Such an operational procedure results in government action with the implicit, if not explicit, assumption that public-sector action improves resource allocation. Both responsible scholarship and citizenship require that consideration be given to the possibility of government failure to improve market imperfections. Government action may instead reflect the efforts of individuals and organized interest groups to manipulate public policy for personal gain even if the policy promotes inefficiency. Indeed, public choice theory reveals that the problem of special interest issues combined with the rational ignorance effect prevents ideal public policy results from being realized.[6] Political expediency often vetoes economic efficiency.

INSTITUTIONAL CHARACTERISTICS OF PUBLIC CHOICE

Adam Smith noted that institutional frameworks matter with regard to human actions. He stated, "Public services are never better performed than when their reward comes only in consequence of their being performed, and is proportional to the diligence employed in performing them."[7] Bureaucrats, like their counterparts in private enterprise, will generally seek to be more efficient when there is a high correlation between effort and reward. Recognition of this does not necessarily make the issue easy to resolve. The Scotsman was aware of the problem; lawyers during his era were paid according to the number of words they wrote.[8]

Decisions of bureaucrats[9] have important effects on the allocation of resources between the private and public sectors given that approximately 40% of the national income is spent through government. Public choice theory postulates that the bureaucrat, like a counterpart in private enterprise, pursues self-interest rather than some vaguely defined notion of public interest. However, the civil servant acts within a different set of institutional constraints.

The bureaucrat, unlike a counterpart in the private sector, does not seek mutually advantageous exchanges directly with the consumer of the product. In this kind of setting the bureaucrat seeks beneficial trades with a third party—politicians who have incentives to supply political goods to meet the demands of voting constituencies. The elected official, being human, tends to view the public interest through the lens of personal interest and must consider, for example, reelection chances, press relations, public image, and possibly a place in history.[10] Neither being subjected to the vicissitudes of the marketplace nor having a residual claimant status, the bureaucrat has less incentive to minimize costs and to satisfy customers. Thus not only is there no carrot in the form of potential profits, but the stick of penalties imposed by inefficient operations is too far removed to be effective.

Fundamental to the economic way of thinking is the notion that changes in expected costs and benefits will cause decision makers to alter their actions in predictable ways. Consequently the bureaucrat will, all other things being equal, perform less efficiently than the profit-seeking entrepreneur. This does not, of course, mean that the bureau chief is any less noble but merely is operating within the confines of a different institutional arrangement that has different, and perhaps even perverse, incentives. A case in point is Niskanen's model wherein bureaus seek budgetary size as their maxim and in the absence of being a residual claimant.[11]

The money calculus of profit-seeking and loss avoidance is a powerful incentive to be efficient. Private enterprise has the essential tools of economic calculation to measure value with considerable accuracy. Public agencies, because they lack such tools, must use other methods to assign responsibilities and monitor performance. Von Mises noted that alternate techniques used by government must specify tedious rules to which all must comply. "Public administration, the handling of government apparatus of coercion and compulsion, must necessarily be formalistic and bureaucratic." The bureau chief has a high degree of risk aversion. In the words of Mises, "he prefers to be on the safe side and to be doubly sure."[12] One example of this has been documented by Peltzman, who cites the Food and Drug Administration as being overly cautious concerning pharmaceutical innovation.[13]

Decision-making by government tends toward categorical rather than incremental decisions of the marginal calculus. Discretion of public decision makers is limited to protect the public as well as politicians and bureau chiefs who wish to avoid political repercussions from decisions made by layers of lower-level civil servants too numerous to monitor. Red tape[14] becomes the trade-off of giving up considerable discretionary activity in an attempt to gain institutional dependability. In the private sector monitoring is done efficiently by the "invisible hand." There is no good substitute for this in bureaucracy.

The symbiotic relations among politicians, bureaucrats, and special interest groups has been called the *iron triangle*.[15] The self-interests of the three groups are interwoven and often set forth as the public interest. This triangle has a strong proclivity to resist any change in the power structure.

Special interest groups are able to wield favors from government. James Madison in the *Tenth Federalist Paper* and George Washington in his *Farewell Address* explicitly warn of the dangers of special interests, or "factions" as they called them. The very process of seeking special privileges from government results in the use of resources that will not be available to produce real goods and services. This phenomenon is often referred to as *rent-seeking*.[16] They undertake actions to design government policy to redistribute income to their particular faction. This can be accomplished by changing the composition of spending, trade regulations, or tax structure. Public choice theory yields a result that contrasts with the mistaken view of the private sector as one based on competitive self-interest (or even selfishness), whereas the public sector altruistically and compassionately resolves difficulties.

It should not be assumed that congressional committees and subcommittees are composed of politicians representing various sections of the nation. Nor should it be assumed that committee members are motivated to formulate policies earnestly in an objective fashion in order to address problems of strictly national concern. To the contrary,

farm-state congressmen dominate the agriculture committees; urban legislators predominate on the banking, housing, and social welfare committees; members with military bases and defense industries in their districts are found on the armed services committees; and westerners are disproportionately represented on the public works, natural resources, and environmental committees. In short, the geographical link, forged in the electoral arena, is institutionalized in the committee system of the legislature.[17]

The symbiosis between bureaus and elected officials is partly a result of the fact that each of the 535 members of Congress cannot possibly be highly informed on all the laws and activities that come within their legislative purview. Similarly, neither can the chief decision makers of the executive branch, the president and his cabinet, be fully knowledgeable about all the activities that branch administers. They are influenced by the advice and opinions of assistants and lobbyists. Consequently many of the actual decisions of government agencies will be made by career bureaucrats.[18]

Differences between private enterprise and public bureaus with regard to forms of ownership and sources of revenue causes systematic differences in conduct. Bureaus do not have a residual claimant status as do private profit-seeking firms; therefore they have no real incentive to spend less than they are appropriated. Indeed, they have the incentive, albeit perverse, to exhaust the entire budget. Should there be any surplus, the bureaucrat is not rewarded for efficiency. To the contrary, the next fiscal year's budget will probably be reduced. Little wonder that it is not the case for bureaus to compete among themselves to return unspent revenues to the treasury.

It seems logical to ask, "What do bureaucrats seek?" The bureaucrat who may be conscientious and may be motivated to pursue a view of the public interest also strives to some extent to achieve such personal goals as status, income, and promotion. These objectives are more readily obtained if agencies are enlarged through bigger budgets and more employees. Furthermore, expansion permits more promotions and salary increments, which, in turn, enhance morale.[19] As the bureau expands, so does the power that accompanies it. Inasmuch as civil service rules make it almost impossible to fire anyone, one way in which management obtains more social cooperation from subordinates is to offer them potential rewards.

EMPIRICAL FINDINGS AND POLICY IMPLICATIONS

Bureaus and private enterprise have provided similar goods, which makes it possible to compare their relative performances. Studies indicate that, on the average, profit-seeking enterprises are more efficient.

The cost of garbage collection by municipalities has been found to be 40% to 50% higher than when it was supplied by business firms that had contracted with city governments.[20] Public housing projects have cost 20% more than similar housing constructed by private firms.[21] Fire protection in Arizona provided by a private firm cost only about half as much as that in comparable communities where such protection was supplied by government.[22]

With regard to government agencies and proprietary firms, Lindsay has stated:

Managers of these two types of enterprise, if rewarded on the basis of actual productivity, would make identical allocative decisions, and there would be no supply-based theory of bureaucracy distinct from the theory of the firm. Actual managerial productivity is not known in either case, however; owners of proprietary firms and members of Congress must discover the productivity of their respective managers. It is precisely because this information must be estimated and estimated differently in these two cases that behavior of the two types of organizations is itself predicted to differ.[23]

Owners of proprietary firms measure their managers' productivity indirectly by monitoring financial statements, particularly profits and losses. Such information factors into the discipline imposed by consumers as they search for valuable goods at what they consider acceptable prices. It would seem appropriate to question why government frequently selects itself to organize the provision of quasi-public goods. It could, instead, finance the purchasing of such goods via subsidy voucher mechanisms and thereby eliminate many of the bureaucratic problems.[24]

In the absence of voucher schemes and without having the profit-loss calculus, legislators must attempt to measure productivity directly. In this scenario bureaucrats have the incentive to employ resources to produce goods or product characteristics that will not be readily monitored. They will, of course, provide those goods that are expected to be monitored. Consequently it is predicted that when private enterprise and government bureaus face identical demand functions, there will be systematic differences in the behavior of individuals in the two separate sets of organizations; and this results from variations in institutional incentives. This is a type of derived demand view of managerial utilization of resources.

Lindsay has noted that some commodity characteristics are more visible and easily monitored.[25] Just as elected officials may avoid supporting policies with hidden benefits for the unorganized majority in order to deliver political goods to special interest groups, bureaus, recognizing politicians' lack of knowledge concerning particular goods, tend to substitute highly visible and easily measured goods for those that might be more desirable. Lindsay, in an examination of the Veterans Administration, noted that large quantities of highly visible services such as patients' average length of stay were increased by trading off invisibles such as quality of service. This is explained by the fact that quality of care is difficult to monitor and is therefore relatively invisible. On the other hand, the number of patient days is both relatively visible and easy to monitor. VA hospitals have tended to keep patients hospitalized for relatively simple illnesses for longer periods than proprietary hospitals. The average length of stay in VA hospitals has been estimated to be 15.3 days for a hemorrhoidectomy, 6.4 days for a tonsillectomy, 26.5 days for gallstones, and 18.6 days for kidney stones; the average stay in proprietary hospitals for each of the same designated forms of surgery were, respectively, 2.1, 2.4, 11.9, and 8.2 days. In the cases of the relatively more invisible good of patient care, which is more difficult for an oversight legislative committee to monitor, proprietary hospitals had staff-patient ratios averaging about 2:5, whereas VA hospitals had a ratio of approximately 1:5. Public choice theory suggests that public administrators will anticipate such bureaucratic behavior as being perceived by a legislative oversight committee as increasing the value of the bureau's output.

The absence of competition among public bureaus engaged in selling the same good reduces the incentive to provide that good efficiently.[26] Therefore it has been argued that this scenario might be improved if several bureaus were allowed to compete for funds to provide a particular good. Competition between bureaus would give each agency an incentive to be more efficient and, simultaneously, make it easier for the agency appropriating funds (e.g., Congress or the Office of Management and Budget) to monitor the degree of efficiency or inefficiency of the competing bureaus. However, a caveat should be considered. It seems possible that the cost of duplicating bureaus could offset potential gains. Also, there would need to be a method of preventing collusion between bureaus attempting to keep prices high and/or to divide the market for public goods—that is, a kind of antitrust policy applied to government. There would be a cost of monitoring such behavior.

Although the characteristics of certain goods may require that they be public goods or quasi-public goods, it does not logically follow that government must produce or supply them. Indeed, the process of supplying such goods can be privatized. Empirical findings show that when and where the supply of public or quasi-public goods is privatized, not only are these goods produced more efficiently but their quality is also enhanced. It may suffice for the state simply to finance them and permit private enterprise to supply. When possible it may be even more desirable to contract out the provision of quasi-public goods with the lowest bidder. User fees could be charged where applicable. In some cases this could result in lower costs and better quality. In other cases, such as education, it could allow competition between public and private suppliers. Financing might be provided by tax revenues, but the user would be able to choose from among those that provide it.

Given the institutional environment within which they operate, bureaus are not only unlikely to minimize costs but they may, by design, attempt indirectly to appropriate profits by intentionally raising expenditures higher than necessary. The manner in which this is accomplished and how the phantom profits are allocated depends on the interests of politicians and bureaucrats.

The very notion of the policy of privatization is a result of institutional obstacles that are inherent in the process of public supply. The process of privatization offers a positive alternative that permits entrepreneurial creativity to help solve public problems.

Regardless of the potential overall economic efficiencies and commensurate societal benefits to be realized by forming contractual agreements with private firms, a legislature might still have a strong preference for giving appropriations to bureaus. The use of bureaus makes it easier to create rents for special interest groups that demand particular goods. Indeed, it seems logical to suppose that if no rents were expected, private firms would be utilized more frequently.

NOTES

1. T. Sowell, *Knowledge and Decisions* (New York: Basic Books, 1980), pp. 114–115. Sowell cites R. A. Dahl and C. E. Lindblom, *Politics, Economics and Welfare* (Chicago: University of Chicago Press, 1976). Dahl and Lindblom contend that government regulation remedies deficiencies in the price system (p. 213); medical care, housing, and other activities are "collectivized because of particular

shortcomings in the price system" (p. 419); government "cannot keep its hands off" wage negotiations because so "much is at stake" (p. 185). Also in A. A. Berle, *Power* (New York: Harcourt, Brace and World, 1969), Berle asserts that government "had to be called in" to education (p. 195); France "found it necessary" to have government control capital markets (p. 252); government regulation of consumption is "the only practicable escape from unendurable congestion and confusion, if not chaos" (p. 252); government must expand economic controls (p. 261).

2. J. Buchanan and M. Flowers, *The Public Finances* (Homewood, Ill.: Richard D. Irwin, 1980), p. 159.

3. Sowell, *Knowledge and Decisions*, p. 146.

4. National defense provides protection for people within the borders of a nation. One person's consumption of national defense does not preclude someone else's consuming the same amount. A second example would be to assume that the provision of a dam to prevent floods is available to all who live within the flood plain. Thus there exists the possibility of the well-known free-rider problem.

5. R. Wagner, *Public Finance: Revenues and Expenditures in a Democratic Society* (Boston: Little, Brown, 1983), p. 31.

6. A special interest issue, such as a tariff or import quota, offers large benefits to a small number of recipients while exacting small individual costs from a majority. The special interest group monitors closely a politician's stance on items in their self-interest. On the other hand, a typical voter seldom invests the time and effort to be informed on issues that he or she expects to affect him or her only indirectly, if at all.

7. Adam Smith, *The Wealth of Nations* (New York: Modern Library, 1937), p. 678.

8. Ibid., p. 680.

9. The term *bureaucrat* refers merely to bureau chiefs; that is, there is no intended invective. Also, the word *bureau* is used herein to identify an agency or organization of nonelected government workers (civil servants) responsible for implementing public programs.

10. A market for legislation is created when citizens and special interest groups express a demand for political goods and individual legislators and political parties supply it. The less the expected costs, the larger the amount demanded. The general theoretical framework of consumer choice is applicable to the market for political goods. In exchange for supporting legislation to meet the demands of various subsets of citizens, tacit payments are received in the form of campaign contributions, reciprocal support of other causes, use of certain law firms, and the like.

11. W. Niskanen, *Bureaucracy and Representative Government* (Chicago: Aldine-Atherton, 1971); and idem, "Bureaucrats and Politicians," *Journal of Law and Economics* 18 (December 1975): 617–643. As a result of observing congressional action over the years, bureau chiefs are able to approximate budgetary levels that Congress is likely to approve. Hence by proposing a budget of a given size rather than utilizing marginal calculus, a bureau receives approval of a budget larger than Congress might prefer. The propensity for this to occur is enhanced

by any given congressperson's dearth of expert information concerning the multitude of proposals on which he or she must act.

12. L. von Mises, *Bureaucracy* (New York: Arlington House, 1969), p. 122.

13. In one example, consider the case of the Food and Drug Administration. When does adequate testing for harmful side affects become adequate? How far should risks be reduced? There are costs as well as benefits attached to more testing. These costs can manifest themselves not only in dollar amounts but in the loss of life and/or suffering that otherwise could be relieved if the new drug were legally marketable. The relative visibility of services becomes significant. Those who become seriously ill or die because the FDA keeps drugs off the market are quite unlikely to blame the FDA; they don't have sufficient information. However, if a new drug is approved and it causes serious harm, cause and effect are more easily visible. Rational human actions faced with these alternatives are predictable. The FDA will tend to be excessively cautious. See S. Peltzman, *Regulation of Pharmaceutical Innovation* (Washington, D.C.: American Enterprise Institute for Public Policy Resarch, 1974). It took ten years for the FDA to establish standards of identity for peanut butter. William F. Peterson, Jr., "Formal Records and Informal Rulemaking," *Yale Law Review* 85 (November 1975).

Arthur Okun stated, "Bureaucratic red tape is neither an accident nor a reflection of bad rules or inept officials: it is the result of the obligation of political decision-makers to be cautious, to avoid capriciousness, to take account of the full range of interest and impacts of the course they adopt. . . . Public officials follow the Ten Commandments of their profession, which proclaim that thou shalt not be experimental or venturesome or flexible." A. Okun, *Equality and Efficiency: The Big Tradeoff* (Washington, D.C.: The Brookings Institution, 1975), p. 60.

14. According to lexicographers, the term *red tape* is derived from the ribbon once used to tie up legal documents in England. It seems the common law gave heavy weight to precedent. Consequently judicial decisions required a thorough search of records for authority and guidance. This would have necessitated large numbers of clerks and lawyers. Red tape is the result of the high information costs of the bureaucracy.

15. M. and R. Friedman, *Tyranny of the Status Quo* (New York: Harcourt Brace Jovanovich, 1984).

16. J. Buchanan, R. Tollison, and G. Tullock, *Toward a Theory of the Rent-Seeking Society* (College Station: Texas A&M University Press, 1981).

17. C. Hardin, K. Shepsle, and B. Wringast, *Public Policy Excesses: Government by Congressional Subcommittee* (St. Louis: Center for the Study of American Business, Washington University, September 1982), p. 10.

18. Okun, *Equality and Efficiency*, p. 61.

19. Although some bureaucrats may be cost-conscientious, there is no inherent motive within the institutional framework of government to reduce the size of bureaus.

20. E. S. Savas, *The Organization and Efficiency of Solid Waste Collection* (Lexington, Mass.: D. C. Heath, 1977). J. Bennett and M. Johnson, "Public versus Private Provision of Collective Goods and Services: Garbage Collection Revisited," *Public Choice* 34 (1979): 55–63; and R. Spann, "Public versus Private Pro-

vision of Governmental Services," in T. Borcherding, ed., *Budgets and Bureaucrats* (Durham, N.C.: Duke University Press, 1977), pp. 71–89.

21. R. Muth, *Public Housing* (Washington, D.C.: American Enterprise Institute, 1973).

22. R. Ahlbrandt, "Efficiency in the Provision of Fire Services," *Public Choice* 16 (Fall 1973): 1–16. Some of these companies had contracts with cities and some with individuals as well. Such firms have developed a new and yet almost obvious way of operating. When someone phones to report a fire, the company asks the extent and kind of fire and then sends the appropriate equipment. This may require only a pickup truck with a couple of fireman and a foam unit rather than two or three large fire engines and a lead vehicle for every fire. The quality of fire protection, if measured by insurance rates, is as good as that supplied by local governments.

23. C. M. Lindsay, "A Theory of Government Enterprise," *Journal of Political Economy* 84 (October 76): 1064.

24. I am certainly not inclined to advocate national health insurance, nor am I arguing for subsidies. The point here is that given the fact that the programs exist, they can be provided in a more efficient way.

25. Lindsay, "Theory of Government Enterprise," pp. 1066–1077.

26. Buchanan and Flowers, *The Public Finances*; Wagner, *Public Finance*; and Sowell, *Knowledge and Decisions*.

3

PRIVATIZATION: A VIABLE POLICY OPTION?

Alan Rufus Waters

THE PRESSURE FOR PRIVATIZATION

Is privatization a viable policy option? First ask how long the state can sustain a role as entrepreneur and producer. If the goal of those in power is for their nations to escape from the bonds of economic weakness that poverty and low productivity define, then the issue is not *whether* but *how* to privatize. Economic theory is quite explicit: because of the nature of ownership and incentives, a state entity cannot be as efficient as a private entity in the production of the same output.

This study indicates some of the technical problems that will arise when a state entity is moved into the competitive sector, suggests ways of minimizing disruption, and develops an initial step-by-step procedure for evaluating state entities and discerning their viability in the free market.

State monopolies and control of the economy by an elite that set the pattern of economic activity have long been justified by the argument that ordinary people, if left to themselves, would not demand or produce enough of what was good for them. State control and regulation transfers wealth to the clerisy; idealists would still use the state to change human nature.

Technology has given us what Simon calls "the age of substitution."[1] Systems of control and regulation are continually and rapidly undermined by technical change. The growing flexibility of the private sector makes it difficult for government officials to control their economies. Communications, lying at the core of every rapidly evolving modern economy, is a prime example. Already small firms (and some individuals) have access to information that has traditionally been the source of state power.

One answer to declining respect for rules and regulations is to increase the degree—and the cost—of enforcement by keeping the communications system—the telephone system in particular—primitive, exclusive, costly, and usually in the hands of the nonprivate sector. The nation that denies its citizens the new individual technology pays by losing a generation of entrepreneurs and by ensuring a future of dependence on foreign innovation. If the desire for economic success exceeds the desire for continued government control, increasing pressure for privatization and reduced official intervention will occur. In the short run there are more visible forces at work.

If one state entity creates a negative cash flow, some other part of the state system must generate the offsetting surplus. A once popular solution—printing money—is now seen to be merely a step in the inevitable progression to inflation, subsequent unemployment, and economic decline. Vigorous economic growth offers a possible escape from the cash constraint. But growth is stunted by the very existence of the state monopolies demanding cash subsidies in the first place. It is a problem with only one viable solution: privatization.

The immediate pressure for privatization may come from the International Monetary Fund, the World Bank, or some other external agency demanding reductions in government expenditure as a price of further indebtedness, or from groups within the government sector who see their welfare threatened by the demands for cash subsidies by other state entities, or even from the increasing cost of extracting additional tax revenue from a slow-growing or stagnant economy. The obvious solution to all these pressures is to dispose of activities in which the cash outflow is greatest. This pragmatic solution is, happily, in complete accord with the best intellectual thinking in economically successful nations.

THE ROLE OF OWNERSHIP

When ownership of property, both real and intangible, is clearly defined and resides with specific individuals, those individuals will benefit from using that property in its most productive manner or will personally bear the cost in the form of reduced returns. Private property rights, coupled to free markets, tie the right to take action, the incentive to take action, and the responsibility for the result of that action.

When ownership is poorly defined, the chain linking opportunities, rewards, and responsibilities is broken. There is a cost to enforcing ownership rights. Before putting forth the time and effort to maintain and protect an asset, a person must be sure that the rewards will accrue to him or her or to someone of his or her choice. This has been recognized for centuries among peasants whose productivity would rise dramatically as soon as they were given clear title to the land they worked. The tenant does not undertake capital improvements or work to improve the wealth of the landlord. This reasoning applies not only to real property and to peasants who refuse to improve land they do not own but to all forms of ownership.

In a world where intellectual capital is the driving force for the future, our thinking cannot be restricted to material assets alone but must take into account the ownership of both tangible and intangible capital. For example, the wealth (the source of income) of the administrative elite may be in the form of the right to control and allocate rewards, deciding who may or may not have access to desirable privileges or services, or allocating reduced penalties or reduced costs. The right to dispense benefits, including reduced penalties, is a function of the government sector and should be called *socialized wealth*. Analysis based upon this reasoning has provided the most significant contribution made by economics in recent decades. Its application represents a direct assault on the concept of the paternal and benevolent state as the engine of prosperity.[2]

THE EFFECTS OF ATTENUATING OWNERSHIP

Economists have spent considerable time trying to compare the performance of state entities (in which rights are poorly defined, if at all) and the performance of private-sector enterprises (in which rights are quite specific). Study of the actual performance of state entities is difficult because their accounting procedures do not treat assets or costs in a manner amenable to rigorous comparison and evaluation. Studies do, however, show clearly the degree to which the rewards and penalties faced by individual decision makers relate to the nature of the ownership arrangements.[3]

Anything that restricts (attenuates) the right of owners or users to do as they wish with an asset reduces the value of that asset. Where ownership is ill-defined, assets will be undervalued. The implications for the nonprivate sector should be obvious: poor maintenance and underuse of assets that are owned by everyone and therefore no one. Even casual observation of the nonprivate sector reveals that this is the case. Nonprivate enterprises tend to be capital intensive, are hoarders of equipment, and have a poor record in maintaining their assets.

In the competititve private sector, as would be expected, assets are more highly valued. The owner can use the asset, perhaps improve it, and ultimately capture the rewards of these efforts by selling the asset (capitalizing it).[4] The private owner will also have to bear the direct cost of replacing an asset, and that alone is an incentive to proper care and maintenance.

Regulations and controls limiting a person's range of options are an attenuation of that person's property rights. The entrepreneur who believes that he can provide a transportation service or a water supply cheaper, and therefore more profitably, than the state entity is thwarted by the law. The value of that entrepreneur's skills, capital, and managerial ability are reduced as he or she is forced to select an alternative occupation.

There is another aspect of the attentuation of ownership rights, however, that may be even more troubling. Where ownership rights are attentuated, the managers of the unowned assets have little incentive to monitor the use of those assets. The cost of monitoring may be heavy in terms of time and personal relations, particularly if it yields no visible rewards. Assets in the nonprivate sector by definition cannot be owned because they cannot be transferred, sold, or otherwise altered by those directly responsible for them. In the state sector there will be a continuing search for privileges, positions, perquisites, pensions, and other benefits and competition for the right to distribute reduced penalties and costs, which will distort the economy and drive resources into less productive activities.

THE RATIONALE BEHIND ATTENUATING OWNERSHIP

Justification for nonprivatization is usually highly intellectual and well argued given that the beneficiaries are often the clerisy. When the arguments for state monopolies become increasingly arcane and complex, moral arguments are substituted for economic ones.

1. Redistribution of Wealth

To increase someone's wealth, the obvious thing to do is give them money. Only the individual can define what will provide happiness, comfort, and wealth. This seemingly obvious statement is shocking to those in authority. It attacks the principle justifying the existence of even the most benevolent elite: that the poor and the unfortunate do not know what is best for them and need to be controlled and guided but never trusted.[5]

The transfer of wealth from one group to another is often the excuse for nonprivatization. It is asserted that the poor, for example, "need" more of a given commodity or service than they are now getting. Because they might not buy what they "need" if we just gave them cash, it is necessary to create an added source of supply and produce whatever output is perceived to be appropriate. The more successful nations have chosen the private sector to produce and the state to purchase and distribute; those less successful have set the state up as producer.

2. Natural Monopolies

The technical definition of a natural monopoly derives only from the theory of perfect competition. A natural monopoly exists where the long-run average cost of production of the first producer in the field declines steadily over the relevant range of output. The biggest producer is in an unassailable competitive position because he or she will always be able to produce at a lower cost than any competitor. The introduction of competition would be a waste of society's resources and a detriment to the whole economy. Furthermore, the sole producer is able to behave as a monopolist: charging a higher-than-market price for a lower-than-market output.

Except as a pedagogical device, and a component of the purely competitive model, the existence of a long-run average cost function is difficult to justify. Cost is a subjective concept.[6] There is also the question of the nature of the long-run cost curve in a situation where constantly changing technology is the norm. One would have to be very secure in one's ability to forecast the future of technology before asserting that a particular activity is a natural monopoly.

Few, if any, so-called natural monopolies seem able to survive without the force of law to keep out competition, and they frequently require direct or indirect subsidies from taxpayers to keep them operating. The natural monopoly concept is little more than a theoretical curiosity. Natural monopoly reigns in the realm of ex post facto justifications of state monopolies benefiting favored groups.

3. Monopolies for "National" Reasons

State control has been justified on the grounds that the product or service is necessary to the basic self-respect of the nation as a whole, particularly when the commodity or service was previously from foreign, or foreign-owned, sources. Arguing about this requires discussion of how the national will is expressed through the political system, and whether or not it is actually the will of a small elite who hold the reins of power.

The acid test for the monopolization of some activity by the nonprivate sector is not that it was created in a surge of emotional support for some popular political cause. Participants in specific causes with a clear and simple goal, such as the elimination of the foreigner, are seldom willing to contemplate alternative means of achieving that end.[7]

A monopoly is a monopoly whether or not it arose through the actions of politicians or businessmen. Yet hope continues that somehow people who operate a state monopoly will behave differently from people who operate one in the private sector. History has shown that monopolies in the state sector produce a less-than-competitive output and generate monopoly profits in the form of excessive costs. Attempts to correct the situation by altering human behavior have only led to deeper problems.[8]

There are two clear distinctions between monoplies in the private and the nonprivate sectors. First, those in the private sector—unless receiving the legal support of government—are subject to continual threats from new technologies, new entrants to their industry, substitute products or services, or changes in the demand for their output. Monopolies in the private sector do not survive. The dreaded giants of yesterday—railroad barons, coal barons, cotton magnates, cattle barons—become the supplicants for public subsidy and protection in a couple of decades. Those in the nonprivate sector survive.

Second, monopolies in the private sector generate visible financial profits or losses. Those in the state sector always generate "profits," seldom in the form of cash, but profits nonetheless.

Monitoring the stewardship of assets is less rewarding in state monopolies where ownership is ill-defined. Managers and operators can obtain direct benefits for themselves only by expanding the costs of the operation and hence their right to perform favors for others. Wages in state monopolies are usually above the market alternative, ensuring loyal employees who know that they cannot earn as much elsewhere and who are aware that there is a line of applicants waiting to fill their positions should they decide to leave. Similarly, the selection of suppliers and customers when prices are above the market alternative will create opportunities for personal benefit even when overt corruption is not present. Conditions of service and perquisites of office will always be better in the state monopoly than in the competitive alternative. Nonmonetary benefits take the place of monetary benefits.

The various stakeholders in the nonprivate monopoly derive their profts in concealed form. Employees, managers, suppliers, and sometimes customers are the beneficiaries. It is difficult at times to see behind the facade of alleged financial losses and appeals for further subsidies. It is difficult, given government accounting practices, to discover whether or not a state monopoly did indeed make a profit or take a loss. Losses are incurred only by those paying direct subsidies or providing indirect subsidies through the absence of an alternative to the monopoly's products.

4. Externalities

Externalities occur when part of the benefits or costs of some economic activity fall upon outsiders—that is, those who were not party to deciding about the activity in the first place. The construction of a golf course, for example, would increase the value of surrounding property and hence the wealth of its owners. There are three possible responses to the sudden gain in wealth by those who were not party to the construction of the course.[9] If the course were constructed by the government, taxes could be imposed upon the property owners to ensure that the resulting increase in wealth is captured by the government. If it were constructed by some group in the private sector, they could capture (internalize) the full benefits of their investment by buying the adjoining property and then selling it after completing the course. The third alternative would be to allow the benefits to flow over to the owners of the adjacent property, thereby undervaluing the course from the viewpoint of the investors.

The problem arises with the inability of the investor or the entrepreneur to capture the full benefits. There is a continual and ongoing process by which externalities are being internalized. As technology provides new means to measure and control access to other people's property, the cost of internalizing externalities falls and more third-party effects are eliminated.[10]

As previously stated, the use of government power frequently comes to mind first when people are faced with a problem of externalities. Nonetheless government power is better utilized through taxation and regulation than by the construction and operation of the gold course. There is seldom strong economic justification for establishing a non-private-sector entity on the basis of the existence of externalities.

5. Shortages of Entrepreneurs and Managerial Talent

Early textbooks frequently argued that a nation in the first stages of modern economic development lacks the basic entrepreneurial or managerial talent necessary to operate complex facilities.[11] The solution to this perceived problem is to use the state as the nation's entrepreneur. Enterprises are therefore established by the state, using the administrative talent concentrated in the government, with very big projects being undertaken so as to economize on the use of the scarce talent. The whole argument about the scarcity of entrepreneurial talent is, however, questionable.

The doubtful argument that some societies generate less entrepreneurial talent than others is not a reason for policies minimizing the uses of such talent. More appropriate policies would encourage the largest possible number of small firms in which the potential entrepreneurs and managers could learn the missing skills. The argument about entrepreneurial talent easily develops racial and ethnic undertones when used to justify the exclusion of successful minorities from the fruits of their efforts. A more rational explanation usually can be found in the excess supply of public administrators and civil servants rather than in the shortage of entrepreneurs and managers.

6. Public Goods

Public goods are those goods for which a private producer cannot charge because the cost of collecting for them is impossibly high. The classic example is the lighthouse.[12] The person who built a lighthouse on a rocky coast would have to spend a great deal to collect fees from all passing ships. The problem, then, is that public goods, once created, are available to all. Hence there is no incentive for the private sector to produce them. The rational answer is for society to determine what goods and services are both truly public in nature and truly vital to the general welfare, and then find the cheapest means of producing them— which may not be government ownership.[13]

Once a public good has been determined, there remains the question of whether the civil service should undertake the production or a franchise should be created and a tax levied to pay the cost. The franchise alternative has everything to recommend it. It can be auctioned off— with well-defined quantity and quality standards—to the lowest bidders; and because it resides in the private sector, there is some assurance that production costs will be kept to a minimum, particularly if the franchise is up for frequent renewal.

COMPARING PRIVATE AND NONPRIVATE ENTERPRISES

Any examination of the performance of nonprivate-sector enterprises runs into several immediate problems. Besides the nature of their accounting systems and proclivity to overcapitalize and overstaff, they have no equity (ownership) component on their balance sheets. The capital structure of the nonprivate enterprise will have no true counterpart in the private sector.

In the cases of uniform services or products being generated by very similar entities, comparing the cost of producing a given level and quality of output would only be conclusive evidence of the superiority of one system over the other. Unfortunately this is seldom possible. Visible overuse of capital exists because there are no capital charges or capital user fees in most state sector enterprises. Therefore there are no depreciation allowances and none of the financial behavior called for by the existence of taxes. Another major problem arises because state entities have traditionally produced what officials determine rather than what customers want. Consequently comparing output is inappropriate.

Nonprivate and private enterprises are seldom allowed to operate side by side. Cases of competition of this nature are few indeed. In making comparisons, the best that can be done is to look at the performance of similar enterprises in other locations and at other times, which raises serious questions of comparability.[15]

Despite all the foregoing, numerous studies have been undertaken to determine the relative cost of productions by nonprivate versus private enterprises. The conclusions of these studies are surprisingly uniform and coincide with those of economic theory, which finds that private enterprises should be more efficient.[16] Most of the work on relative cost of nonprivate versus private production has been done in the more economically successful nations, but a growing number of studies involve the less developed countries and indicate a uniformity of outcome that would be overwhelmingly conclusive evidence in any other field.

Evidence accumulated about the relative efficiency of state and private sectors in performing the same function should include nonquantifiable factors. The traveler who spends time in several countries inevitably begins to develop some sense of the relative cost and quality of various services and products provided by the nonprivate sector in one nation and the private sector in another. There is a pool of such people who are amenable to sophisticated survey techniques from which useful evidence could be drawn. Such external surveys could then be used as reference points for similar surveys of various groups at the national level.[17] This technique should not supplant the more usual statistical evaluation of the existing data (usually accounting data) but provides useful added evidence if decisions are to be based upon objective criteria.

THE ECONOMICALLY SUCCESSFUL NATIONS

Ever since the British government began a policy of selling off state-owned companies such as British Telecommunications PLC,[18] there has been much talk in Europe of moving commercial enterprises out of the nonprivate sector.[19] So far, however, most of what has occurred outside Britain is only talk.[20] Despite a few isolated cases, Europe has not yet come to terms with the fact that its increasingly encrusted nonprivate economy is unlikely to have the flexibility necessary for success in rapidly changing global markets.[21]

The United Kingdom should be an exception the inflexibility of the European situation. First, the United Kingdom has moved major enterprises out of the nonprivate sector by using the well-developed British financial markets. Complete state entities have been moved into the private sector with little restructuring. Nevertheless there are few indications that regulation of competition will be relaxed, or that the full range of ownership rights will actually be transferred. Until there is secure evidence that the new owners of a former state entity can go bankrupt, be taken over by another entity, or dispose of their assets and close the operation, the kind of ownership that the British discuss is rather thin. Furthermore the opposition party in Parliament remains committed to reverse much of what has been done if it should return to power.

Preoccupation with the enterprise, instead of with the function it is designed to fulfill, must be abandoned. Instead of state entities, the products and services they provide should be the central issue. A more open environment—with greater competitive access to the sources of capital—might allow a totally different productive system to arise and satisfy the wants of the consumer group. In the United Kingdom, however, there is still a regulatory atmosphere totally alien to the widespread practice of entrepreneurial skills. The foreign visitor senses a continuing commitment to the paternal state, not the entrepreneurial state.

One plan in the United Kingdom is different and exciting: a program to privatize state-owned dwellings by selling them to their current occupants. The implications of this are far-reaching, for with the new owners' need to maintain their homes and the incentive to improve and to trade, there will emerge a whole new arena for specialized and decentralized service firms in the private sector.

Privatization's greatest impact in Britain, and in the rest of Europe, will come with the return of many of the local services—for example, water supply, sewage, and garbage disposal—to the private sector from which they were removed decades ago. The sale of intact state entities with the prospect of continuing indirect subsidies and with detailed regulation of competition alone is not significant.

Innovative local capital markets are a key factor in rapid economic development. Privatization in the United States is driven by the provision of services and products to meet distinctly local demand and can be of significance in generating and sustaining local capital markets. Currently less developed nations should emulate this local initiative based upon locally raised funds. A growing number of institutions and firms in the United States are involved in helping local government officials make the transition to the private sector.[23] There are no preconditions or central government rules about how funds may be raised. Each local entity stands or falls on the basis of its own credit and financial situation. There is no attempt to equalize services, and yet the level of service in general is among the highest in the world.

It is not, however, in the more developed nations where the process of privatization is likely to bring the greatest rewards. The burden of the nonprivate sector is greatest in the poorer nations, and it is in these nations that the most remarkable changes are occurring.

THE LESS DEVELOPED NATIONS

The latest and most interesting moves in privatization have occurred in the foreign-aid-receiving nations of the Third World. A visitor may complain about the quality of public transport in cities of the poorer nations, but in fact the privately operated urban transport systems of Manila, Bangkok, Nairobi, and Abidjan are more available, more efficient, and more relevant than the heavily subsidized public systems of any major U.S. or European city. Example after example shows that private-sector transport services work and nonprivate-sector transport services do not, despite subsidies and legal protection from competition. Too often public transport becomes a showpiece of bureaucracy.[24]

While public transport in the United States—and most of Western Europe— seems to be inextricably entangled in a vicious circle of rising costs and declining ridership, other countries provide many examples of urban public transport that combine financial viability with higher service quality.[25] According to the Bureau de Circulation of the Ivory Coast, informal services provided by Gbakas, 14- or 22-seat vehicles, have a daily traffic of 15,000 vehicle-trips carrying about 200,000 passengers on two main routes, while the public bus company carries 160,000 on these same two routes. . . . Costs per seat-kilometer are roughly equivalent for the Gbakas and for the public standard buses. However, the public service operates with a heavy deficit while the privately owned Gbakas seem to be making comfortable profits.[26]

In 1962 the situation became intolerable, and Transportes de Buenos Aires was dissolved. All transport services, except the underground railway, were turned over to private companies. The trams and trolley buses were dropped out of service and were replaced by regular full-sized buses. It is significant, however, that many of these were subsequently replaced by 23-seat microbuses.[27]

People want personal transportation if they can get it at a reasonable price. The automobile—and the freedom it offers—is the continuing ideal of most of the world. Where public transport systems are the only available alternative, those most flexible and diverse appear to succeed. A wide range of quality is obviously a major factor. As in every other market, alternatives and competition guarantee care for what the consumer wants.

Gabriel Roth (see chapter 13) provides examples that are documented for Cairo, Calcutta, Hong Kong, Istanbul, Khartoum, Kuala Lumpur, Nairobi, Puerto Rico, Singapore, and other cities. He concludes that the transportation system will be efficient and productive and provide the services more people want when ownership is private, vehicles and operating units are small, and route associations for voluntary sharing of information about schedules and routes exist.

Sadly, in the less economically successful nations there are few cases of the private sector being allowed to compete in telecommunications services. The role of the communications system in the development of an information-based economy is crucial for the poorer nations that seem most likely to cling to state telephone monopolies. The successful economies of the future will be those allowing greatest individual access to international communications networks—those offering their citizens top-quality, low-cost means of communication by both voice and computer connection. The Philippines, Brazil, and Bolivia provide examples of local telephone companies that serve small towns with varying degrees of success. In each case, however, the constraints of regulation, equipment standards, or controlled access to a central state monopoly of national transmission lines exclude serious competition.

National coordination by several competing private companies—as in the United States—has not been tried in any other major nation, although there are examples in some of the island nations of the Caribbean. Also, surprisingly little use has been made of the possibilities offered by competing franchises.

Urban water supply, education, sewage disposal, and other services are usually classified as public goods. Until recent decades this was not so. In most cases the process of transfer to the nonprivate sector began with price controls and regulations that made private firms no longer profitable. As the quality of service declined, the government stepped in and transferred production to the nonprivate sector. Subsidies replaced the missing profits. There are now strong indications that this trend is reversing itself.

Shortage of public money and the growing contrast between public waste and private thrift provide the domestic impetus for giving private enterprise more rope. Meanwhile the media and travellers' tales proclaimed to the Chinese and South Asians the success of such nearby free enterprise economics as Japan, Hong Kong, South Korea and Singapore in beating poverty and scarcity and reaching European levels of the good life.[28]

Even profound faith must ultimately be shaken when faced with a visible and contradictory reality. Perhaps a sense of national pride as well as a desire for personal and family well-being are the reasons why authorities in more nations are talking about returning state-controlled activities to the private sector.

THE COST OF PRIVATIZATION

There are two barriers to action. The first is a group of objections classified as political. In actuality, such defense of the status quo merely indicates that the true list of stakeholders in the public enterprise is not being recognized or valued appropriately.

The second objection to change is more respectable: little work has been done on the actual process of making the transition from nonprivate status—specifically on how best to achieve minimum disruption and subsequent commercial success in the private sector. In part the problem centers on the question of how to define success. The proper focus should be on the product or service wanted by the users. The private sector cannot tolerate products and services that are of arbitrary quality, provided at less than optimal times in less than desirable locations, or packaged in greater than desired quantities. The crucial test must be that the provision of the product or service be attractively profitable at levels of output and quality supported by consumers in their purchases.

Those advocating privatization have often been guilty of oversimplification. Sensing the strength of their argument for removal of commercial enterprises from the nonprivate sector, they have failed to work through the mechanics of the actual transfer. It is easy to advocate the sale of a state company; it is more difficult to specify how the sale should be conducted, to whom, and for how much.

Similarly those with a stake in a nonprivate company have often exaggerated the difficulties of moving to the private sector because they have not thoroughly considered the process by which that transfer would take place.

Human nature resists change. Inertia must be overcome by the hope of reward or the threat of penalty. In the case of nonprivate enterprises, there are factors that reinforce inertia and that must be overcome if progress is to be made. The state entity is not structured to compete in the private sector for reasons rooted in the way they were established and in the pattern of the subsequent operation.

FAILED ACCOUNTING SYSTEMS

State-sector accounting practice actually causes the state entity to behave in perverse economic fashion because it fails to account for capital assets in a manner recognizing their true cost to society. Only if there is an annual usage cost or interest payment will capital assets be valued appropriately by operators of state entities. If capital assets are not accounted for through an annual charge, there is an incentive for managers and operators to hoard capital. Similarly, without some appropriate valuation of all capital assets under the control of the entity, and a consistent method of computing depreciation as an offset to some equivalent of pretax income, an effective capital management program is not possible. The accounting systems operated by many state companies have resulted not only in accumulation and hoarding of capital but caused a visible lack of maintenance and a consequent high level of capital consumption.

Accounting developed as a profession operating within a well-defined system of ownership. Where ownership has not been well defined, accounting systems have compensated by an emphasis on control systems that have been required to bear more weight than they can stand in the face of perverse incentives. As a result they have become ends in themselves and an additional element leading to higher operating costs, less flexibility, and lower productivity. Only with the introduction of ownership (equity in some form) can state entities be made accountable in any positive way. State entities moved to the private sector must be evaluated in terms of private-sector accounting systems, not from the perspective of government accountants.

A further problem lies in the fact that the traditional state systems ignore several important groups of stakeholders in the entity. For example, the nonpecuniary wealth (socialist wealth) created by state entities—that is, the net present value of titles, positions, and perquisites granted through employment on various regulatory or management boards—must be explicitly recognized and assessed as part of the liability side of the company's balance sheet.

Failed Project Analysis or Capital Budgeting

Many nonprivate entities in less developed nations were established after exhaustive analysis by economists and others. The problem lay with the use of analysis based upon the concept of a cost/benefit ratio, which acknowledged selected nonmarket factors. Social cost/benefit analysis was frequently a justification for undertaking activities that could not generate the cash needed to keep them afloat without subsidies. Arguing that a particular project runs a cash loss but generates a positive net marginal social benefit may, in some arcane sense, be a valid use of logic, but such reasoning flies in the face of common sense when talking about state commercial activities.

Advisers and aide officials from the more economically successful countries have failed the poorer nations by not emphasizing commercial techniques of investment analysis based on realistic estimates of market-generated cash flows. For the purely commercial world, in which the developing nations must ultimately learn to survive, social cost/benefit analysis has little operational content. Furthermore, social cost/benefit analysis has resulted in the accumulation of a stratum of capital-wasting and resource-consuming industries in the less developed countries.

In these countries perhaps the most damaging result of the era of social cost/benefit analysis—as an alternative to standard capital budgeting techniques—has been the creation of an influential intelligentsia whose well-being depends upon the continued application of noncommercial methods using nonmarket prices as their guide.

Cash flow is the key to survival in the private sector. High expected net earnings after tax or significant growth in equity are useless if the firm cannot meet its immediate commitments. In addition, economic rather than engineering time horizons in developing an appropriate life span for estimating the net present value represented by company's future earnings, realistic and representative interest rates for the cost of capital are necessary. Within the private sector it is pointless to manipulate the discount rate for "social" reasons when one must live with the outcome of one's analysis and without the hope of subsidies to cover mistakes.

For those entities to be released to the private sector, project analysis must be objective. Buyers will certainly evaluate the situation in terms of strict market analysis. They will be interested in revenue estimates derived from what people are prepared to buy, not "perceived needs." Thus if any valuation of an entity for transfer to the private sector is to be realistic, it must be done by people who are in touch with the market and the local business situation at the most operational level. Outsiders from the higher echelons of government, international institutions, or foreign aid agencies may have some fascinating and convincing methodology, but they too often substitute knowledge for information.

In too many cases project analysis has dealt cavalierly with risk. To the private-sector operator risk is the key element. Risk is present in every decision about how to serve the market. Survival, let alone profit, depends upon the ability to judge risk. We need to take account of the risk preference of the potential purchaser when we package an entity for transfer to the private sector. The preferred level of risk is represented in the private sector by the debt-equity ratio, or the degree of leverage indicated by a given capital structure. Inflation, which is endemic in many less developed nations, is another risk factor.[29]

The three basic components of risk in the private sector are commercial risk, foreign exchange risk, and sovereign or political risk. State enterprises are ill-equipped to analyze commercial risk and frequently barred by law from hedging operations (the normal way such risks are reduced). The basis for analysis of various aspects of foreign exchange risk lies in an ability to integrate into corporate planning the most realistic estimates of future exchange rates. The problem from an operational standpoint is that such estimates are frequently at variance with the estimates upon which current government policy is based. Manipulated and controlled exchange rates are the norm in most of the nations of the Third World. Under these circumstances no state entity could publish—or admit to the existence of—exchange rate forecasts indicating that current government exchange rate policy is unlikely to work. Such forecasts would create further justification for speculators to sell short the nation's currency in the foreign exchange markets and hence bring present policies into even greater disrepute.

Sovereign, or political, risk refers to the possibility of an unanticipated decline in net income streams or a reduction in asset values resulting from unanticipated government action. Political risks are carefully evaluated by any prudent management in the private sector. The collection and analysis of information may lead to conclusions very unflattering to the present government. To be valuable, political risk analysis requires a high level of objectivity. Open and critical discussion of government personalities and policies by private organizations is not encouraged by authorities in most of the Third World nations. For government departments and state firms to undertake critical analyses of the activities and policies of other government entities is practically unheard of.

Even if political risk analysis were possible for the state company, the actions necessary for reduction of such risk could only be seen as directly counter to current government policy. Managers in state enterprises cannot submit budgets containing estimates of the likelihood of self-destructive government activities or estimates of the likelihood that the government will be removed and replaced at a certain time in the future. The management of a state enterprise cannot, therefore, evaluate risk appropriately. The state company will always undervalue its assets and overvalue its estimates of future income.

FAILED MARKETING STRATEGY

Any plan to create a new entity must first discover what the resulting revenue will be. Only then is it worth spending the time and money to discover exactly how, and at what cost, the product or service can be produced. Marketing analysis precedes technical analysis. The last step, financial analysis, should be undertaken only when it is known that the necessary financial streams exist. In state projects the process has frequently been reversed: hypothetical financial scenarios are first analyzed; technical information about production is then sought; and at some point during the process a few casual and gross assumptions are made about the market for the output.

Marketing specialists use sophisticated analytical techniques to estimate the quality of product or service potential customers want, where they would like it delivered, the time or season of highest demand, the most wanted size and type of package, and approximately how much they are willing to pay for it. From all this the marketing analyst produces estimates of sales and revenue. Marketing is a combination of all management and economic skills, with specific emphasis on logistics. Not-for-profit or government activities particularly need the services of marketing specialists.

To the degree that existing state corporations have not used marketing analysis in a professional manner they are suspect. Because they will have only a vague idea of their customers' wishes, or how those wishes would surface if competitive alternatives existed, there is no guarantee that their product or service will be relevant to the private sector. Major rethinking will have to be undertaken before state entities are thrown out of the state cocoon and into the harsh world of customer choice.

THE MECHANICS OF PRIVATIZATION

Studying the transfer of state entities to the competitive private sector is a relatively new activity. The process by which new private enterprises are established can give some points of reference; much of what remains can be learned only from actual practice.

Once the decision to privatize a given state entity has been made, the next decision is whether to privatize the entity as a going concern or to write off its liabilities, liquidate its assets, and allow it to emerge again as a private-sector activity. The basic issue is quite simple: the product or service provided. If the output of the state entity can be better and more economical if provided by the competitive private sector, and there is no way that the company could possibly compete, then it is better for society and the government if the state entity is terminated and its assets put on the block.[30]

The rule dictating whether to sell or dismember is this: if estimates of the present value of future net cash flows are consistently negative under differing but realistic scenarios, the state entity should be shut down at once. Scenarios considered should contain objective estimates of future cash flows—both revenues and costs—over commercial time horizons and should use discount rates that truly reflect local scarcity of capital. For the moment reserve the issue of how to restructure a state entity for viability in the private sector and consider instead the problem of valuing the assets to be sold if the disposal option is selected.[31]

The following factors are particularly important in considering a state entity's disposal value:

1. The estimated local market value of the physical assets. (Historical cost will be of no help here, only real cash flows and therefore current market values.)

2. The net market value of financial assets.

3. Anticipated future obligations—both legal and implied—that will exist even if the state entity ceases to exist.

4. The recorded current liabilities (Accounts Payable, etc.).

5. Intangible obligations of the state entity, such as the vested interest of the
   various parties in its continued existence as a unit.

Simple techniques can be used to organize the information: pro forma
balance sheets, income statements, and other financial statements. For
a state entity, however, it will be necessary to include both liabilities
and assets not normally found in commercial analysis. Nonpecuniary
assets and liabilities will play a significant part in the outcome.

A potential demand for the output of a privatized state entity at viable
market prices makes a case for outright sale to private investors. It is
now time to restructure the company and create a new operating framework out of its existing assets. The first step in restructuring for sale to
the competitive private sector is to create a thorough catalogue and
realistic appraisal of existing assets and liabilities.

Appraisal of Existing Assets

Assets must be catalogued by someone having an intimate knowledge
of the local market and the history of the state entity. (As mentioned
earlier, there are individuals and groups within the state interested only
in protecting selected assets, and few state enterprises have maintained
appropriate records of their assets.) Once all the assets have been catalogued, they must be appraised at realistic market value by a professional with the necessary skills and knowledge. The appraiser must
represent the private sector, not the state or the particular entity to be
restructured. Above all, the state must be prepared to accept the valuation the market puts on the assets to be sold. Preconceptions abound
concerning the worth of assets acquired at significant cost but having
little market value in real terms.

Estimating the Full Cost of Disposal

Frequently those who have not been close to markets in which alternatives exist will be shocked at the cost to the government of disposing
of a state entity. It is never possible to shut down an ongoing enterprise
and walk away, but in the state sector the problem is compounded by
additional factors. Commitments remain with the ending of any enterprise; in the state sector they have a peculiar importance, including actual
and implied contracts with management and employees; commitments
to suppliers, contractors, and customers; and implicit commitments
emerging with the apportionment of net capital gains or losses.

Some actual implied contracts with the management and employees
of a state entity are explicit and quite usual; others, less so. A standard
responsibility would be the continuation of existing pensions plus ac-

ceptance of liability for any vested pension. Less obvious are those other elements of the total income received by state employees which may have become contractual through tradition and common usage. The fact that such implicit contracts have no legal standing is hardly significant if state income recipients can enforce their claims through political means.

Anticipated perquisites from working for the state (e.g., generous medical benefits, below-market loans for homes and cars, and other allowances) may have to be negotiated to avoid employee resistance to privatization. Similarly, the amount by which state salaries exceed market income for the same job description may represent a perceived claim on the state entity. The net present value of the anticipated future stream of such excess incomes over a given period is the appropriate measure of their value for negotiating purposes.

Even less obvious than other implicit contracts that the states must recognize are the strictly nonpecuniary rewards accruing to people not currently employees and whose positions may appear purely honorific or titular. Appointments to various boards and committees, although not salaried, carry the right to make real or implied judgments affecting the potential wealth of other stakeholders in the state entity. Many of these claims can be reconciled by the creation of similar positions elsewhere in the government sector. There will, however, remain those having to be bought out in some way if full cooperation in the privatization process is to be obtained.[32]

As a result of its past policies a state entity may have implicit contracts with suppliers, contractors, and customers. An implicit—or even legal—commitment may exist to continue buying from some given supplier at prices above the current market level. The commitment may be to buy a quality or quantity of input that creates a better-than-market return for the supplier. The timing and quantity of purchases may create economies of scale for a chosen supplier.

There may be commitment by the state entity to sell at favorable prices to certain groups—agricultural, industrial, or governmental—whereby the government is providing them a subsidy. With privatization the subsidy will have to be provided in some other way. Direct cash payments are the most efficient means, but if this is not acceptable, tax deductions or other indirect means will have to be employed.

Net capital gains or losses will result from the first stage of privatization because state entities do not maintain capital assets on their books at market value. It may not be possible to convert capital gains into cash flows that can be used to finance the new private-sector company. On the other hand, the state can usually write off capital losses if no cash outflow is required.

The state has no tax obligations to itself. Gross capital gains to the state are automatically net. Even though capital gains that occur because assets were previously undervalued on the books may generate no cash for possible distribution, political claims may arise. Just as in the process of setting up a state entity, wealth is transferred from the populace to favored groups—"socialist wealth"—so at liquidation other groups with influence may wish to capture any pool of perceived assets. This is a real problem. The solution lies in the process of financial restructuring. If the process of liquidation and re-creation is well planned and totally integrated, so as to ensure that the uses of specific funds are identified clearly and ahead of their appearance, the problem of apparent surpluses will not arise.

Sources and Timing of Cash Flows

The timing of anticipated cash flows is most important. Two factors must be considered in this respect: first, the timing, as well as the potential sources, of future credit needs; and second, the tax implications of the new private firm's chosen capital structure.

There are several advantages to credit received from government sources and international agencies. First, such funds have traditionally been available at below-market cost. This is true even for so-called hard loans whereby the cost, although commercial in name, is below what would be available on the basis of a given firm's own credit standing. Second, funds from official sources—such as the World Bank and various regional development banks[33]—are not subject to the same sense of urgency and commitment as funds borrowed from commercial sources. They carry a lower level of perceived risk because the threat of foreclosure is less. Governments, government entities, quasi-government entities, and, in a few cases, large corporate borrowers that have the blessing of the government are the initial recipients of official international loans.[34] This immediately means that the government's credit standing and implied coercive authority are involved. Political factors now enter into any negotiations about debt management problems, and governments have seldom been the first to foreclose and force a borrower into bankruptcy.

Due to the terms on which they are provided, most forms of official funding provide a competitive and operating advantage for the new firm. The disadvantages arise from the inevitable political intervention that will follow and the loss to society of competitive benefits—the fundamental reasons for privatization in the first place.

The timing of cash flows is important even without tax considerations. It may be possible to time some of the cash outflows to coincide with a return on investing the proceeds of the sale of assets. The usual government procedures of paying no interest on taxes withheld from personal or corporate income and delaying payments until the end of any payment period have set a useful precedent for managing the final cash transfers associated with the closure of a state entity.

The New Capital Structure

The financial structure of the new company will be determined by the best estimates of what has the greatest potential for survival and success in the competitive private sector. The complexity and size of the new company and the nature of the markets in which it will compete are important. What is financially feasible in creating the firm's capital structure will also be determined by the nature and state of local financial markets.[35]

As a first approximation of a desirable capital structure the state should sell equity and incur long-term debt in approximately the ratio that exists for similar companies already in operation. As the new company begins to operate and its equity stock changes hands several times, an appropriate capital structure will emerge as its own.

Capitalization is best handled by local private-sector financial agents. Commissions should be determined on the basis of the savings achieved in raising given quantities of funds, thereby providing incentives to minimize costs. There is no point in complaining that organized local financial markets do not exist in many of the less developed nations. The process of raising funds for privatization can be the means of recognizing the existence of unofficial financial markets and an incentive to permit the emergence of official ones. It provides an opportunity to create the missing organized financial structure.

Raising local funds offers scope for imagination. For example, shares of stock can be sold initially through retail stores if the denominations are sufficiently small, and major loans can be raised from private sources and from various forms of small savings accumulation if the hope of attractive returns is offered. Loans should be marketed in small units with sufficient guarantees for their security.

Finally, in the process of refinancing the role of the state enterprise's current employees and management should be minimized. If there is no other way of buying them out, it may be realistic to issue present stakeholders with shares in the new company. If the present employees are to share in the new company, they should be offered stock on the same terms as other citizens whose savings have gone to support the entity during the years it was in the state sector.

The actual process of financial restructuring is best handled by local businesspeople on a competitive basis. Large international accounting firms are well equipped to bid on refinancing jobs but poorly equipped actually to carry through if the money is to be raised locally. Government and international agencies should be kept out of the process, except as suppliers of funds. Managers of government agencies have conflicting goals, making it difficult to induce them to innovate and take risks at the local level. International and foreign aid agencies have a very poor record with any but the largest—and usually quasi-governmental—elements in the private sector. After decades of working through government officials and agencies they have lost their once recognized local knowledge, and are unlikely to be successful in helping to restructure for the private sector.

Implementing Financial Moves

Any means of ultimate funding will be easier, and the process of financial restructuring will cost less, if well-defined planning techniques are used from the start. Critical path method (CPM) and performance evaluation and review technique (PERT) are two forms of network analysis that are particularly appropriate for planning and control of a financial restructuring project. These techiques have traditionally been applied to physical construction or manufacturing projects; their application to financing projects is relatively new but most appropriate.[36] There is a tendency for financial planners to take account of the time value of money in every activity but their own. Wherever outside information is required, and whenever the skills of outside consultants must be used, there is a case for using some type of scheduling technique.

Preconditions for Ownership

If a financially restructured state entity is to be successful in the competitive private sector and truly separate from the government, assurance of ownership must be clear and definite. The new owners must have credible guarantees of the right to alter the product and its price as they see fit in reponse to competitive conditions, and freedom to restructure the new firm in any way they feel is appropriate. They must be able to change the nature of the new firm's activities, such as by ceasing some lines of activity and by using subcontractors. Above all the new owners must have the right to sell or shut down the firm if they so desire in the light of alternative investment opportunities.

Well-defined ownership is the single most important precondition for a market system to exist at any but superficial levels. In addition, government regulation and ownership are not separate issues; government regulation is an element of ownership. Regulation attenuates the right of the owners to use their property as they see fit. Therefore it reduces the value of ownership and lowers the price people are prepared to pay for privatized assets.

Although it is quite appropriate for the government to require pre-determined price and quality standards for the things it buys from the private sector, it is not appropriate to set those conditions for other customers. Similarly, it is appropriate for the government to require specific behavior of all producers in a particular industry, but it is most inappropriate to require and enforce such behavior for single firms or specific segments of an industry. The essence of a market system is the individual customer's right to choose his desired level of quality and risk, and the right of the producer to cater to customers' desires.

It has proved extremely difficult for government to relinquish control of state entities it is supposed to have sold, particularly when central governments are involved but also for local governments. Privatization requires that politicians and government officials relinquish assets valuable to their careers without any visible reward. It is only to be expected that they will try to retain control.[37] But continued regulation—or the mere creation of a private monopoly to replace a government one—does nothing to encourage people to be more productive. The sale of state monopolies complete with monopoly rights is nothing more than a revenue-raising action; it has nothing to do with the establishment of a free and competitive economic system.

Two more steps must be taken if the financially restructured state entity is to be successful as a competitive private firm: first, develop a business strategy that will convince potential investors that the firm has a future; and second, demonstrate clearly not only that the new firm has a sound capital structure but also that it can generate the short-run cash flows necessary for survival. This second point demands evidence that business risk has been fully considered.

Developing a Business Strategy

A business strategy requires that a firm understand and define its role explicitly. It requires a definition of the industry in which it will compete and a determination of the nature of existing and anticipated competition within the industry. A good strategic plan also requires examination of potential new entrants into the industry, possible substitute products that may emerge, and the role played by customers and suppliers in the life of a firm. A marketing strategy then becomes the key to implementing the plan.

Developing a strategic plan for a new firm demands data and information gathering and analysis, but the first step is to outline what will be required. There are professional strategic planners, but they are mainly creatures of the major corporations and unlikely to be of much help in working with privatization. Strategic planning requires a range of skills that cross the usual academic boundaries. The most fruitful approach is to read at least one standard work on the subject and then contact the American Management Association or almost any graduate school of management in the United States for help in finding the desired consulting assistance. This is not a job for amateurs; it requires skilled people with the capacity to work cooperatively with local businesses.[38]

Accounting for Risk

An estimate of risk must be brought into every business decision. In financial decisions I have argued earlier that risk is best taken account of by reducing estimates of future cash flows. There are technical reasons why raising discount rates—the usual alternative—leads to unduly pessimistic results. In situations of extreme political uncertainty it may be desirable to demand shorter payback periods as insurance, but in general the discounted cash flow (DCF) model produces the most realistic results.

The timing and regularity of cash flows determine the ability of the business to offset liabilities and assets on its balance sheet. Thus the pattern of cash flows largely determines the proportion in which the company will choose to issue debt and equity and the nature of its debt structure. On the one hand, when diversification of investment assets is difficult due to a lack of well-developed financial markets, both debt and equity will cost more. On the other hand, the same cost faces all business and does not affect the relative competitive position of a given firm.

Subjective estimates of risk must be left to the buyers and operators of the firm whom privatization has created. It is not for the seller to say what level of risk the buyer should perceive. Furthermore, there are no techniques that can substitute for the buyer's estimate of risk. In situations in which markets are not perfect and the flow of information is uneven, there is a clear advantage to the individual with local knowledge. This information differential is one of the key reasons for privatization. In competitive markets the individual with the best estimate of actual risk may be prepared to pay more for an asset than appears reasonable to the outside observer. We must be prepared to see unexpectedly high and low bids for the assets offered in the privatization process.

Marketing the New Firm

The government stands to gain in every respect by using expert financial and investment advice in marketing the newly restructured firm in the private sector. The type of expert advice and the type of financial marketing services needed will depend upon a series of considerations. First, is the sale to be by direct offering or not? Second, are equity sales to be restricted—for example, to domestic markets? Third, is there an existing network of efficient brokers? And fourth, are foreign brokers to be used for the placement of equity?

In the case of debt we should know that even relatively small firms can gain access to international capital markets thanks to the current globalization of finance. It is very important to have information about the alternative sources of debt; this information is available only from a relatively few brokers and bankers involved with state-of-the-art communications and the latest changes in the financial markets. Traditional bankers and placement brokers are not the best source of advice about finance for small to medium-sized firms.

CONCLUSIONS

The goals of those controlling the government determine whether or not privatization is a viable policy option. If their goals include rising national prosperity, national economic power, and an open competitive society, privatization will be attractive. If their goals include personal gain, personal power, and a controlled society, privatization will be anathema. Privatization transfers ownership—and therefore control—away from the state and into the hands of others. It is not possible to operate a closed society and an open economy.

Privatization has nothing to do with whether or not the poor have access to goods and services. Those who live by the public sector will always introduce equity to obscure the real issue. The real issue is between private (competitive) and public (noncompetitive) production. Who gets the output is a separate issue, an issue of public finance.[39] The question about privatization is a question of efficiency: can the competitive private sector produce a desired output at lower cost to society than the state sector? If the answer is yes, privatization should take place.

The process of privatization requires skills not normally found in the public sector. The first task is to conduct a thorough market study to determine if there is a demand for the output of the entity to be privatized, and hence a revenue stream. If there is a demand, the next step is to determine if the necessary supply can be generated in the private sector. If the supply can be created, it is worth undertaking the financial analysis. Marketing is the first step, technical analysis second, and financial analysis last.

When privatization is decided upon it becomes necessary financially to restructure the state entity. This is needed because of the nature of ownership—or the lack thereof—in the public sector. The basis of success in privatization, as in every other economic activity, lies in recognizing that the structure of ownership in society determines the pattern of incentives. Private ownership provides incentives for people to create wealth rather than merely concentrating on the distribution of what already exists. The illusion that an economic system can function without equity ownership is the basic difference between the successful and the unsuccessful nations.

The current wave of interest in privatization is an exciting step in the direction of a rapid escape from poverty through the use of the competitive free-market system. The process of implementation represents new ground for many nations to explore and will require serious study. But we now know the outcome of the major alternative economic systems—competitive markets versus various forms of state control—and the argument that less developed nations cannot afford free markets is a hideous distortion of the truth. They cannot afford the state entities that strangle their progress. Knowing this, it behooves people of sincere goodwill to recognize that privatization is not just a policy option. Privatization is a vital necessity for societies in which the escape from poverty is moving too slowly for decency.

NOTES

1. J. L. Simon, *The Ultimate Resource* (Princeton, N.J.: Princeton University Press, 1981).

2. Arbitrary rules and regulations are also a necessary but not a sufficient condition for a corrupt society. N. Sanchez, A. R. Waters, E. G. Furobotn, and S. Pejovich, eds., *The Economics of Property Rights* (Cambridge, Mass.: Ballinger, 1974), pp. 279–296.

3. The literature is now voluminous and encompasses most of the major journals in economics. A good point of departure is the first major survey of work in the field: E. G. Furubotn and S. Pejovich, "Property Rights and Economic Theory: A Survey Article," *Journal of Economic Literature* 10, no. 4 (December 1972): 1137–1162. Subsequent contributions of significance have been made by numerous others, including A. A. Alchian and H. Demsetz, "Production, Information Costs, and Economic Organization," *American Economic Review* 62, no. 5 (December 1972): 772–795; L. D'Alessi, "Managerial Tenure under Private and Government Ownership in the Electric Power Industry," *Journal of Political Economy* 84, no. 3 (May-June 1974): 645–653; idem, "The Economics of Property Rights: A Review of the Evidence," *Research in Law and Economics* 2 (1980): 1–47; M. W. Crain and A. Zardkoohi, "Public Sector Expansion: Stagnant Technology or Attenuated Property Rights," *Southern Economic Journal* 46, no. 4 (April 1980); S. H. Hanke, "The Privatization Debate: An Insider's View," *Cato Journal* 2, no. 3 (Winter 1982): 653–662; B. Klein, R. G. Crawford, and A. A. Alchian, "Vertical Integration, Appropriable Rents, and the Competitive Contracting Process," *Journal of Law and Economics* 12, no. 2 (October 1978): 279–326.

4. It has even been suggested that the right to increase the value of an asset and then capitalize on the result is the only proper definition of pluralistic capitalism.

5. For a clear, thorough, and readable technical argument, see R. C. Amacher, R. D. Tollison, and T. D. Willett, "A Menu of Distributional Considerations," in *The Economic Approach to Public Policy* (Ithaca, N.Y.: Cornell University Press, 1976).

6. This is easily seen if we recollect that cost—opportunity cost—must refer to the foregone alternative use of resources. This in turn requires that we rerun history and find out what the outcome would have been had we undertaken some other activity instead of the one we chose. The classic work on this is James M. Buchanan, *Cost and Choice, an Inquiry in Economic Theory* (Chicago: Markham, 1969).

7. We assume here that the reason for monopolization is not based in pure socialist faith but rather is the ad hoc answer to a demand for change in a particular situation. The range of alternatives is as broad as the ability of the human mind to conceive forms of business organization. The dividing line is the intervention of the law to retain the activity in the nonprivate sector. See R. C. Amacher et al., *The Economic Approach to Public Policy* (Ithaca, N.Y.: Cornell University Press, 1976).

8. Positive or scientific economics is particularly precise on this crucial point: "A first major element of the economic approach is the tendency of economists to look for mechanisms that harness self-interested behavior by individuals. This concern dates from the early classical economists, and its beginnings are usually associated with the work of Adam Smith (*The Wealth of Nations*). This view of individual motivation typically leads economists to give policy advice that emphasizes the manipulation of incentives rather than individual values." Amacher et al., "The Economic Policy Approach to Social Policy Questions: Some Methodological Perspectives," in *The Economic Approach to Public Policy*, p. 19.

9. The example is from A. A. Alchian and W. R. Allen, *University Economics*, 2d ed., (Belmont, Calif.: Wadsworth, 1968), p. 476.

10. For a rigorous technical discussion of the issue, see S. Cheung, "The Structure of a Contract and the Theory of a Non-Exclusive Resource," *Journal of Law and Economics*, 4, no. 1 (April 1970). For a more general discussion of the issue, see R. Staaf and F. Tannian, eds., *Externalities, Theoretical Dimensions of Political Economy* (New York: Dunellen, 1972).

11. The historical fashions in economic development are well discussed in I. M. D. Little, *Economic Development, Theory, Policy and International Relations* (New York, Basic Books, 1982), p. 111.

12. It is interesting to note that the ancient lighthouses that can be seen on the islands in the Red Sea were put there by charitable Arabs of old; they were abandoned by the governments that followed. It is also interesting that modern technology has made the lighthouse problem trivial by providing electronic communications and satellites enabling the producer of the service to monitor his or her property (the service) and charge for it if he or she chooses.

13. The creation of public goods has income and wealth distribution effects that can be properly analyzed only within a general equilibrium framework. Unfortunately much of the justification for the government undertaking partic-

ular productive activities is based upon partial equilibrium analysis, which fails to take account of the second-round effects. For a useful analysis of the theoretical basis for public goods, see M. B. Krauss and H. G. Johnson, *General Equilibrium Analysis, A Micro-Economic Text* (London: George Allen & Unwin, 1974), chap. 5, "The Theory of Public Goods."

14. The franchise option is well described in S. H. Hanke, *The Private Provision of Public Services and Infrastructure*, a report commissioned by the U.S. Agency for International Development (unpublished, 31 May 1984), pp. 16–24. The franchise option was proposed in E. Chadwick, "Results of Different Principles of Legislation and Administration in Europe; of Competition Within the Field, as Compared with Competition Within the Field, of Service," *Journal of the Statistical Society of London* (March 1959). The option was redeveloped and extended by H. Demsetz, "Why Regulate the Utilities?" *Journal of Law and Economics* 2, no. 1 (April 1968). The issue of effective competition is developed in O. E. Williamson, "Franchise Bidding for Natural Monopolies—in General and with Respect to CATV," *Bell Journal of Economics* 7, no. 1 (Spring 1976).

15. For example, cross-section or time-series regression studies that use as their reference points coefficients (parameters) derived from other locations or other times (or both) have serious methodological flaws. Descriptive case studies using simple and robust statistical techniques may be more significant and useful at this stage.

16. The best and most recent summary and compilation of work in this area is to be found in S. H. Hanke, "The Private Provision of Public Services and Infrastructure," a report submitted to the Agency for International Development, U.S. Department of State, (Washington, D.C., 31 May 1984), pp. 26–78.

17. Quite sophisticated analysis of survey and interview data is now possible with relatively limited-capacity microcomputers. For example, see C. Chase et al., *Solving Marketing Problems with Visicalc* (Quantitative topics from *Marketing Problem Solver* adapted for Visicalc on Apple II and IIe computers), (Radnor, Pa.: Chilton Book Company, 1984). At a much deeper level, see *NWA STATPAK, Multifunction Statistics Library*, Version 3.1 (Portland, Ore.: Northwest Analytical, Inc., 1984).

18. Given the constraints imposed by the state in the British Telecommunications sale, the retention of regulation and control by officials, and the government holding the "golden share," it is stretching things to talk of this as a true case of privatization. It is more a case of government revenue-raising by unusual means. But the policy and ramifications are of interest.

19. See for example "Britain's Successful Sale of State Owned Firms Sparks Denationalization Talk Around Europe," *The Wall Street Journal*, 18 December 1985, p. 39.

20. For an example of bold statements about impending actions, see "Europe for Sale: Why State-Owned Businesses Are on the Block," *Business Week*, 14 January 1985, pp. 28–31.

21. There are utilities throughout Europe (e.g., water supply in France, garbage collection in Switzerland, and various other activities) for which the private sector is still a provider of public services. The overall trend to the private sector alternative is, however, not gaining momentum. The literature on the subject is extensive. For representative works, see S. H. Hanke, "De la crise actuelle

en matiere de distribution d'eau urbaine," *Techniques et Sciences Municipales* (Janvier 1982); E. S. Savas, "Public vs. Private Refuse Collection: A Critical Review of the Evidence," *Journal of Urban Analysis* 6 (1979): 21–27.

22. Derived from Advisory Commission on Inter-governmental Relations, *The Challenge of Local Government Reorganization*, vol. 3 (Washington, D.C.: Government Printing Office, February 1974), appendix table 3-A.

23. For example, the Local Government Center of the Reason Foundation is dedicated to the process of privatization and offers seminars, publications, a directory of private service providers, and a data bank of all the public services that have been privatized by specific local governments across the country.

24. G. Roth (this volume) is the source of these quotations.

25. G. Roth, "The Overseas Experience," in *Urban Transit: The Private Challenge to Urban Transportation* (San Francisco: The Pacific Institute, 1985).

26. Ibid.

27. Roth, "Enterprise in Developing Countries: A Strategy for Economic Growth" (Paper delivered at the U.N. Conference on the Role of the Entrepreneur in Economic Development, 17 November 1984).

28. D. Wilson, "Privatization of Asia," *The Banker* (September 1984): 47. The quotation continues: "The great divide is between the American-influenced eastern fringe of Asia which looks up to Rockefeller and Henry Ford and the continental westerly areas which emerged from European imperialism seduced by Lasky and the Marxists. While the countries at the eastern edge—Japan, South Korea, Taiwan, Hong Kong and the five Asian Countries—have followed the road of free enterprise and private ownership, India, China, Burma, Vietnam and North Korea have followed the star of state-owned enterprise, central planning and even collective agriculture."

29. There is an extensive literature on the issue of capital budgeting during inflation. For a state-of-the-art approach, see D. R. Mehta, M. D. Curlee, and F. Hung-Gay, "Inflation, Cost of Capital, and Capital Budgeting Procedures," *Financial Management* 13, no. 4 (Winter 1984): 48–54.

30. The issue of using DCF techniques in evaluating projects in situations in which higher than usual levels of uncertainty prevail is discussed in J. E. Hodder and H. E. Riggs, "Pitfalls in Evaluating Risky Projects," *Harvard Business Review* 63, no. 1 (January-February 1985): 128–135.

31. President Hastings Banda of Malawi placed in receivership Spearhead Limited, a state conglomerate that had consistently lived off bank overdrafts. He instructed an accounting firm to sell the profitable parts of the operation and dispose of the rest as best they could. There are other examples from Somalia, Cameroon, and the Ivory Coast. See A. Rabushka, "Free Markets and Economic Development in Postwar Developing Countries" a report commissioned by the U.S. Agency for International Development, August 1983, pp. 124–126.

32. Only when a state entity is liquidated can we see the full cost to which the taxpayers were committed by the establishment of such concerns in the first place. The universal desire of political decision makers to give all associated with or employed by the state an above-average income lies at the heart of a problem that can no longer be avoided in the less developed nations. As with the repeal of the Corn Laws in England in the mid-nineteenth century, the

adjustment to economic reality may be less painful than political decision makers believe. There will, however, be an inevitable cost.

33. We should include the IMF as a development bank now that it has shifted to general-purpose loans for periods of up to ten years (called "structural adjustment loans") for balance-of-payments purposes.

34. The degree to which governments can raise loans is based upon their future tax revenues and not the worthiness of any particular project. It is also based upon their anticipated willingness to use those future tax revenues to fulfill their borrowing commitments.

35. Government officials will find it difficult to accept unorthodox methods of financing. This is another reason why they should be excluded from the refinancing process. Early discussions of the government approach to competitive financial markets in less developed countries can be found in A. Bottomly, *Factor Pricing and Economic Growth in Underdeveloped Rural Areas* (London: Crosby Lockwood and Son Ltd., 1971); and U. T. Wai, "Interest Rates Outside the Organized Money Markets of Underdeveloped Countries," *Staff Papers of the International Monetary Fund* 6 (1957–1985).

36. There are numerous excellent sources for network analysis. Software now exists in all the important formats. Among the good programs are *Milestone, A Project Management and Scheduling Program*, from Organic Software, Livermore, California; also *VisiSchedule*, from VisiCorp, San Jose, California *GANT-IT*, by A+ Software Inc., of Skaneateles, New York.

37. Government officials and politicians in the United Kingdom and Canada have been particularly tenacious in holding onto entities that have allegedly been privatized. In this regard, see A. Peacock, "Privatization in Perspective," *The Three Banks Review*, no. 114 (December 1984): 3–25. Also see "Selling State Fossils" and "Privatization in Britain," both in *The Economist*, 23 February 1985, pp. 11–12 and 76–78; and "National Freight Keeps on Trucking," *The Economist*, 23 February 1985, pp. 80–81. In addition, see T. Kierans, "Commercial Crowns, The Canadian Situation Calls for Privatization if Necessary But Not Necessarily Privatization," *Policy Options Politiques* 5, no. 6 (November/December 1984): 23–29.

38. The best book on the subject for our purposes is M. E. Porter, *Competitive Strategy, Techniques for Analyzing Industries and Competitors* (New York: The Free Press, 1980). In particular one should read the first forty-six pages before deciding what moves to make in seeking a consultant. Also, in the realm of starting new businesses it would be unwise to seek help elsewhere than in the United States. Europeans, for example, have proved particularly unsuccessful at this activity in recent history.

39. This argument is well made by S. H. Hanke in "Privatization: Theory, Evidence and Implementation," *Proceedings of the Academy of Political Science* 35, no. 4 (1985): 101–113.

II.   PRIVATIZATION: DOMESTIC ISSUES

4

ECOLOGY AND ENTERPRISE: TOWARD THE PRIVATE MANAGEMENT OF WILDLIFE RESOURCES

John Baden and Tom Blood

INTRODUCTION

The demand for environmental quality and environmental amenities is growing and will continue to grow. Political economists expect this movement; conservationists applaud it.

Those of us who were active participants in the great ecological awakening of the 1960s view the first Earth Day as a watershed in American history. Clearly appreciation for environmental values is a superior good; that is, demand for environmental quality increasing disproportionately with increases in income and wealth. Thus demands for environmental quality are analogous to those for gourmet foods, foreign travel, and opera. Unless increased centralized planning and the drift toward socialism reverses our economic progress, this continuing shift toward preferences for higher environmental quality is likely to be permanent. Failure to understand this fundamental fact plagued James Watt during his brief career as secretary of interior.

A new conservation movement is indeed emerging. This movement is based upon a coalition of conservationists, fiscal conservatives, and those who place a high value on individual freedom and responsibility. From the perspective of the New Resource Economics, the paradigm holding the intellectual high ground in scholarly circles—the Progressive Era of the later nineteenth and early twentieth centuries—was a noble but hopelessly naíve and fatally flawed effort at reform. It relied upon centralized planning and "scientific management." In contrast, the new conservation movement, known as "free market environmentalism," is based upon private property rights, the rule of willing consent, and the market process. In this paradigm the primary function of government is to define and defend property rights, provide a system of laws and courts for the adjudication of conflict, and deal only with those areas in which the market cannot currently work—areas such as air and water pollution, the regulation of migratory wildlife and other fugitive resources—and otherwise serve as a detached umpire.

Beginning with the Progressive Era, the United States has conducted a series of experiments involving governmental ownership management and/or control of resources. A hundred years of data are now in—the conclusion is clear, compelling, and irrefutable. The conclusion, most simply stated, is of tremendous importance: bureaucracies are run for the benefit of the bureaucrats in them. Bureaucratic entrepreneurs, special interest groups, and elected officials form an iron triangle intended to benefit this trio of interests. A direct result of this is an abused environment and assaulted taxpayers.

As a result of this ecologically perverse and economically inefficient system, Americans have been subsidizing the destruction of their environment through taxes coercively extracted. Only a masochist with a preference for poverty, misanthropes antithetical to the goals of St. Francis, and those who use ecology for an excuse for advancing socialist/fascist ideals can possibly support the current system. The litany of Forest Service deficit timber sales, Army Corps and Bureau of Reclamation dams that are environmentally destructive and economically inefficient, Bureau of Land Management (BLM) overgrazing, federally subsidized wildlife habitat destruction, compliments of the Department of Agriculture and the Department of the Interior, produce a chorus crying for reform.

The first rule of policy analysis is simply stated: Not all good things go together. The second has greater constructive utility: decisions are made on the basis of information and incentives. This provides a key for analyzing our current environmental problems and designing constructive reforms consistent with fiscal responsibility, conservation, and individual liberty.

The overwhelming preponderance of the officials in the resource administration agencies of the federal government are intelligent, well trained, and dedicated. The problem, most emphatically, is not one of bad people. Rather, it is one of institutions that systematically generate bad information and perverse incentives. These problems are inherent to socialized/collectivized organizations.

Given that the problem is not one of bad people, the council of perfection recommending replacing bad people with good ones is hopelessly naive. Rather, constructive reform sensitive to ecological and economic considerations must accept the fundamental realization that decisions are, in fact, made on the basis of information and incentives. In our few thousand years of recorded experience with human organizations, one fact stands out. At the national level no other mode of organization approaches the perfection of private property rights and the market process in efficiently coordinating and conserving resources. This system was eloquently described by Adam Smith and accepted by our founding fathers in drafting the U.S. Constitution.

We are witnessing the development of a new conservation movement, free market environmentalism. This movement's intellectual foundations become ever more secure as the record of governmental mismanagement demonstrates economic inefficiency compounded with environmental atrocities. The alternative conservation paradigm based on private property rights and the market process becomes ever more attractive to conservationists, fiscal conservatives, and those who support the traditional American values of individual freedom and responsibility.

Of all the challenges faced by the New Resource Economics, that of private wildlife management and habitat provision is commonly perceived as the most difficult. Both theory and data, however, strongly support the superiority of the new conservation movement—the movement based on private property rights, the rule of willing consent, and the market process. A brief overview of that problem is presented below.

PRIVATE MANAGEMENT OF WILDLIFE RESOURCES

People complain, and the legislature passes game laws, and nobody pays any attention to them after they are passed. Why? Because we insist on considering wild animals as our remote forefathers considered them, when men were scarce and wild animals were plenty. In a new country, the first settlers may properly have, not only liberty, but in some things license; license to till land anywhere, to cut wood anywhere, to shoot and trap game anywhere, to catch fish anywhere and in any way. All such things are then too plenty. As population increases, land and wood become PROPERTY. . . . This is the march of civilization.[1]

On farms and ranches across the country, wild animals and their habitat requirements conflict with crops and domestic livestock. In the Western states big game is a fugitive resource, ranging across state and federal grazing allotments and private farms and ranches. Both state and federal lands tend to be at higher elevations, whereas the valley floors and gentle slopes usually are privately owned. In general deer and elk summer at higher elevations and winter on private land at lower elevations. Further, given that nutritional needs are extremely high during late gestation and early lactation, spring grasses on lower slopes are especially important for wildlife. Thus in many regions private land is critical for wild game survival. In fact, it is estimated that 85% of the wildlife habitat that is economically feasible to improve is on private land, and 80% of the game harvested is on private land.[2]

The cause of the conflict can be stated quite simply. The majority of land is owned by private individuals and corporations and its associated wildlife is owned by the state. At present less than 4% of national hunting expenditures goes to private landowner/managers. Under current institutional arrangements, then, wildlife is usually a positive externality that is being produced by the landowners. It is no surprise that a recent survey in Colorado showed that 67% of the private land documented was posted against free hunting.[3]

In this chapter we will show how entrepreneurship and innovative contracts can be used to benefit wildlife, sportsmen, and landowners. We have found that by looking at these problems from a perspective focused upon the economics of property rights it is possible to go beyond current arrangements to find solutions that are more productive, efficient, and ecologically sound.

Two hundred years ago the government placed no restrictions on hunters and trappers; much wildlife had a negative value. Today many believe that the federal government must take an active role to protect wild game before hunters, trappers, and habitat modifiers destroy them all.

It is important to remember that wild game populations are subject to dynamic forces and evolve over generations, continually adapting to their environments. Forms of human organization are subject to analogous pressures and behavior and institutions change in response to changing relative scarcities and opportunities. All good things do not go together, so it is not surprising that there is often conflict and competition between wildlife and human action.

Even as pressures increase and as land use intensifies, it is possible for both human and wildlife well-being to improve. Examples of the conflicts that arise under current institutional arrangements will be presented to demonstrate that there are ways to resolve them in an ecologically and economically sound fashion.

ECOLOGY, ECONOMICS, AND INSTITUTIONAL EVOLUTION

There is little question that state regulation has been beneficial in maintaining many species of wildlife. Given relative scarcities, the fugitive and common pool character of goods, and existing technologies, such actions were appropriate. But because all these characteristics are in flux, new institutions are evolving. We hope to help advance this evolutionary process.

In many regions of America one problem associated with wildlife management is an overabundance of game relative to existing habitat. Another problem is that private landowners are subject to costs imposed by the states' wildlife; however, they are usually unable to capture the benefits. This is not because game animals have little or no value, but because existing institutional arrangements made it illegal or awkward for producers to capture wildlife values.

Although many people believe that wild game is a free good (aside from a small license fee for residents), it is not costless to produce. Cattle and elk compete for the same forage, and antelope and deer compete with sheep. To various degrees the feed spectrum of each of these animals overlaps each of the others. Thus there is a trade-off between wildlife and domestic stock. When a range operates at carrying capacity (i.e., at the margin), the opportunity cost of feeding one elk is .8 that of feeding a cow, and each deer or antelope displaces one sheep.[4] A sheep is worth from $35 to $55, but many hunters will pay several hundred dollars for one deer—and far more for a trophy buck. Obviously there are opportunities for increased efficiency in the joint production of wildlife and domestic livestock.

Current institutional arrangements inhibit moves toward a more highly valued mix of outputs.[5] When the state owns the wildlife, ranchers rarely benefit from managing their land to optimize the mix of wildlife habitat and feed for livestock. In most situations farmers and ranchers face the costs—negative externalities associated with the state's wildlife management practices—but they are unable to capture the benefits. Thus in accord with Demsetz and Anderson and Hill, we expect to develop innovative contractual arrangements leading to more efficient institutions.[6]

Such contracts would allow individuals to equate private and social marginal costs and benefits, whether it be between beekeepers and orchard owners and lighthouse operators and sailors or sportsmen and landowners. As the following examples demonstrate, these contracts increase efficiency, including that associated with conserving resources.

For years lighthouses were used as a classic example of a public good because they contain the following characteristics. First, once the lighthouse is constructed, the cost of providing services for one ship or one thousand ships is the same—that is, the marginal cost of providing lighthouse services to an additional ship is zero. Second, exclusion is virtually impossible. It would be extremely difficult and very costly to prevent a ship from benefiting from the lighthouse beacon.[7]

Due to public good characteristics, lighthouse construction and operation have typically been funded by tax dollars as a service to these vessels. In the British Isles, however, lighthouses have been privately built and operated. Contracts can be enforced because the ships sailing from port to port through waters protected by these lighthouses are required to pay a toll at their destination. This revenue is collected by customs agents and is transferred back to the lighthouse operators.

The benefits from this system are obvious. Not only are costs previously borne by society now paid by those who use the services (except customs official salaries), but one would expect lighthouse services to improve as lighthouse entrepreneurs become the residual claimants by identifying increased opportunities for gain—for both themselves and seagoing vessels.

Similar contractual arrangements have developed between beekeepers and orchard owners.[8] For practical reasons it is impossible for an orchard grower to prevent a hivekeeper's bees from gathering nectar from his orchard blossoms. Conversely, a bee owner cannot prevent his bees from gathering nectar without cross-pollinating the entire orchard. When these two positive externalities are combined and the marginal costs of pollinating and nectar gathering are summed, a market demand and supply curve develops. With this information the optimal hive quantity and price can theoretically be derived.

Although few beekeepers and orchard growers are economists, they have developed complex contractual arrangements whereby a carefully selected number of hives are strategically placed throughout the orchard to allow nectar gathering and pollination to occur. Rents are paid in either money or honey. Most important, property rights are established, and more honey and fruit are produced while human welfare is increased. Thus innovative contracts can push the production possibility frontier on a northeastern expansionary path.

For such contracts to evolve in the field of wildlife management institutional changes must also occur. There are both theoretical and empirical reasons to believe that opportunities exist to move the production possibility frontier of wildlife outward. Transferring property rights to wildlife from the state or federal governments to the landowner is expected to yield substantial improvement for certain species. It is our contention that efficiency will be enhanced and that wildlife and habitat will benefit from such arrangements.

There are, of course, cases in which this arrangement would be inappropriate. Migratory wildlife such as waterfowl certainly cannot be controlled by a single landowner. When dealing with such true common pool resources, governmental jurisdiction may be justified, at least until new technologies permit neoteric contractual arrangements to evolve. But in many cases property rights to wildlife can be easily defined. This is especially true when private landholdings are large, animal movement in those holdings is minimal, terrain is relatively open, and only small amounts of public land are available for hunting at zero user charge.

The following cases, which vary geographically from the northwest to the southeast and ecologically from coniferous forest to the grasslands, help illustrate the viability of private wildlife management.

NORTH CENTRAL MONTANA—SEMIARID GRASSLAND[9]

The first example can be found on two adjacent ranches in north-central Montana. One range is 6,500 acres and consists mostly of cultivated grain with some pasture and grassland. The topography of the land provides prime resting and holding areas for a herd of 350 to 400 mule deer. The other ranch is 10,000 deeded acres consisting of both cultivated and pasture land, with foothills on the upper margins where the productive farmlands rise into higher country. These foothills provide excellent holding habitat for a nonmigratory herd of 300 to 350 mule deer.

An outfitter in the area recognized an opportunity to use the deer herds for economic gain for himself and the landowners. He proposed that the three of them manage the deer herds to provide quality hunting for those willing to pay trespassing privileges. Both landowners considered the proposal and agreed to experiment. During the planning process, the outfitter agreed to allow hunters to shoot only certain deer, such as spike-horned bucks, three-point bucks, and does—only on predetermined occasions would hunters be allowed to bag a trophy buck. The landowners agreed to deny access to all hunters not booked with the outfitter.

The compensation plan was relatively simple. Hunters paid the outfitter for each day in the field; the price included transportation, meals, lodging, horses and guiding, and trespass privileges. In turn, the outfitter paid the landowners on a per-day basis for his trespassing privileges. The outfitter also agreed to be available when help was needed for such jobs as branding, haying, and rounding up.

The hunting program was designed to increase the proportion of four-point bucks, average antler sizes, and the average buck/doe ratio by culling certain classes of animals. Data gathered over the first five-year period indicate that these targets were realized.

This case indicates that wildlife was successfully converted into a commodity with a positive value. Not only was the outfitter paid for being the entrepreneurial middleman ($1,000 for a five-day hunt), but the landowners were compensated more than $400 for each trophy buck taken on their land.

The landowners realized other than monetary benefits as well. They now know who is on their property at all times, how long they will be there, and what game will be taken. It is the outfitter's responsibility to be certain that gates are left open or closed as directed and that no livestock are killed. Obviously the outfitter has a stake in minimizing the negative impact of the hunting expeditions, as he is faced with the long-run consequences of his actions. In addition, landowners have an automatic answer to anyone who wants to hunt on their property: The land is leased, please contact the outfitter.

Most important, the landowners began to manage the deer herds positively much as they manage other valuable assets. Where they had once rationally discounted the deer's importance, now they meet regularly with the outfitter to discuss deer herd management plans and optimal hunting procedures. The deer are no longer pests; they are a valuable resource worthy of the landowners' consideration in their overall stock/land management plan.

INTERNATIONAL PAPER—SOUTHERN YELLOW PINE[10]

International Paper (IP) is a giant in the paper industry, with approximately $5 billion in annual sales and seven million acres in land holdings. In this highly competitive forest product industry, IP has initiated and developed an extensive habitat management/lease-hunting program. At times IP actually suspends logging and other resource extraction activities in order to protect game habitat. Why? Simply because managing for the production of wildlife has become profitable for the corporation. Consequently timber and wildlife have become joint products.

IP began leasing land out for hunting in 1957 as a public relations gesture. At the time few deer roamed the area, and small game populations were also relatively low. Today the situation is quite different. Thriving populations of deer and other game and nongame species roam the 1.65 million acres that IP leases out for hunting. In 1982 average lease fees ran from 62¢ per acre for individual hunters to 83¢ per acre for hunting clubs. As the quality of the habitat and hence the hunting improved, fee revenues have increased accordingly. IP's income statement reveals that hunting leases have developed into one of the corporation's best products in terms of return on investment.

As a result IP has committed more acreage for the production of game and nongame species than has any state agency in the United States. However, obtaining information about IP's wildlife program has become extremely difficult since an upper-management turnover in late 1982. Current policy includes a ban on releasing any information about the lease program or the wildlife development program. IP is apparently attempting to protect its future returns as the lease-hunting program evolves from a semiprofit, positive public relations phase to a program oriented toward efficiency and protection of their research.

According to confidential company sources, the lease program is predictably becoming more sophisticated. IP constantly upgrades its computer simulations and refines cost-benefit analysis to optimize hunting habitat, conditions, and yields. Since the program's inception improved management has led to a doubling and even tripling of game populations on some leased tracts.

As the leased lands become increasingly productive, hunters have begun to criticize the condition of adjacent public land because of low game population densities, poor habitat management, trash dumping, and abuse by off-road vehicles.

ST. REGIS CORPORATION—HARDWOOD FORESTS[11]

St. Regis Corporation also experienced difficulties on their public access lands that were adjacent to the land they lease out for hunting. Hunters complain of overhunting, poaching, vehicle abuse, trash dumping, and, in some cases, even arson. As a result St. Regis may gradually include these lands in their own lease programs.

St. Regis initiated its wildlife program in 1956 in eastern Texas and, like IP, has successfully improved wildlife populations and habitat while maintaining timber production. To increase wildlife populations and improve habitat, the company established a wildlife department, which began making improvements by altering the shape and distribution of clearcuts, leaving crucial stands of deciduous trees for habitat, and establishing brush and timber zones between clearcuts and highways. The company makes some compromises during periods of intense timber demand, just as it suspends certain logging operations for the sake of wildlife. It is not that St. Regis managers have a preference for wildlife; rather, they are weighing marginal costs and benefits.

St. Regis has also set aside its 23,000-acre Brushy Creek tract, which lies in the heart of the company's leased Pineywoods region in Texas, for timber production, customer and guest hunting, and experimental game management. Forest management on Brushy Creek involves state-of-the-art technology and has become the testing ground for the company's newest developments in timber and wildlife production, including thirty-year pulpwood rotations, innovative clearcutting, site preparation and planning, protection of streamside management zones, and careful prescription burning. Security measurements, including occasional helicopter patrols, have been initiated to control illegal hunting. A study comparing deer on the Brushy Creek tract to those on adjacent public lands revealed that Brushy Creek deer had larger antlers and that the Brushy Creek tract supported a higher deer population than did the open-access public lands.

St. Regis has effectively incorporated the management of wildlife into its timber management program, generating profits, a quality environment, and positive public relations. Success is contagious, and in time we expect similar corporate programs to develop.

DESERET RANCH—SALT DESERT TO SUBALPINE FIR[12]

The Deseret Ranch is a 350,000-acre enterprise near Woodruff, Utah, that was consolidated by a sheepman in 1891 who wanted to control his winter sheep range. The ranch has evolved into much more than a sheep operation. Today Deseret manages for deer, elk, and moose in addition to sheep and cattle. Deseret's general manager, Greg Simonds, described the ranch as comparable to one Bureau of Land Management land district and having six ecosystems, ranging from salt desert to subalpine fir. Simonds said he is no better educated than the average BLM manager, and "most of the folks working under me aren't well-educated at all. However, we are operating under an entirely different incentive structure, and the numbers speak for themselves."

Even though full-time staff was reduced by 30% between 1968 and 1974, the following trends have emerged since 1978: (1) hay production per acre has more than doubled; (2) the Deseret cattle herd has increased from 4,000 to 9,000; and (3) the ranch produces 3% of Utah's total sheep output.

Certainly these statistics are impressive, but perhaps more surprising is the fact that the common livestock/wildlife conflicts have not arisen. Under the Deseret management system they are complementary joint products. Elk numbers have increased more than fourfold since 1978—from 350 to 1,600 animals. In 1978 an average Deseret buck deer had two points with a 14-inch antler spread. Today Deseret data indicates that a five-point buck with a 23-inch antler spread is the norm.

Simonds explained,

Many people think that this ranch has some sort of magical quality. Scientists have conducted research on our land in attempt to explain our success with abstract regressions and other formulas. But we have the same water, dirt, and grasses as public lands do. The people here are Deseret's highest and most valuable investment. The difference being that we are operating under different incentives, and therefore are encouraged to innovate.[13]

Deseret water run-off during the late 1970s, for instance, used to be muddy and sporatic, with flow usually terminating by mid-July. The ranch adopted a new cattle grazing system that encouraged intensive grazing before the cattle were rotated—similar to bison grazing on their natural range. Run-off now percolates through the root network rather than draining over the ground surface. Since the practice was initiated vegetation density has increased three- to fivefold, and the "water is clear and runs year-round," Simonds reported. According to one of the older ranch hands, water is running where none existed fifty years ago. Improved forage and water quality benefit the wildlife populations.

The BLM managers may be better educated, said Simonds, but they manage game by a different set of incentives or, more appropriately, pressures: namely, those generated by special interest groups. These programs are telling on game populations. Deseret's hunter success ratio has varied between 75% and 90% during the previous three seasons, fluctuating with the intensity of the previous winter. Hunter success ratios on public land, however, hover between 20% and 30%.

Simonds believes that although state game management agencies are becoming increasingly cooperative, the state should give landowners more control over wild game when property rights can be defined. "There are tight restrictions on what we can do," he said. "If they were removed, it would greatly improve our ability to accentuate game populations. We could economically justify monitoring winter range and improve it. Right now, someone else is providing winter range and we benefit from it."

Simonds would like to see contractual arrangements that give landowners more control and more certainty. "Deseret has proved that proper incentives can lead to responsible game management," Simonds concluded. "With more certainty and control, we could increase management quality and thoroughness to benefit both sportsmen and wild game."

CONCLUSION

We appear to be on the forefront of the development of landowners' property rights to wildlife. The current legal doctrine permits landowners to charge a trespass fee for hunting. On some Montana ranches in the 1984 hunting season, for example, this fee was graduated—that is, $X per day to trespass, $X + $Y to trespass and take an animal, and $X + $Y + $Z if the animal taken was of trophy quality.[14] If the landowners are permitted to charge the Y + Z components of this price, we have come close to recognizing private property rights in live wildlife.

Given genetic endowments, wildlife is a manmade resource; man is the primary influence on habitat. If wild animals have positive social value and if land is privately owned, then the owners must face incentives to manage for wildlife if efficiency is to be achieved. A system of private property rights will foster this objective.

It may be argued that such a system will only work for animals that have a severely limited home range, such as the white-tailed deer. It is, however, quite risky to bet against the contractual genius of entrepreneurs. One can learn a lot from observing nature—and lighthouses, and bees, and the contracts that unite them in theory.

NOTES

1. J. A. Tober, *Who Owns the Wildlife? The Political Economy of Conservation in Nineteenth-Century America* (Westport, Conn.: Greenwood Press, 1981), fronts-piece.

2. R. D. Teague, "Wildlife Enterprises on Private Land," *A Manual of Wildlife Conservation* (Denver: *Wildlife Conservation Manual Committee*, 1971), p. 140.

3. Ibid.

4. Animal forage is measured in AUMs, or animal unit months. The amount of forage required to carry a domestic beef cow and her calf is one AUM. Five domestic sheep equal one AUM. An elk equals .8 AUMs, and one deer or antelope equals one sheep or .2 AUMs.

5. We are now operating well within the production possibility frontier.

6. The literature on the evolution of property rights provides an explanation of the process of property rights definition in the area of American wildlife. Most simply, property rights develop when it becomes economical to implement institutions that internalize benefits and costs. Pejovich noted: "The creation and specification of property rights over scarce resource is endangerously de-termined. . . . Some important factors which govern changes in the content of property rights are asserted to be: technological innovations and the opening of new markets, changes in relative factor scarcities, and the behavior of the state." S. Pejovich, "Towards an Economic Theory of the Creation of Property Rights," *Review of Social Economy* 30 (1972): 309–325.

It is obvious that this perspective is applicable to wildlife in the developing economy of the United States. It is increasingly clear that establishing and pro-tecting property rights in wildlife is a production activity toward which resources are drawn. For a discussion of this process in the American West, see Garrett Hardin & John Baden (chapter 20 in *Managing the Commons* [San Francisco: W. H. Freeman, 1977]). A more general statement is Harold Demetz, "Toward a Theory of Property Rights," *American Economic Review* 57 (May 1967).

7. R. H. Coase, "The Lighthouse in Economics," *Journal of Law and Economics* 17 (October 1974): 357–76.

8. S.N.S. Cheung, "The Fable of the Bees: An Economic Investigation," *Journal of Law and Economics* 16 (April 1973): 11–33.

9. J. Baden, T. Blood, and S. Taylor, "Innovation, Incentives, and Posterity: Wildlife and the Entrepreneur" (Paper prepared for the Elk Management Sym-posium at Utah State University, 19–20 April 1984).

10. This case study was rewritten from a study presented in T. Blood and J. Baden, "Wildlife Habitat and Economic Institutions: Feast or Famine for Hunters and Game," *Western Wildlands* 10, no. 1 (Spring 1984).

11. Ibid.

12. Phone conversation with Greg Simonds, general manager of the Deseret

Ranch, 2 November 1984.

13. Ibid.

14. On at least one Gallatin Valley Ranch Z = \$400. This is obviously far below the market clearing price for 4+ bull elk.

5

PRIVATIZATION OF URBAN PUBLIC SERVICES

Cliff Atherton and Duane Windsor

INTRODUCTION

This chapter will discuss entrepreneurial opportunities associated with the privatization of local public services in urban areas of the Unitied States.[1] Although our focus will be on instances of successful privatization at the local level of government, we will draw on concepts and evidence from the larger literature as well. Entrepreneurs can be an important part of local privatization programs, but to function properly in their role they must understand the practical and theoretical complexities underlying privatization transactions.

A variety of circumstances support our emphasis upon privatization at the local level as a locus for potential entrepreneurial activity.

1. The motives underlying privatization activities at the local level differ significantly from those operating at the federal level.
2. The Gramm-Rudman-Hollings (1985 Balanced Budget and Emergency Deficit Control) Act imposes financial hardships on state and local governments which are different and more severe than those experienced by federal government agencies.
3. Policy concerns and expenditure patterns at the local level are considerably different from those at higher levels in the federal system.
4. The combined effects of policy devolution, fiscal austerity, and the "housekeeping" focus of local government create a positive attitude toward privatization at the local level.
5. There are close similarities between benefit taxation employed by local governments and full-cost pricing.

Privatization at the local level of government solves a problem that has two basic components. First is the fiscal austerity produced by the twin pressures of policy devolution and taxpayer resistance. Seeking funds for essential services and infrastructure, local government entities are increasingly looking to the business sector to provide investment capital and supply services. Questions arising in this component focus on profitability (through pricing or subsidy), contracting, and franchising. The second component, though more philosophical in character, is equally important. Officials have begun to reevaluate the proper role for private-public cooperation at the local level of government.

The term "privatization" needs some careful scrutiny before we proceed to an examination of theory, evidence, and cases. Privatization serves as a buzzword for the Reagan administration's policy of shrinking the federal government through sale of assets, policy devolution, and spin-off of activities to the private (business or nonprofit) sector.[2] The term has come to embrace contracting, vendor financing, and a variety of other specialized techniques. The broader question of private-public cooperation in the provision of services and infrastructure is vital to the functioning of local communities. Privatization has been used correctly to describe the full range of options by which we may increase private participation in the provision of urban services and in the development and maintenance of infrastructure. In adopting this definition we do not explicitly prejudge issues concerning the sale of public assets or the spin-off of public activities. We argue, instead, that a richer mosaic of private-public interaction is conceivable in part by differentiating the policy, financing, ownership, operation, and management aspects of public services. At the local level in particular these dimensions may be combinable in a multitude of ways.[3]

FACTORS FOSTERING PRIVATIZATION AT THE LOCAL GOVERNMENT LEVEL

There are significant differences between the underlying motives for privatization of public services at the local and at the federal level. We view the Reagan administration's broad strategy of privatization and deregulation (including sale of federal properties, spin-off of various activities such as Amtrak and Conrail to the business sector or social welfare programs to private charity, and devolution of domestic policy responsibility to the state-local level) as an element of political philosophy. The federal administration is ideologically oriented toward privatization, on the one hand, and toward reallocation of federal resources for defense activities on the other. Local concern with privatization is driven by fiscal austerity and by the resistance of taxpayers in the post-Proposition 13 environment to higher public expenditures. Local governments are caught in a fiscal squeeze between their taxpayers and falling federal grant assistance.

The Gramm-Rudman-Hollings Act may have differential effects on the state and local levels. This thesis is argued by Collender.[4] The automatic spending cuts ("sequestration") mandated by the statute for fiscal year 1987 may well fall more heavily on state and local interests than on other federal activities. Although the act calls for a uniform percentage cut across the board, with a 50–50 split between defense and nondefense programs, it also exempts almost half the budget and limits automatic reductions for another quarter. Most of the federal aid to state and local governments falls in the remaining quarter of the budget.

Policy concerns and expenditure patterns are considerably different among levels of the federal system. Local governments are in their service as distinct from their political functions,[5] best thought of as "housekeeping" units. They provide basic public services (police, fire, water, sewage, refuse collection, land use control, education, transit, parking) and basic community infrastructure (roadways, flood control, parks, utilities, stadiums). In addition, local governments are at the bottom of the pipeline for grant assistance funds from higher levels of the federal system. A major concern of local government is economic development (in the sense of the spatial location of economic activities and employment), which is at least partially dependent on public services and infrastructure. The latter, as illustrated by governmental assistance in various forms to canals, railroads, highways, and air transportation, has always been a critical factor in national economic growth.

The close similarities between benefit taxation and full-cost pricing should make the effects of privatization transactions less visible to local consumers. Generally local government's housekeeping activities occur in the allocation branch of the public budget. Stabilization and redistribution functions are carried out at the federal level. The latter may "flow down" to the local level through assistance programs. Housekeeping services, although not necessarily physical infrastructure as are roads, are very similar to commercial services. The distinction between ability to pay and benefit taxation fades away under these conditions. Under the former, tax liability is based on income and wealth. The ability-to-pay principle is prominent at the federal level in the personal and corporate income taxes. The local property tax may, under certain conditions, represent a price for services as distinct from a pure levy on wealth. It is not surprising that user charges are prominent at the local level, accounting for perhaps 15–20% of locally generated revenues. At the local level, we can focus readily on allocation activities suitable for direct, full-cost pricing and thus for privatization and deregulation.

Tocqueville concluded that the roots of American democracy lay in the local self-government and administrative decentralization.[6] In many respects the existing theory of local government is ill-defined. Local government is not mentioned in the U.S. Constitution, and it exists as a legal creature of the states based on our traditional political and administrative practices.[7] As a practical matter, democracy, business-government relations, and both political and administrative experience arise in large measures at the local level. It has been argued that "urban regimes" of local governance are dependent on a given city's business concerns. The late 1960s saw a diversion from that traditional pattern through federal fiscal assistance; the late 1970s may have precipitated a new "regime" due to fiscal austerity and subsequent federal concern for policy devolution.[8] In a broad sense, what must be judged at the local level in each city is the relative role of public bureaucracies and private (free or regulated) markets. The housekeeping activities of local government may be especially susceptible to a broad spectrum of private-public cooperation methods. Hospitals and schools, for example, are widely provided by the public, the nonprofit, and the business sectors as competitors.

THE EMPIRICAL EVIDENCE

There would be little point in discussing the merits of privatization without some evidence of practical success at the local level. However, one must proceed cautiously in this regard. As one critic has pointed out, much of the popular literature on privatization is theoretical at best (and ideological at worst) in touting the advantages of privatization.[9] Much of the message boils down to the presumption that government bureaucracies are inherently inferior to privately owned business enterprises. The privatization issue is much more complicated. A single hard and fast ideological rule is almost certainly meaningless. With this caveat in mind, we will first examine the results of the empirical studies.

Two basic summaries of the empirical literature are available in Borcherding et al.[10] and Bennett and Johnson.[11] The Borcherding study evaluates the evidence on the relative efficiency of private and public production in the United States, West Germany, Australia, Canada, and Switzerland. The other study looks at a variety of governmental activities in the United States. Both studies accept the use of unit production costs as an indication of the efficiency of organizations in providing services to customers. The Borcherding piece was prepared with knowledge of the Bennett and Johnson article.

Borcherding et al. examined more than fifty studies, which are classified and summarized, covering nineteen public activities.[12] "The findings in most of the studies are consistent with the notion that public firms have higher unit cost structures."[13] Only three studies found less costly public operations, and five found no difference.

The literature seems to indicate that (a) private production is cheaper than production in publicly owned and managed firms, and (b) given sufficient competition between public and private producers (and no discriminative regulations and subsidies), the differences in unit cost turn out to be insignificant.[14]

Bennett and Johnson reviewed empirical studies (with some overlap) of refuse collection, fire protection, debt collection, health care and hospital services, claims processing, ship repairs, electric utilities, and airlines. The evidence was generally in favor of significant cost reductions through privatization.

The literature reviewed by these two major studies includes analyses of some classic national experiments. The most significant experiments involved the operation in direct competition of transportation services by both a public and a private enterprise. In Australia domestic air service is restricted to a single private company and a single public authority. Both are constrained by public policy to compete on essentially equal grounds (fares, routes, equipment, contracts, etc.).[15] Operating under similar conditions, the private firm generates a profit through higher productivity per employee and lower labor costs. In Canada the public Canadian National Railroad and private Canadian Pacific Railroad compete directly.[16] No significant differences in cost and performance were found. It is likely that competition has forced the public railroad to utilize efficient production methods. In any case, the public entity exhibits no advantage over the private company. Nothing in this particular evidence implies that public enterprise cannot be efficient under competitive conditions. Both experiments seem to reinforce the expectation that both types of firms respond to competitive conditions with entrepreneurial innovation. However, the typical rationale for public production concerns natural monopoly, public goods, scale economies, and externalities—not competition.

There are a number of studies comparing private and public provision of municipal services, particularly in urban transportation, electric and water utilities, fire protection, and especially refuse collection. All are essentially housekeeping services provided largely at the local level in the United States. Borcherding cites three studies of water utilities which collectively examined at least 150 suppliers; public entities were found to be less productive and more expensive. Similar results have been found for the electric utility industry. It should be noted that private utilities are regulated by public commissions in terms of rates and costs.

Probably the classic success story at the local level is reported in Ahlbrandt's study of fire protection in Scottsdale, Arizona.[17] The Rural/Metro Corporation provides contract fire-fighting service for about 20% of Arizona and certain other areas. Based on data for Washington State, which correctly predicted Arizona costs, Ahlbrandt estimated the per capita cost for Scottsdale to be 48% of the average cost for similar 100,000-population cities. Cost was estimated as a function of population, area, fire insurance rating index, number of personnel, and other variables. Ahlbrandt's empirical study shows that a bureaucratic producer would cost $7.10 per capita as against the contract cost of $3.32 per capita. Scottsdale's fire insurance rating, a quality of service indication, was unaffected.

Although cost and performance are not readily available, there is an interesting contracting service in Harris County (Houston, Texas) for police patrol service. The county constables, who are currently independent of the sheriff's department, provide contract patrolling for neighborhood civic associations. Privatization of public services is a common device in Texas, as illustrated by contracting patrolling, municipal utility districts,[18] and substitution of deed restrictions (enforceable by private action in court) for municipal zoning.[19] Civic associations maintain boulevard landscaping, provide mosquito spraying, and handle other quasi-governmental services.

The most intensely studied local governmental function is refuse collection, in part because contracting and franchising have been common practices. At least three studies in St. Louis County, Missouri, and Minneapolis, Minnesota, found no significant cost difference between private contractors and municipal enterprises.[20] A study of 26 cities in Montana concluded that municipal suppliers were more efficient.[21] An equally impressive body of reports found private suppliers to be more cost-effective, including studies of cities in the Midwest,[22] Connecticut,[23] Canada,[24] Switzerland,[25] Fairfax County, Virginia,[26] and Monmouth County, New Jersey.[27] Estimates of higher costs for public operations ranged from 14% to 60%. An interesting finding in some of these studies was that private monopoly franchise (as distinct from competitive private contracting) was slightly more expensive than private nonfranchised collectors.[28] The Connecticut study, by contrast, concluded that in 101 cities private nonfranchised collection was 25% to 36% more costly than municipal collection, which in turn was 14% to 43% higher than private monopoly contract. Stevens found private competition 26% to 48% more costly than private contract monopoly in a sample of 340 firms.[29]

Critical for evaluation of the refuse collection example is the determination of cost comparability. In addition to organizational arrangement, at least four other factors probably affect the cost comparison. The first is variation in service conditions. Per unit or per capita average costs of collection may depend on population size and density, area, terrain, factor prices, weather, and a number of other influencing variables for which one must control (typically through multivariate regression analysis). Most studies tackle this problem directly. But clearly regression model misspecification, variable multicollinearity, or differences in interpretation may significantly affect the relative cost results.

The second factor is that cost data are not generally comparable between private and public entities or across political jurisdictions. Profit-oriented firms presumably incorporate all internal costs in their pricing. Municipal collection is usually organized on the basis of a budget-based agency rather than a full-cost recovery public enterprise. Because budget procedures vary widely in this regard, the agency's costs may well not be fully internalized. Kemper and Quigley calculated for their Connecticut sample that the Hartford fiscal year 1972–1973 budget underestimated true cost by 41% together with 2% to 3% in foregone property tax revenues (a measure of the opportunity cost of municipal collection).

Savas conducted a more detailed and systematic study, which found that for a sample of 68 cities, actual cost calculated using a standardized cost-accounting model exceeded budgeted cost by 30% on average with wide variation among cities.[30] Of this sample, 50 cities levied a user charge. For contract collection the charge was equal to calculated full cost; for municipal collection, calculated full cost exceeded the user charge by 26% on the average. The actual cost of refuse collection is substantially understated by nominal budget data that typically fail to include costs for vehicle purchase, operation, and maintenance; fringe benefits, including pension contributions and share of unfunded pension liabilities; for borrowed supplementary workers; garage and office facilities; foregone property taxes of municipally owned real estate; allocated administrative overhead costs; and self-insured liability claims and insurance premiums.

A third problem is that private firms must presumably generate an after-tax profit that is determined in part by tax code definitions of revenue, deductions, and credits and depreciation of assets. Municipal collection is not on the same economic or accounting basis.

Finally, scale economies may be improperly defined. Cost calculations for bureaucracies are made within the context of fixed political jurisdictions not adopted on any grounds of economic efficiency. Therefore we are comparing actual (budgetary) rather than "engineering" costs. Whether the results would be affected by varying jurisdictional boundaries is unknown. Private firms are not necessarily constrained and may operate across existing boundaries.

After controlling for these various factors, what is the relative cost efficiency of the organizational alternatives? The set of alternatives includes public enterprise or agency (the two devices are not necessarily the same, but this distinction has not been made in the literature), private competitive contracting (to a public agency), private unregulated competition (firms and customers contract directly as is typically the case for commercial and industrial as distinct from residential collection), and private monopoly franchise. The organizational alternatives at the local level across the broad range of housekeeping activities is quite complicated. In refuse collection the empirical evidence comparing monopoly franchise to competitive contracting is mixed. Studies generally have not differentiated between public agencies and public enterprises. It is not immediately clear why the latter should not function like private monopoly franchises considering that both will be confronted with "fair" pricing issues as distinct from unregulated profit maximization.

THEORY AND PRACTICE OF PRIVATIZATION

The empirical evidence on privatization of urban public services yields conflicting results, due in part to methodological difficulties. But there certainly are studies that find significant cost and performance advantages in privatization. At a minimum there is no consistent finding in favor of public-sector superiority that is, in our view, the critical test. Consequently we interpret the empirical evidence as favoring privatization when privatization is defined in broad organizational terms to include relatively unregulated private firms operating in competitive or oligopolistic markets, regulated public utilities, private competitive contracting, or a private monopoly franchise in lieu of provision by a public agency or a public enterprise.

To tackle the theory and practice of privatization at the local level, we will concentrate on mass transit.[31] This industry has several significant features. It has switched organizational structure from locally regulated utilities (prior to the 1964 Urban Mass Transportation Act) to public authorities receiving federal capital and operating subsidies. It faces incentives from a growing federal devolution and state-local fiscal austerity to both innovate and privatize its operations and its financing activities.[32]

The 1964 UMT Act contains provisions (sections 3(e) and 8(e)) that stress the importance of private participation service delivery. Some interesting experiments have taken place around the country in both regards. The Houston Transportation Authority has contracted with private parties for both bus maintenance services and turnkey park-and-ride lots. The Tulsa Authority has contracted with ATE Management Company for the provision of managerial personnel. Special assessment district financing has been used to build the downtown circulation component of the Miami-Dade County rail system. Joint development of rail stations is gradually being considered more widely throughout the country. A French firm has received a franchise from Orlando County, Florida, to build and operate a twelve-mile light-rail system. Dallas is planning to contract all its bus services (supported by a 1¢ sales tax and bonding authority) based on the success of its contract suburban express bus services. Private buses carry 5,000 commuters to Chicago (on a subscription club basis) and 100,000 to New York City (through chartered carriers).[33]

There have been two private proposals for a sixteen-mile rail line from Dulles Airport to the Washington, D.C., subway.[34] It has been reported that some transit authorities are saving 20% to 60% by contracting for bus and paratransit services.[35] A private contractor took over an unprofitable public bus line in Portsmouth, Virginia, and operated it for half the cost previously incurred by Tidewater District Transportation Commission.[36] Tidewater also replaced suburban subscription bus service with subsidized private taxis and vans operating at lower cost. Enterprise Transit Corporation of Paramus, New Jersey, competes at higher prices with New Jersey Transit by using small buses to eliminate transfers and offering various amenities such as the morning paper.[37] In Westchester County, New York, the private Liberty Lines Transit, Inc., operates at $3.18 per mile compared to Nassau County's public bus authority at $4.09 per mile. Recent experience with delivery of transit services by private operators is probably greatest in the paratransit (taxis, vanpooling, special services)[38] and express bus areas.[39] Privatization of urban transportation services is more advanced in cities of developing countries, although service conditions and performance standards are clearly quite different.[40]

The decision to incorporate privatization in the delivery of local services should be separated into its political and economic dimensions. The economic dimension focuses on the relatively productive efficiency of different forms of organization. In addition, these organizational forms will behave differently as market conditions vary. Private firms operating in oligopolistic markets may be no more efficient than bureaucracies. The political dimension is concerned with the level of private-public cooperation in a decentralized social system.

The standard theoretical explanation for public provision of transit services draws on the economic concepts of public goods, natural monopoly, scale economies, and externalities—together with the conceptually different question of the city-shaping efforts of rail investments. Because these concepts are generally used in the analysis of public services and infrastructure, we can examine their application to the transit situation as a case illustration.

Transit is not a natural monopoly; in a broad sense it faces competing modes such as the auto (64% of 1980 urban work trips) and paratransit (20%). Transit obtained only 6% of 1980 trips.[41] It may exhibit monopoly characteristics in the narrowest sense that mass transit is widely delivered by a single public agency in each urban area; but bus services are probably divisible. The same data vitiate the expectations that transit significantly reduces congestion, pollution, or energy consumption or that city land use and travel patterns can be dramatically reshaped. Transit is ~~not a classic public good~~. Although the marginal cost of an additional rider on a given vehicle is essentially zero, price exclusion is feasible. Fare recovery is only about 39% of operating costs due to subsidy arguments. It is not even clear that large rail or bus systems achieve lower unit costs due to scale economies. They may, in fact, generate diseconomies due to unionized labor, bureaucratic management, large vehicles, and fixed assets.

As a broad generalization, regulated utilities were driven into the public sector by auto competition and the availability of subsidy under the 1964 UMT Act. Operating deficits have risen steadily over the last two decades. The justification for continuing subsidies of public entities has become a vague rationale of "balanced transportation" and mobility for specific transit-dependent populations. This rationale has a political rather than an economic basis. It does not address whether alternative organizational arrangements might provide better services[42] or whether alternative subsidy schemes might better help transit-dependent populations.

The literature addresses the theoretical issues of privatization from two perspectives. First, it is argued that a market containing competing suppliers is likely to be more efficient than on containing a monopolist. This is a market structure argument, and Canadian railroad and other examples provide it with empirical support. A second argument is that public bureaucracies involve weaker incentives for managerial performance than private firms. "Unless the public sector producer is directly rewarded for using the least cost production techniques, he will not automatically be motivated to do so."[43] This is an organizational form argument. Both the market structure and organizational form arguments are incorporated implicitly when the theoretical performance of a government-owned monopolist is compared with that of an industry populated by competing privately owned firms. The application of this theoretical literature is flawed.

With regard to the market structure argument, most real markets are populated by private firms engaged in oligopolistic rather than perfect competition. Oligopoly has been addressed only through what has been described as an oral tradition despite a long history of formal modeling of duopoly and oligopoly dating from Cournot.[44] There is simply no unified analytical theory of oligopoly; there is only a variety of models that are not used for the study of real markets.

From the empirical evidence we know that market structure is a critical determinant of the performance of government bureaucracies relative to that of private firms. In fact, Borcherding et al. argued that the presence of competition was more important than organizational form. The

Canadian railroad and the Australian airline examples provide support for this proposition.

The organizational form argument focuses on the lack of incentives for managers in the public bureaucracy to reduce costs. The cost-reducing efforts that are adopted as a standard for comparison are those found in the owner-controlled firm. We find two flaws in Borcherding et al.'s evaluation. First, most real firms are manager-controlled firms. An entire body of literature called *agency theory* has arisen to address the incentive structure faced by managers in the manager-controlled firm. Second, in our review of the evidence on the economic performance of producers of local government services, it was clear that a wide variety of organizational alternatives are being employed. This complexity has quite simply been given short shrift in the theoretical literature, and importance of organizational form clearly cannot be concluded from field data that have not controlled for it.

The issue of organizational form also introduces contracting activity. Agency theory is an example of a contracting problem, but its focus is much narrower than the broad range of problems encountered by all contracting theory. The development of a specialized organizational form will involve legal, administrative, and political facets of the contracting problem. Contracting activities will include negotiation, specification, and monitoring of a set of private rules that will govern the behavior of a number of parties. An implicit assumption in most of the economics literature is that contracting is a mere technical appendage. Both legal theory and field experience demonstrate otherwise. Our own studies of privatization in the mass transit industry showed that the contracting requirements presented the greatest challenge to the success of many privatization activities.

THE ROLE OF THE ENTREPRENEUR IN PRIVATIZATION TRANSACTIONS

The real issue in evaluating privatization transactions is not whether a private firm can handle some activity better than government. Instead, the question is whether the private firm is markedly inferior to government in that activity. Whenever circumstances allow a market to develop and persist, the philosophical presumption in economic theory, social tradition, and political experience is in favor of competing privately owned firms. This philosophical presumption creates a favorable environment for entrepreneurs as long as no major obstacles are present in the market. We have already discussed a number of factors that currently impinge upon local governments and provide them with a positive predisposition toward privatization. There can be little question that opportunities currently exist for entrepreneurial efforts to remove economic activities at the local level from the public sector to the private.

However, it is crucial that the entrepreneur act as an initiator, as an agent of change in the privatization process. Initiators must both investigate opportunities and become pliable negotiators, identifying opportunities to reduce costs or to increase demand without dramatically reducing quality or increasing unit prices, and communicating with government officials whose objectives and constraints may be quite different from those of the business world. Consequently the entrepreneur's initial role is one of convincing government officials of the feasibility and desirability of privatization transaction.

Government officials are not likely to identify privatization opportunities and make available the information necessary to evaluate them. Government officials may be motivated to support privatization in principle, but they may be ill-prepared to foster its implementation because primary knowledge about activities amenable to privatization resides in the very employees whose jobs could be eliminated by it.

To evaluate the profit potential of a privatization transaction, the entrepreneur must evaluate the current and potential demand for the service or product, analyze the cost structure of existing producers and technologies, and consider the relationship of demand and production to potential organizational forms.

Although identification of opportunity may not be unusual for the entrepreneur, the process of presenting the idea to government officials will be very different from presenting a business proposal to potential investors. Certainly the entrepreneur, in striking a bargain with local officials, must preserve the profit potential of the venture by securing control over the major variables that affect profitability. However, in the presentation the entrepreneur must ensure that the plan also is fair to the customer/constituents and politically acceptable to government officials. Perceived fairness has as much political significance as genuine fairness.

In negotiating a contract with the local government, the entrepreneur must be flexible because political circumstances may arise that make it impossible for government officials to compromise on individual issues. Political pressures make the negotiations different from those between private businesses whose concerns are primarily economic. Government officials will have multiple objectives, both economic and noneconomic, may be influenced by short-term considerations, and may have hidden agendas.

The review of the theoretical analysis of privatization cited two major defects: first, an unrealistic definition of market conditions, and second, a failure to consider adequately the relationship between organizational form and performance. Our review of the experience with privatization identified two potential sources of superior performance by private firms: the presence of competition and a management incentive structure that encourages cost savings. First, given that entrepreneurial firms tend to be owner controlled, the incentives of the management team will not present obstacles to reducing costs of production. Second, proper attention to market characteristics, the organizational form of the private firms, and the governing rules allow one to structure the revised industry so that competition provides adequate discipline of the participating private firms. In the absence of competition, a set of rules can be established to govern performance.

Privatization presents entrepreneurs with unusual opportunities to enhance the venture's chances of success. A privatization transaction redefines market conditions and creates a new organization that will operate under new conditions. In developing a business plan to pursue a privatization objective, the assumed market conditions and organization form are essential for the projected success of the venture. At the planning and negotiation stage of a privatization transaction, the entrepreneur can shape the operating rules for the market and can fashion an organization that meshes readily with those market conditions. Similar opportunities to affect the success of a venture will be found in few other circumstances.

Obviously time and experience will judge the viability to privatization as a means of reorganizing the production of services at the local government level. The entrepreneur can function as an important change agent in the transfer of services from the public to the private sector and, by attending to the factors we have cited, can play an important role in the ultimate success of privatization.

SUMMARY AND CONCLUSIONS

This chapter has reviewed the literature on privatization of urban public services in the United States. Our objective has been to evaluate the role of the entrepreneur in the privatization process. We have taken a broad view of privatization, defining it as any steps that move away from exclusively public ownership and operation of services or infrastructure. Service contracts, franchise arrangements, joint ventures, sale and leaseback arrangements, and operating leases all qualify as privatization under our definition.

There exists a privatization debate in the true sense of the word, with valid arguments for and against the transfer of economic activity from the public to the private sector. Privatization is a movement that originated in political ideology and fiscal austerity, and the literature and field experiments inevitably reflect its origins. Privatization involves complex economic (efficiency), political (equity and business-government relations), and managerial (performance) issues. Whenever circumstances allow a market to persist, the philosophical presumption in economic theory, social tradition, and political experience is in favor of competing privately owned enterprises. The key question is not whether business can do it better, but why government should be involved. We believe that this question implies the appropriate standard to be applied in evaluating privatization opportunities: economic activity should be performed by private businesses unless, from an efficiency standpoint, private provision is markedly inferior to provision by a government entity.

For several reasons the urban level of government is a particularly rich locus for privatization activities. First, at the local level one encounters motives to consider privatization that differ from those found at the federal level. Second, federal deficit reductions may have differential effects at the local level. Third, policy concerns and expenditure patterns are different at the local level, where the focus is on housekeeping activities. Fourth, American cities are currently engaged in considerable experimentation with privatization. Finally, there are important similarities between benefit taxation and full-cost pricing.

Much of the available evidence that compares private provision with public provision of a variety of urban services clearly supports mixed conclusions. Much of the confusion stems from methodological problems. Empirical studies have not differentiated very well the broad range of organizational alternatives that must be compared and evaluated. The empirical studies also need to control for a variety of other variables, such as differences in accounting practices and the role of scale economies, especially as affected by political boundaries. Both types of variables will affect conclusions regarding the efficiency of either public or private provision.

The studies do show two variables to be important. The presence of a private competitor results in lower costs and prices for government providers. The use of an organizational form that incorporates incentives for managers to cut costs, a category that does not include the government bureaucracy, also is important. From the existing empirical evidence, it is unclear which of the two is most important. However, it is clear that privatization opportunities that take advantage of both of these variables should result in economic benefits for all concerned.

We have argued that the theoretical literature is of little help in resolving the privatization debate or in identifying a role for entrepreneurs. In the case of functioning markets, competitive pressures and managerial incentives may encourage private enterprises to outperform a public enterprise or agency. The usual rationale for public provision lies in concepts of public goods, natural monopoly, scale economies, and externalities. We used the transit industry as a case study to illustrate these concepts and found that it qualified under none of them as an industry in which government provision is appropriate. In our analysis of the economy as a whole, we find few industries that are populated by owner-controlled firms engaged in perfect competition, which theory clearly demonstrates is superior to government provision. Also, we find that theory treats contracting—in our opinion the most critical dimension of privatization—as a mere technical appendage, a problem that will solve itself once the parties understand their respective economic interests.

Several factors imply the entrepreneur must act as an initiator, an agent of change.

1. Government officials may be limited in their ability to identify opportunities and make available the information necessary to evaluate them.

2. Political factors make negotiating with government decision makers different from negotiating with businessmen.

3. The entrepreneur's efforts should be positively received given that privatization through the use of entrepreneurial firms will ensure the presence of the two major sources of superior economic performance by private firms: competition and a management incentive structure that encourages cost reduction.

4. Finally, the contracting phase of a privatization transaction presents entrepreneurs with the unique opportunities to affect (and possibly to effect) their own destinies by shaping the conditions under which they will operate.

The privatization debate clearly has ideological overtones. However, there is a much larger agenda at stake. Some 50% of public output in the United States and Canada is probably contracted to private producers.[45] At stake is whether the various forms of privatization might reduce service costs while providing better services through entrepreneurial innovations. No one should ignore the fact that there have been some failures in the privatization effort.[46]

Resolution of the debate would be facilitated by the conceptual separation of policy, financing, ownership, operation, and management. Many combinations of these dimensions are possible, and the academic literature provides no conclusive guidance as to the best way to combine them. Because of the state of economic theory, the empirical evidence plays a more important role. Regarding the impact of these five dimensions on competition and managerial incentives, one can draw some positive inferences. These inferences, when combined with the political pressures bearing upon local government officials, create a strong case in favor of entrepreneurial innovation through privatization.

Until the theoretical and empirical deficiencies are resolved, local officials will be unable to rely on academic results to determine the appropriate course of action in a specific fact situation. Consequently the debate will be resolved through experimentation and experience rather than a theoretical breakthrough. The problem is more amenable to an engineering than a laboratory solution. Officials will have to develop workable contracts with entrepreneurs rather than optimal arrangements. In negotiating privatization agreements political considerations may frequently arise in conflict with so-called pure economic considerations. When they do, entrepreneurs need to yield to the political considerations in order to negotiate a contract successfully. If this sounds like a "half-a-loaf" theory of privatization and entrepreneurship, it is better than the "big loaf" theory (exclusive government provision) or the "sweet roll" theory (perfect competition among owner-controlled firms).

NOTES

1. See W. J. Baumol, "Urban Services: Interactions of Public and Private Decisions," in H. G. Schaller, ed., *Public Expenditure Decisions in the Urban Community* (Washington, D.C.: Resources for the Future, 1963), pp. 1–18; D. M. Pinderhughes and L. F. Williams, "Urban Government Policy," in S. S. Nagel, ed., *Encyclopedia of Policy Studies* (New York: Marcel Dekker, 1983), pp. 246–265; and W. Z. Hirsch, "The Supply of Urban Public Services," in H. S. Perloff and L. Wingo, Jr., eds., *Issues in Urban Economics* (Baltimore: Johns Hopkins University Press, 1968).

2. D. Russakoff, "Deficit Worries Bolster New Push for 'Privatization,' " *The Washington Post*, (13 January 1986).

3. This argument is developed further in C. Atherton and D. Windsor, "Privatization of Public Services: A Model Applied to Urban Transit" Journal of Private Enterprise Vol. 2 (Fall, 1986) pp. 116–122.

4. S. E. Collender, "Gramm-Rudman-Hollings: Fiscal Armageddon for State and Local Governments," in *Public Sector Review* (Washington, D.C.: Touche Ross, January 1986).

5. This distinction between the service and political functions of local government is made in E. C. Banfield and J. Q. Wilson, *City Politics* (Cambridge: Harvard University Press, 1963).

6. A. de Tocqueville, *Democracy in America* (1835).

7. See the discussion in D. Windsor and F. J. James, "Breaking the Invisible Wall: Fiscal Reform and Municipal Land Use Regulation," in L. H. Masotti and R. Lineberry, eds., *Urban Problems and Public Policy* (Lexington, Mass.: Lexington Books, 1975), pp. 87–105.

8. S. L. Elkin, "Twentieth-Century Urban Regimes," *Journal of Urban Affairs* 7, no. 2 (Spring 1985): 11–28.

9. H. Henderson, "Can Business Do It Better?" *Planning* 51, no. 11 (November 1985): 12–21.

10. T. E. Borcherding et al., "Comparing the Efficiency of Private and Public Production: The Evidence from Five Countries," *Zeitschrift für Nationalokonomie/Journal of Economics*, suppl. 2 (1982): 127–156.

11. J. T. Bennett and M. H. Johnson, "Tax Reduction without Sacrifice: Private-Sector Production of Public Services," *Public Finance Quarterly* 8, no. 4 (October 1980): 363–396.

12. Borcherding et al., "Comparing the Efficiency," Table 1, pp. 130–133. The activities include airlines, banks, buses, cleaning, debt collection, electric utilities, fire protection, forestry, hospitals, housing, insurance claims processing, insurance sales/servicing, ocean tanker repair, railroads, refuse collection, savings and loans, slaughterhouses, water utilities, and weather forecasting.

13. Ibid., p. 134.

14. Ibid., p. 136.

15. D. G. Davies, "The Efficiency of Public versus Private Firms: The Case of Australia's Two Airlines," *Journal of Law and Economics* 14, no. 1 (April 1971): 149–165; "Property Rights and Economic Efficiency: The Australian Airlines Revisited," *Journal of Law and Economics* 20, no. 1 (April 1977): 223–226.

16. D. W. Caves and L. R. Christensen, "The Relative Efficiency of Public and Private Firms in a Competitive Environment: The Case of Canadian Railroads," *Journal of Political Economy* 88, no. 5 (October 1980): 958–976.

17. R. S. Ahlbrandt, "Efficiency in the Provision of Fire Services," *Public Choice* 16 (Fall 1973): 1–15; "Implications of Contracting for Public Service," *Urban Affairs Quarterly* 9, no. 3 (March 1974): 337–358.

18. R. E. Peiser, "The Economics of Municipal Utility Districts for Land Development," *Land Economics* 59, no. 1 (February 1983): 43–57.

19. See B. H. Siegan, *Land Use without Zoning* (Lexington, Mass.: Lexington, Books, 1972).

20. J. N. Collins and B. T. Downes, "The Effect of Size on the Provision of Public Services: The Case of Solid Waste Collection in Smaller Cities," *Urban Affairs Quarterly* 12, no. 3 (March 1977): 333–347; W. Z. Hirsch, "Cost Functions of Urban Government Services: Refuse Collection," *Review of Economics and Statistics* 47, no. 1 (February 1965): 87–92; E. S. Savas, "An Empirical Study of Competition in Municipal Service Delivery," *Public Administration Review* 37, no. 6 (November/December 1977): 717–724.

21. W. J. Pier, R. B. Vernon, and J. H. Wicks, "An Empirical Comparison of Government and Private Production Efficiency," *National Tax Journal* 27, no. 4 (December 1974): 653–656.

22. W. M. Petrovic and B. L. Jaffee, "Aspects of the Generation and Collection of Household Refuse in Urban Areas" (mimeo, Bloomington: Indiana University, 1977), cited in Borcherding et al., "Comparing the Efficiency."

23. P. Kemper and J. M. Quigley, *The Economics of Refuse Collection* (Cambridge, Mass.: Ballinger, 1976).

24. H. M. Kitchen, "A Statistical Estimation of an Operating Cost Function for Municipal Refuse Collection," *Public Finance Quarterly* 4, no. 1 (January 1976): 56–76.

25. W. W. Pommerehne and B. S. Frey, "Public Versus Private Production Efficiency in Switzerland: A Theoretical and Empirical Comparison," in V. Ostrom and F. P. Bish, eds., *Comparing Urban Service Delivery Systems* (Beverly Hills, Calif.: Sage Publications, 1977), pp. 221–241.

26. J. T. Bennett and M. H. Johnson, "Public versus Private Provision of Col-

lective Goods and Services: Garbage Collection Revisited," *Public Choice* 34, no. 1 (1979): 55–64.

27. R. M. Spann, "Public versus Private Provision of Governmental Services," in T. E. Borcherding, ed., *Budgets and Bureaucrats: The Sources of Government Growth* (Durham, N.C.: Duke University Press, 1977), pp. 71–89. Bennett and Johnson, "Tax Reduction without Sacrifice," caution that this study (showing average per capita costs 70% higher for public provision) does not hold other factors constant across observations.

28. F. R. Edwards and B. J. Stevens, "Relative Efficiency of Alternative Institutional Arrangements for Collecting Refuse: Collective Action vs. the Free Market" (mimeo, New York: Columbia University, 1976), cited in Borcherding, "Comparing the Efficiency"; E. S. Savas, "Municipal Monopolies vs. Competition in Delivering Urban Services," in W. D. Hawley and D. Rogers, eds., *Improving the Quality of Urban Management* (Beverly Hills, Calif.: Sage Publications, 1974), pp. 437–500; E. S. Savas, ed., *The Organization and Efficiency of Solid Waste Collection* (Lexington, Mass.: Lexington Books, 1977); "Policy Analysis for Local Government: Public vs. Private Refuse Collection," *Policy Analysis* 3, no. 1 (Winter 1977): 49–74; "Comparative Costs of Public and Private Enterprise," in W. J. Baumol, ed., *Public and Private Enterprise in a Mixed Economy* (New York: St. Martin's Press, 1980), pp. 234–294; B. J. Stevens and E. S. Savas, "The Cost of Residential Refuse Collection and the Effect of Service Arrangements," in *Municipal Year Book 1978* (Washington, D.C.: ICMA), pp. 200–205.

29. B. J. Stevens, "Scale, Market Structure, and the Cost of Refuse Collection," *Review of Economics and Statistics* 60, no. 3 (August 1978): 438–448. An explanation is advanced in D. R. Young, *How Shall We Collect the Garbage?* (Washington, D.C.: The Urban Institute, 1972), p. 73.

30. E. S. Savas, "How Much Do Government Services Really Cost?" *Urban Affairs Quarterly* 15, no. 1 (September 1979): 23–41.

31. D. Windsor and C. Atherton, "Administrative Impacts of Private Financing Techniques for Urban Transportation," Rice Center's Joint Center for Urban Mobility Research (Washington, D.C.: U.S. Department of Transportation, Research and Special Projects Administration, Office of University Research, January 1984), DOT/RSPA/DMA–50/84/19; "Public vs. Private Ownership of Transit Systems," Rice Center's Joint Center for Urban Mobility Research (Washington, D.C.: U.S. Dept. of Transportation, UMTA, University Research and Training Program, February 1986).

32. See J. A. Dunn, Jr., "Transportation Policy," in Nagel, *Encyclopedia of Policy Studies*, pp. 667–685; R. F. Kirby and C. T. Everett, "Transportation," in J. L. Palmer and I. V. Sawhill, eds., *The Reagan Experiment* (Washington, D.C.: The Urban Institute Press, 1982), pp. 419–437.

33. See the report in Rice Center's *A Guide to Innovative Financing Mechanisms for Mass Transportation* (Washington, D.C.: U.S. Dept. of Transportation, UMTA, Office of Planning Assistance, December 1982), DOT-I-82-53.

34. R. L. Stanley, "Transit Needs a Touch of the Market," *Wall Street Journal*, 26 May 1985.

35. "Investors Consider Building Trolley Line in Washington Area," *Wall Street Journal*, 21 February 1985.

36. Stanley, "Transit Needs."

37. C. Conte, "Resurgence of Private Participation in Urban Mass Transit Stirs Debate," *Wall Street Journal*, 27 November 1984.

38. C. K. Orski, "The Changing Environment of Urban Transportation," *Journal of the American Planning Association* 48, no. 3 (Summer 1982): 309–314; R. F. Kirby et al., *Para-Transit: Neglected Options for Urban Mobility* (Washington, D.C.: The Urban Institute, 1982).

39. See E. K. Morlok and P. A. Viton, "Self-Sustaining Public Transportation Services," *Transportation Policy Decision Making* 1 (1980): 169–194; P. A. Viton, "Eliciting Transit Services," *Journal of Regional Science* 21, no. 1 (February 1982): 57–72.

40. See G. Roth and G. G. Wynne, eds., *Free Enterprise Urban Transportation* (New Brunswick, N.J.: Transaction Books, 1982).

41. P. N. Fulton, "Public Transportation: Solving the Commuting Problem?" (Paper delivered at the Transportation Research Board annual meeting, January 1983).

42. Consider P. S. Florestano and S. B. Gordon, "Private Provision of Public Services: Contracting by Large Local Governments," *International Journal of Public Administration* 1, no. 3 (Summer 1979): 307–327; W. J. Murin, "Contracting as a Method of Enhancing Equity in the Delivery of Local Government Services," *Journal of Urban Affairs* 7, no. 2 (Spring 1985): 1–10.

43. Ahlbrandt, "Efficiency in the Provision of Fire Services," p. 3. A different position is argued in G. U. Downs and P. D. Larkey, *The Search for Government Efficiency: From Hubris to Helplessness* (Philadelphia: Temple University Press, 1986).

44. P. L. Joskow, "Firm Decision-Making Processes and Oligopoly Theory," *American Economic Review* 65, no. 2 (May 1975): 270–279.

45. Borcherding, "Comparing the Efficiency," p. 144.

46. Henderson, "Can Business Do It Better?" p. 20, cites two examples: (1) Chicago saved $1 million by taking over contracted parking meter maintenance; and (2) in 1970 a private contractor did not improve the scholastic standing of a Gary, Indiana, elementary school (which may well prove only that public education is a difficult production function to manage).

6

PRIVATIZING MEDICARE

John C. Goodman

Federal spending on the elderly (mainly through Social Security and Medicare) currently consumes about 25% of the federal budget. As we move into the next century these two programs threaten to become a financial nightmare. By one estimate, in the year 2060 the payroll tax may need to be as high as 42% of income just to pay for benefits now written into law.[1]

Quite apart from the looming financial burden of these two programs, they involve an arbitrary and unfair redistribution of income. They take money out of the pockets of some Americans—many of whom are poor—and give it to other Americans—many of whom are quite wealthy. They are run on a pay-as-you-go basis, similar to a Ponzi scheme or a chain letter. Those on the receiving end did not earn the benefits they now enjoy. Young people on the paying end realistically expect that they will never be able to cash in on future benefits they are being promised.

Under Social Security and Medicare, the longer one lives, the more benefits one receives. As a result these programs discriminate against minorities and others who have low life expectancies. The raising of the retirement age under Social Security and the prospect of a similar change under Medicare will make the effects of this discrimination even worse. In addition, the Medicare program has been the chief cause of spiraling health care costs, waste, and inefficiency in the medical marketplace.

The National Center for Policy Analysis has proposed a way to privatize Medicare through health IRAs, also known as medical IRAs or MIRAs.[2] Privatization of Social Security is already under way in Chile and Britain, and the programs of these two countries are viable options for the United States.

Because the problems of Social Security are more widely known and understood than those of Medicare, this chapter focuses on the Medicare program. In this age of $200 billion budget deficits, Congress is supposed to give each of the items in the federal budget careful scrutiny. Some items in the federal budget are intended to help the needy. Other programs are designed to strengthen the national defense or to promote the general welfare.

Some federal spending on medical care is consistent with these objectives. Medicaid, for example, is designed to help the poor. Veterans Administration hospitals are related to national defense, and programs for medical research allegedly promote the general welfare. Yet the big ticket item, Medicare, cannot be explained by reference to any of these goals.

Medicare, which pays medical bills for the elderly, consumed about $69.7 billion in fiscal year 1985, according to the Department of Health and Human Services. Between now and 1995, the cumulative Medicare deficit may be as high as $130.9 billion.[3]

Why do we have Medicare? When the Medicare program was enacted in 1965 it was part of the War on Poverty, and ever since it has been viewed as a poverty program. This perception is incorrect, however. Medicare does not take from the rich and give to the poor; if anything, it does the reverse.

MEDICARE IS NOT A POVERTY PROGRAM

On the average, the people who are receiving benefits under Medicare are better off than the people who are paying for those benefits. The disposable income of the elderly is higher than the disposable income of the nonelderly. In 1980 the elderly had an average of $6,300 in after-tax income per capita, whereas the nonelderly had $5,910 in after-tax income.[4] Not only do the elderly have more income than the nonelderly, but they also have more assets.[5]

Medicare provides people over 65 years of age with a health insurance policy. Its value to recipients is about equal to what they would have to pay in the private market for a similar policy. This is equal to the amount of money Medicare is paying per beneficiary. Currently that is about $2,000 per year. So the value to each enrollee of being covered by Medicare is about $2,000 per year, on the average.

A BONANZA FOR THE BENEFICIARIES

The people who are receiving this health insurance paid far less into the system than the benefits they can expect to receive. Take a man earning the average income who retired last year at age 65. Within three years the benefits he will draw from Medicare will exceed the amount of taxes he paid into the system during his entire working life. The Department of Health and Human Services estimates that this retiree can expect to receive about $28,255 in Medicare benefits before he dies.[6] Yet he paid only $2,640 in Medicare taxes. If the retiree has a dependent spouse, the expected benefits from Medicare will approach $62,360. In essence, the American public is writing a $62,360 check to this couple. Strangely, we don't do that for people who are 62, 63, or 64. But we do it for those who are 65.

Even if there is no increase in Medicare spending per beneficiary in the future, and ignoring the time value of money,

- A male beneficiary, age 65, can expect to receive 10 times more in Medicare benefits than he paid in taxes.
- A male, age 70, can expect to receive 21 times more in benefits than he paid in taxes.
- A male, age 75, can expect to receive 53 times more in benefits than he paid in taxes.
- A male, age 80, can expect to receive 291 times more in benefits than he paid in taxes.
- If these beneficiaries have a dependent spouse, the expected benefits relative to taxes will more than double.

MEDICARE IS UNFAIR TO MINORITIES

The latest life expectancy statistics from the National Center for Health Statistics show that a black male born today has a life expectancy of 65.5 years. Although he will pay taxes into the system throughout his working life, he can expect to die *the same year* he becomes eligible for benefits. If the eligibility age is raised to 67, as recommended by the Advisory Council on Social Security, a black male can expect to die well over a year *before* he becomes eligible for benefits.

A Hispanic male at birth has a life expectancy of 66.6 years. A white male has a life expectancy of 71.8 years. Both pay the same payroll tax rates, yet the white male can expect to receive Medicare benefits five times greater than those received by his Hispanic cohort.

A study done by the National Center for Policy Analysis (NCPA) showed that the future increase in the Social Security retirement age from 65 to 67 is devastating for minorities.[7] The same will be true if the eligibility age under Medicare is increased to age 67.

- A black male, age 20, will lose 100% of his expected benefits if the Medicare eligibility age is increased. His white counterpart will lose only 25%.

• A black female, age 20, will lose 19% of her expected benefits. A white female will lose only 14%.

The Advisory Council on Social Security recommended not only to raise the age of eligibility from 65 to 67 but to index it as well. This proposal would mean that whenever there is a general improvement in life expectancy, the eligibility age would go up. This would make it almost impossible for blacks and Hispanics ever to reach a point where they can expect to receive any substantial benefits under the system.

Medicare discriminates against minorities in another way. Under the program minorities are overrepresented among taxpayers and are underrepresented among Medicare beneficiaries. About 14.4% of the population of taxpaying age is nonwhite whereas only 8.6% of Medicare beneficiaries are nonwhite.

MEDICARE IS UNFAIR TO THE YOUNG

The enormous benefits received by today's elderly are made possible by the taxes being paid into the system by the working population. Yet young workers who are paying these taxes will never receive anything like the "deal" the elderly are receiving today. In fact, most young workers entering the labor force right now will pay considerably more into Medicare than they can expect to receive in return.

The NCPA has calculated the present value of Medicare for workers at different age levels under the conservative assumption that Medicare spending per beneficiary will grow at about the same rate as the rate of growth of nominal wages.[8] Under these assumptions:

• A white male, age 20, can expect to pay about $8,500 more in taxes than he will receive in benefits.

• A black male, age 20, can expect to pay about $14,000 more in taxes than he will receive in benefits.

Moreover, almost anything Congress is likely to do to relieve the financial crisis of Medicare—raise the payroll tax, raise the eligibility age, raise deductibles or coinsurance rates—will lower the expected benefits to young workers and make the return on their Medicare investment even lower than it is now.

Under existing law the combined payroll tax on employers and employees is scheduled to rise from the current 2.6% to 5.08% by 1995. If Congress also raises the eligibility age to 67, the penalty imposed on young workers will be substantial:

- With a 5.08% Medicare payroll tax and an eligibility age of 67 a white male, age 20, can expect to pay about $33,171 more in taxes than he will receive in benefits.
- Under the same conditions, a white female worker, age 20, can expect to pay about $6,685 more in taxes than she will receive in benefits.

THE CRITERIA FOR ELIGIBILITY UNDER MEDICARE ARE HIGHLY ARBITRARY

The basic requirement for eligibility is to reach 65 years of age. One need not be poor. There are 254,000 millionaires in the United States who either are covered by Medicare or who could be covered if they wanted to be. The president of Exxon cannot get social security benefits until he retires, but he can get Medicare when he reaches age 65. Nor does one have to have paid Medicare taxes to be able to draw Medicare benefits. There are people over 83 who didn't pay a dime into the system, and yet receive full benefits. People who are retiring today without having paid Medicare taxes can get covered simply by paying special premiums, and for most of them that turns out to be a very good deal.

Medicare is a system that takes billions of dollars from the working population and hands it over to people who by and large are not working. It gives billions of dollars in medical benefits to people who did not earn those benefits. It takes taxes from the working poor and pays the medical bills of retired millionaires. It is a system that is structurally unfair. It distributes costs and benefits in a highly arbitrary way. It is costly and is going to get more costly. The time has come for reform.

THE NEED FOR RADICAL REFORM

Medicare needs major reform, not just minor alterations. The Advisory Council on Social Security[9] took the same approach toward Medicare that the National Commission on Social Security Reform (the Greenspan Commission)[10] took toward Social Security. The assumption was that the system can be salvaged. However, when we look at the long run we can see that unless major reforms occur, the system cannot avert disaster in the next century.

Under the pessimistic projections of the Social Security Administration, 40 years from now the payroll tax will have to exceed 30% of income in order to pay for the Social Security and Medicare benefits now written into law; 65 years from now it will have to be in excess of 40%.[11] These projections by no means represent the worst case, for they ignore the likelihood that life expectancy will dramatically increase. Researchers in gerontology tell us that before the end of this century, life expectancy might well be extended to 150 years. If that happens, it will spell disaster for the Social Security and Medicare programs, clearly putting our children and grandchildren at great risk.

Medicare also suffers from a special financial problem that does not plague Social Security: inherent waste and inefficiency. Social Security money goes directly to the recipient. Medicare money, by contrast, goes to the providers—physicians, hospitals, and nursing homes. Medicare beneficiaries are not spending their own money in the medical marketplace. They are spending someone else's money. As a result the people who make the decisions on how and where the money will be spent do not bear the financial costs of their bad decisions or reap the financial benefits of their good ones.

Moreover, Medicare benefits are open-ended and potentially limitless. The pattern has been that if you can show that a technique or procedure (no matter how expensive) contributes to health, Medicare will buy it. Small wonder the system is going bankrupt.

About 78% of all the money spent under Medicare is spent on behalf of only 11% of the beneficiaries. About one of every three dollars spent under this program is spent on patients in their last year of life.[12] If people were spending their own money, they might be making different choices.

PRIVATE ALTERNATIVE TO MEDICAL CARE

The National Center for Policy Analysis has developed a proposal based on a concept developed by Jesse Hixson to give Americans a private alternative to Medicare.[13] Under the proposal individuals would be allowed to make annual contributions to qualified individual retirement accounts called medical IRAs (MIRAs). Funds that accumulate in these accounts would allow individuals to pay for their own medical expenses and to purchase private health insurance for their retirement years. Individuals choosing this option will have opted out of the basic Medicare and will be covered only in case of very large catastrophic medical expenses.

The plan has a thirty-year phase-in period. An individual who contributes to a medical IRA for only one year will receive 29/30ths of whatever Medicare pays once he reaches age 65. An individual who makes fifteen contributions to an IRA will be entitled to only half of whatever Medicare pays. After thirty years of contributions, the individual will be completely opted out.

The choice to opt out of Medicare is voluntary. However, individuals who choose the IRA option will get tax credits for their medical IRA contributions. We calculated that a tax credit of $500 per person will be sufficient to encourage all members of each new generation of workers to choose the private IRA alternative to Medicare.

For poor Americans a special provision would be made. Individuals with no earnings would be granted an income tax "refund" equal to the amount of the allowed tax credit. The refund will be placed in their medical IRA. This would give people with little or no income a source of funds from which to purchase their own medical care during the retirement years.

Money deposited in a medical IRA is the private property of the individual who deposits it. Moreover, this money is part of the individual's estate and can be passed on to his heirs. As a result, when individuals spend their MIRA money they will be spending their own money, not someone else's. This gives individuals an incentive to make rational choices in the medical marketplace.

The plan would relieve the long-term financial crisis of Medicare. With fewer Americans paying into the system, there would be fewer retirees making demands on Medicare as we move into the next century.

The plan also provides a practical means of reaching an important social goal: that individuals can be and should be responsible for providing for their own health care during retirement. Adherence to this principle is the best way to provide future generations of elderly citizens with the financial security they need. It is the best way to ensure that elderly citizens retain their dignity and self-esteem. And it accomplishes these objectives in a manner consistent with the spirit of a free society.

PRIVATIZATION OF SOCIAL SECURITY

The medical IRA alternative to Medicare can also be used to privatize Social Security. In fact, this has been happening in Chile since 1981. In Chile individuals are allowed to opt out of Social Security by putting at least 10% of their income into the Chilean equivalent of an individual retirement account. The IRA is managed by private companies, such as insurance companies, banks, or other thrift institutions. As in the United States, there is competition among these institutions. At the same time, there are some restrictions on what kinds of investments the institutions can make with their clients' money.

For Chilean workers who had been under the state system in the past and chose to opt out, the government gives them nontransferable bonds to cover their past contributions to the system. These bonds can be redeemed when the workers retire. The system has been enormously successful. Almost 50% of all Chilean workers have exercised the option to be out of the state-run system.[14]

Among the developed countries the most extensive privatization of Social Security has occurred in Britain. Private companies may contact workers out of Britain's second-tier Social Security program by providing private pensions as substitutes. As in Chile, workers are given tax incentives to choose the private option. About half of all British workers are now contracted out. Although this may sound like an idea of the Conservative party, it was the British Labour party that passed the act that put the current system into effect in 1978. Not only did the Labour party endorse the proposal, it has no significant opposition from the socialist trade unions. The trade unions realized their workers would benefit.

If such a development can occur in one of the world's preeminent welfare states, cannot a more capitalist country such as the United States follow suit?

NOTES

1. U.S. Department of Health and Human Services/Social Security Administration, the 1986 Annual Report of the Board of Trustees of the Federal Old-Age and Survivors Insurance and Disability Insurance Trust Funds, and the Annual Reports of the Medicare Board of Trustees, 1986.

2. P. Ferrara, J. C. Goodman, G. Musgrave, and R. Rahn, "Solving the Problem of Medicare," Policy Report No. 109 (Dallas, Tex.: National Center for Policy Analysis, January 1984), p. 12.

3. Calculated by Gerald Musgrave, Economics America, Inc., based on the annual report of the Medicare Board of Trustees, 1986.

4. U.S. Bureau of the Census, *Current Population Reports*, Series P–23, No. 126, "Estimating After-Tax Income Distributions Using Data From the March Current Population Survey" (Washington, D.C.: U.S. Government Printing Office, 1983), Table 1, pp. 20–23.

5. *The Wall Street Journal*, 28 April 1982, p. 30.

6. Based on information provided by the U.S. Department of Health and Human Services.

7. J. C. Goodman, "The Effect of the Social Security Reforms on Black Americans," Policy Report No. 104 (Dallas, Tex.: National Center for Policy Analysis, July 1983).

8. "Solving the Problem of Medicare," p. 6.

9. Social Security Administration, Advisory Council on Social Security, *Social Security Financing and Benefits: Report of the 1979 Advisory Council on Social Security* (Washington, D.C.: Government Printing Office, 1979).

10. *Report of the National Commission on Social Security Reform* (Washington, D.C.: Government Printing Office, 1979).

11. The 1986 Annual Report of the Board of Trustees of the Federal Old-Age and Survivors Insurance and Disability Insurance Trust Funds, and the Annual Reports of the Medicare Board of Trustees, 1986.

12. "Solving the Problem of Medicare," p. 12.

13. Ibid.

14. J. C. Goodman, "Private Alternatives to Social Security: The Experience of Other Countries," in *Social Security: Prospects for Real Reform* (Washington, D.C.: Cato Institute, 1985), p. 111.

7

PRIVATE OWNERSHIP INCENTIVES IN PROFESSIONAL SPORTS FACILITIES

Dean Baim

Social scientists often debate what motivates individual behavior. One of the hypotheses is that private property ownership provides incentives that will promote behavior different from that promoted by alternative methods of resource management. Proponents of these incentives argue that the private proprietor, who is responsible for earning and enjoying a profit, will have more incentive to see that the resources are used efficiently. Other social scientists argue that the existence of private property is demeaning and leads to inefficiency by wealthy owners. In its weakest form the argument against private property incentives is that the incentives are too weak to alter an individual's behavior, or that these incentives compete with other, stronger forces that lead owners to behave in ways that are contrary to those predicted by private ownership.

The private property argument is not to be interpreted as indicating that public employees are more wasteful or lazy than public-sector employees with the same responsibilities. Instead the hypothesis is that the incentives faced by a private manager are significantly different enough to foster different behavior.

Because sports facilities that are privately and publicly owned and/or operated professionally exist simultaneously, they offer a fertile ground to test the incentives, if any, provided by private ownershsip. Proponents of the existence of private property incentives would predict that private owners will have reason to be more aggressive in securing bookings, be more concerned about consumer welfare, and be more vigilant in the use of resources to achieve these ends and in constructing the facility.

This study will test the competing hypotheses by comparing publicly and privately owned stadiums and arenas to determine if there are significant differences in the utilization, customer amenities (as measured by available parking), and cost of construction. In addition to comparing privately and publicly owned sites on these criteria, the inquiry will compare two ownership techniques for their contribution to franchise stability.

ARENAS

Thirty-eight facilities have been used as the home court for National Basketball Association (NBA) teams and/or the home ice for National Hockey League (NHL) teams since 1953. All thirty-eight arenas were surveyed and are included in this report except when, because of unavailability, unreliability, or incompatibility of data, meaningful inclusion was not possible for a particular criterion.

Construction Costs

Twenty-four arenas were surveyed for construction costs. The fourteen sites omitted (four private and ten public) were not included because reliable data source could not be found; or the arenas were built at a date that preceded accurate deflators, making inflation adjustments difficult; or they were built coincidentally with other facilities and the division of costs was impossible. Of the remaining arenas, four were privately owned and twenty were owned by public entities.

Original construction costs were supplemented with major renovation costs, although maintenance costs to replace aging equipment were not included. When evidence showed renovation had been undertaken but reliable data regarding costs were not available, only the original construction costs and capacities were used. All cost figures (original and renovation) were either inflated or deflated using the Department of Commerce's composite index of construction costs.[1] As a result all costs were adjusted to 1977 dollars. Because this index begins in 1947, only arenas constructed after 1946 are included in the analysis.

To allow for different-sized facilities, the inflation-adjusted construction costs were divided by the current seating capacities. Because capacities differ in the same arena for hockey and basketball, basketball capacities were used for arenas that host an NBA team and hockey capacities were used when the site was used only as an NHL home ice. These calculations yield a cost-per-seat figure that is in 1977 dollars for all arenas.

The respective average inflation adjusted cost per seat to construct (AIACPS) of $1,333 for privately and $1,946 for privately constructed arenas strongly supports the theory that facilities built by private parties are done so with a lesser use of resources than are arenas built by public agencies. Statistically the chances for these averages coming from the same distribution is less than 5%.

An alternative approach is to test to see if the privately constructed mean is significantly less than the aggregate mean of all arenas. The aggregate mean is $1,843. The $510 difference in the means is significant at the 93% confidence level. Given the large number of public arenas relative to private arenas, it may not be surprising that the aggregate mean is not significantly different from the public mean, but the significance between the private mean and the public aggregate means indicates that the incentives provided to proprietors do lead them to build an arena more inexpensively than their counterparts in the public sector.

Days Used

Sports facilities can be used for noncompetitive events when the home team is on the road or in the summer and early autumn, when the NBA and NHL teams are not competing. The more intensively an arena is used, the more events can share in the fixed costs of debt amortization and routine maintenance. Similarly, a "dark" arena has little value to the owners and no positive impact on the local community's economic or cultural development. Any event that at least covers the additional cost to the owners of hosting the event should be sought and accepted.

To test the proposition that privately owned arenas will be more aggressive in recruiting business, data on the days used were gathered on all arenas. When available, days used included move-in and move-out days, as the facility was not available for an alternative use. Seven of the eight private arenas in the study were able to provide data on the days used. Seventeen of the thirty publicly owned arenas were able to provide data that could be used.

The test of the hypothesis is complicated by the fact that seven of the publicly owned arenas were operated by private management firms. These firms pay the public owners a specified amount or a percentage of the arena's revenues to the city and keep any residual payments. Where these "hybrid" arenas are placed has an interesting impact. For example, if the test is privately owned arenas versus publicly owned arenas (including hybrids), the respective means are 254 days used and 197 days used per year. These means are significantly different in excess of the 98% confidence level. When the hybrid arenas are included with the private facilities, the difference between privately and publicly owned usage remains significant at the 98% percent confidence level.

Although this would indicate that hybrid managers experience many of the incentives of the private arena owners, comparing the hybrid mean with the privately owned mean indicates that there are significant differnces between these two populations. This may reflect the fact that many private management companies share the profits with the municipal owners, rather than paying a lump sum and keeping all residual payments. As a result the actual benefit of booking additional events received by the manager is diluted.

When testing the private arena's average days used against the aggregate average days used, the results continue to testify to the strong impact of private enterprise incentives. The privately owned arena's mean was different enough from the aggregate mean that any hypothesis suggesting similarity could be rejected at a confidence level exceeding 97%. Adding hybrids to the private arenas reduces the level of confidence in rejecting the hypothesis of similarity to 94%. It should be noted that when the hybrids are added to the privately owned arenas, our sample sizes for privately and publicly owned arenas is twelve each. Thus this 94% confidence level is not tainted by the aggregate being made up of mostly public arenas.

As suggested earlier, an arena would be operated efficiently if it accepted all events in which rental receipts exceed the additional costs of hosting the event. The fact that privately owned and, when included, operated arenas are utilized more intensively suggests that these arenas either more aggressively recruit events and/or have lower operating costs, allowing them to accept events that public facilities cannot accommodate. Neither alternative speaks well of the incentive structure available to employees of public agencies.

Further support of this can be inferred from an informal and unscientific survey of once publicly operated arenas that are now privately operated. In the two cases for which data were received, operating companies that took over arenas that were financial liabilities to their owners are now able to pay the cities an amount equal to the debt maintenance on the arena and within a reasonable period of time earn a profit. This would be a fruitful area for further investigation.

Parking Facilities

Amenities for patrons play a crucial role in the decision to attend any event. The easier it is to reach one's destination, and the nicer the facility, the more likely a customer will return for another event. Lack of these amenities will result in lower attendance, leading to lower arena revenues, and dissatisfaction with the event promoter and patron.

Ample parking is one of those amenities that is readily apparent and, when there is a lack of it, can ruin an otherwise pleasant outing. On the other hand, too many parking spaces means that too many resources have been devoted to parking. Several studies have been made to estimate the average number of fans arriving in each car.[2] Most agree that the average is between 2.8 and 3.2. Parking demand is further eased by the observation that 5% of the fans generally take public transit to the games and another 5% take leased buses. Obviously these numbers will vary from city to city, but they do provide a basis of comparison.

Reliable parking information was available for twenty-three arenas (eighteen public and five private). Off-site parking within walking distance of the site was included in the survey when available. For each facility the seating capacity was divided by the parking spaces available. This capacity-per-space figure was then reduced by 10% to allow for patrons who did not drive to the game. To allow further for differences in transportation and concurrent use of the facility, those arenas with a capacity-to-parking ratio of 2.5 to 3.5 were considered "acceptable," as opposed to the 2.8 to 3.2 previously mentioned.

Of the eighteen public arenas, only four had acceptable ratios. Nine public arenas had more parking spaces than would seem necessary. By contrast, three of the five private arenas had acceptable parking ratios. If the seven hybrid arenas are placed with the private arenas, then only one public arena has an acceptable capacity-to-parking ratio. It was not possible to determine whether this means that privately operated arenas will provide better parking facilities or if private management companies are interested in operating only those arenas with adequate parking facilities.

A note of caution in interpreting this data. The acceptable parking ratio was computed on a capacity-to-parking ratio. In the likely event that the home team does not play to a full house, the computed ratio is an overestimate of the parking demand placed upon the facility. This means that those arenas with ratios that are below 2.5 are providing still more excessive parking facilities than a first glance would suggest.

STADIUMS

Construction Costs

Twenty-eight stadiums were used in analyzing construction costs. Like the arenas, these stadiums were excluded because reliable data could not be found, the arenas were built at a date that preceded accurate deflators, making price adjustments impossible, or they were built concurrently with other facilities and the allocation of costs was not possible.

Because of the different field configuration for football and baseball, the seating capacities vary greatly in some instances. For stadiums that are used for both major-league baseball and the NFL, the baseball capacity is used. If a stadium is used by only the NFL, then the football capacity is used.

Reliable data were found for twenty-four of the thirty-six publicly owned stadiums listed. The 1977 AIACPS range from a low $303 for Florida's Tampa Stadium to a high of $2,388 for the Houston Astrodome. The AIACPS for the four private stadiums ranges from a low of $221 for Sullivan Stadium in Foxboro, Massachusetts, to a high of $1,187 for Busch Stadium in St. Louis.

The average AIACPS for publicly constructed stadiums is $1,066, which compares with the average AIACPS of $623 for privately constructed stadiums. The standard deviations for publicly and privately constructed stadiums are $517 and $417, respectively. The chances of these two means coming from the same distribution is less than three in one hundred.

An alternative approach is to compare the private mean with the combined mean of $1,003. The combined standard deviation is $521. The likelihood of these coming from the same distribution is less than five chances out of one hundred.

There is some debate as to the real costs of one of the privately built facilities, Dodger Stadium. Some reports place the actual construction costs at $18 million rather than the $10 million used in the foregoing calculations. Substituting the higher figure will lead to an average AIACPS of $708 and a standard deviation of $397 for private stadiums. Even with this higher cost estimate for building Dodger Stadium, the probability that the construction costs are the same is less than six in one hundred.

Because construction costs have a large fixed costs factor, the capacity sizes were compared to see if this difference in AIACPS could be explained by private facilities being larger and thus spreading the fixed costs out over a larger number of seats. The publicly constructed stadiums have an average capacity of 59,607 and the standard deviation is 12,419. This compares with the private average capacity of 60,853. The standard deviation for the private capacities is 4,581. It is safe to conclude that the explanation of the significant difference in construction costs is not due to different facility sizes.

Another explanation is that perhaps the privately built stadiums are influenced by a "sunbelt" factor. That is, because one-half of the privately owned stadiums are located in the sunbelt states of California and Texas, perhaps the construction costs are artificially low because of lower labor or other construction costs in the southern and southwestern states. Casual comparison of the construction costs of the privately and publicly built stadiums in the sunbelt would tend to refute this explanation.

For example, the AIACPS for Dodger Stadium is somewhere between $425 and $765 depending upon the true cost of construction. Even the higher figure is lower than the AIACPS of $898 and $1,227 for the publicly constructed Anaheim and Jack Murphy Stadiums. Similarly, in Texas the AIACPS of privately constructed Texas Stadium is $660, whereas the AIACPS of the Astrodome and Arlington Stadium are $2,388 and $1,205, respectively.

Statistically, comparing the means of the privately constructed sunbelt stadiums of Los Angeles and Dallas with the eight publicly constructed sunbelt stadiums (Anaheim, California; Arlington, Texas; Atlanta, Georgia; Houston, Texas; San Diego, California; and Tampa, Florida) yields means of $610 and $1,337, respectively. The standard deviation of the private distribution is $262; the distribution for the public stadiums is $699. The likelihood of these distributions being the same is less than two chances in one hundred. Using the higher cost estimate for the construction of Dodger Stadium does little to affect the results. The new sunbelt private mean and standard deviation become $728 and $95, respectively, indicating that the chances of the two distributions being equal is still less than two in one hundred.

A final explanation of the difference has been that the public stadiums are predominantly downtown stadiums where real estate and labor costs are more expensive than in the suburbs. Two of the four private stadiums, Texas Stadium and Sullivan Stadium, are located in the bedroom communities of Irving, Texas, and Foxboro, Massachusetts.

Actually the opposite effect may be occurring. The location of many public stadiums is not always determined solely by the comfort and convenience of the patrons of the facility but by other criteria. For example, many of the publicly owned stadiums are constructed as part of an urban renewal project. In this case the property on which the stadium is built is in a depressed area. The land values may be depressed below what similar land would sell for in the suburbs. In many cases the property has been abandoned.

To test the downtown versus suburban hypothesis, the AIACPS of five publicly owned suburban stadiums were compared with the AIACPS of the two privately owned suburban stadiums in Irving and Foxboro. The publicly owned suburban stadiums used in this comparison are Anaheim Stadium, Arlington Stadium, Giants Stadium in East Rutherford, New Jersey, Rich Stadium in Orchard Park (a suburb of Buffalo, New York), and the Silverdome in Pontiac, Michigan.

The mean and standard deviation of the public suburban stadiums is $786 and $344, respectively. For the two private stadiums, the mean and standard deviation are $441 and $310, respectively. This indicates that there is still a better than 91% chance that these means do not come from the same distribution.

Days Used

To test the proposition that privately owned stadiums will be more aggressive in recruiting business, data on the days used was solicited on all stadiums. When available, days used included move-in and move-out days, as the facility was not available for an alternative use on those days.

Data on the number of days used in 1984 for sixteen public and six private stadiums were studied. "Days used" included days on which parts of the facilities other than the stadium was used when that could be determined. Therefore if a convention center or parking lot is part of the stadium complex and can be utilized to host an event, those days used are included in this total.

The means of 96 days for the private stadium and 107 days for the public stadiums are not significant to any meaningful levels of confidence.

These results may not be altogether surprising. There are few events of the magnitude that justifies a stadium as a site. Furthermore the operators of stadiums, particularly those with no dome, face a practical consideration of a shortened season when the stadium would be appropriate for use, especially in the northern part of the country. Another consideration for a stadium with a natural grass field is that there may not be enough time to repair turf after an event before the sports team, presumably the principal tenant, returns. These constraints exist regardless of ownership, so it is not surprising that there is little difference between the number of days a privately owned and publicly owned stadium is used.

Parking

Stadium managers face a classic peak load problem if their facilities are used by major-league baseball teams and NFL franchises. This is because most NFL teams play before capacity crowds, whereas most baseball teams do not. For this reason owners must be able to provide parking for the football enthusiasts, even if doing so will lead to excessive capacity for most baseball games. A happy solution could arise if the stadium were located in a business district where surrounding parking facilities in office buildings could provide an elastic supply of parking spaces that expands for peak Sunday NFL demand but contracts for baseball games.

Because of the peak load issue, capacity is used as the appropriate measure for stadiums that were used as football stadiums. For stadiums that were used solely as baseball stadiums, average attendance for the first five years the stadium was in use is used as the measure of parking demand.

One fact working in favor of the stadium manager facing the peak load problem is that football fans average about 3.5 occupants to a car whereas baseball fans average about 2.5 occupants per car.[3] Thus even if more fans attend NFL games than baseball games, they tend to use their cars more intensively.

In total, data on parking facilities were found for forty stadiums (nine private and thirty-one public).

The capacity (for football facilities) and/or average attendance (for baseball) was divided by the number of parking spaces within walking distance of the stadium to compute the capacity per parking space (CPS) and average attendance per parking space (AAPS), respectively. The computed number was then reduced by 10% to account for fans taking mass transit or chartered vehicles to the game.

In order to be considered acceptable the CPS had to be between 3.0 and 4.0 for football stadiums. Using this standard, eight of the public and one of the private stadiums had acceptable parking. Twenty-one of the public and two of the private had too little. Three of the public but none of the private had too many spaces.

There is not much to recommend parking in either ownership category. There is a tendency for most NFL stadiums to have too few parking spaces in the probable event of a sellout. This could be explained by the fact that the NFL home season usually includes only eight home games, not counting playoffs. Given that most stadiums are not so intensively used on other occasions, it would be unwise to allow for a sellout, which would only happen eight times a year.

A patron of a privately owned NFL stadium is more likely to be in a stadium with acceptable parking than if he was in a publicly owned stadium. One-third of the private NFL stadiums have acceptable ratios, while only one-fourth of the publicly owned stadiums have acceptable parking facilities.

None of the privately owned facilities devote too many resources to parking, whereas almost one in ten of the public facilities do provide too many parking spaces. Because the comparison is against the capacity of the stadium, it is not conceivable that this excess supply of parking can be explained by a desire to accommodate future growth in demand.

Privately owned facilities may have more appropriate parking facilities than their publicly owned counterparts, in that there is a tendency for public planners to provide for parking spaces that most likely will not be used.

In order to be considered acceptable, a baseball stadium's AAPS had to be between 2.0 and 3.0. The number of public major-league baseball stadiums that have too many totals twelve; four have an appropriate number of parking spaces. None had too few. Only one of the private stadiums had too many, but two had less than the desired number. Three should be classified as acceptable.

Again the numbers do not speak well of the parking facilities of either type of ownership. Of twenty-two stadiums, only seven have acceptable facilities, and thirteen have devoted too many resources to parking.

A look at the percentage of the stadiums with acceptable parking ratios in each ownership category is, as before, revealing. A patron of a privately owned stadium is twice as likely to be attending a facility with acceptable parking ratios than a fan at a publicly owned stadium. Half of the private stadiums have the appropriate number of parking spaces, whereas only one-fourth of the publicly owned stadiums have the acceptable levels.

The privately owned baseball stadiums make up less than 28% of the total number of baseball stadiums, but they contribute almost 46% of the stadiums with an acceptable parking ratio.

Of the total NFL and major-league baseball stadiums considered, some counted twice as both a home for both a football and a baseball team. When combined, sixteen stadiums are found to have the appropriate level of parking. This represents 28% of the stadiums surveyed. Of the private stadiums, 44% had acceptable levels of parking, whereas only 25% of the public stadiums were in this category. Both types of ownership have the same proclivity for providing too few spaces, in that in each type of ownership, 44% of the facilities do not have enough parking spaces to cater to the demand of their patrons. The inference is, therefore, that private owners tend to guess more accurately than public owners, who tend to be more overly optimistic as to the potential number of fans who will attend a team's home games.

TEAM LOYALTY

Many current sports headlines do not deal with competition among professional sports teams from different cities, but rather with the competition between cities for professional sports teams.

Recent legal decisions[4] will increase the pressures on host cities as disenfranchised cities build new facilities in hopes of taking advantage of team owners' new-found freedom to move their clubs. New York, San Francisco, Miami, Phoenix, and St. Louis are just a few of the cities that are either planning or constructing new facilities in hopes of securing, keeping, or attracting a major-league sports franchise. One survey shows that in the two years following the Raiders' case, at least thirteen of the forty-two municipalities that host a major league sports team have been requested to make facility improvements or provide tax incentives as a condition to keeping the team in the city.[5]

Since the decision in the Raiders' case, the threat of teams leaving a city has become so real that at least four bills have been introduced in

Congress to limit a team's ability to change venues. It is not surprising that these proposals have been sponsored by representatives of districts that have just lost, or are in the danger of losing, a major-league sports franchise. Each of these bills would require that certain deficiencies be proven by the sports franchise before it is permitted to move. Another aspect of this issue, now being heard by the courts, is whether localities may use their power of eminent domain to keep professional sports teams in a locality. All of these proposals would lead to costly litigation and years of indecision if a team desires to move.[6]

Arthur T. Johnson[7] suggests that another alternative to these costly methods is to provide franchise owners with an economic tie to the community. The purpose of this financial tie is to create costs to the team owner who moves from the city. One way of ensuring an economic stake in the community is to have team ownership of playing facilities.

Table 7–1 reviews the history of franchise moves from one city to another beginning in 1953. This table shows only the interurban franchise moves and does not consider intracity moves from one facility to another. In this way the analysis will capture the proclivity of team owners to leave one city for another, but it overlooks the efforts of a city to keep an existing team by building a stadium that the team then occupies rather than move to a new stadium in another municipality. In this respect the analysis may overstate the stability provided by private ownership.

Table 7–1 shows that Johnson's reasoning is sound. In the period from 1971 there have been twenty franchise moves. Of these, only one has involved a team moving from a private facility—the Cincinnati Royals' move to Kansas City. In fact, the 1950s is the only decade in which more moves were made from privately owned facilities than publicly owned facilities. It is useful to keep in mind that during the 1950s five baseball teams moved from privately owned facilities that ranged in age from 47 to 67 years old.[8]

Property Tax Considerations

Besides increasing team stability, another positive aspect of private ownership is that the property remains on the tax roles, thus easing the fiscal burden of the municipality. To illustrate the magnitude of these foregone tax revenues, the 1986 assessed valuation of the land and structures that make up the Superdome complex in New Orleans is $16,896,580.[9] Given the property tax rate of 13.232% of assessed valuation, public ownership of the Superdome costs the city of New Orleans $2,235,755.47 in property taxes annually.

Table 7–1
Moves by Professional Sports Franchises by Ownership and Sport

Sport	Moves from Public Facility	Moves from Private Facility
	1953–1961	
Baseball	0	5
Football	0	1
Hockey	0	0
Basketball	2	2
	1961–1970	
Baseball	4	2*
Football	2	0
Hockey	0	0
Basketball	2	3
	1971–1984	
Baseball	1	0
Football	9	0
Hockey	3	0
Basketball	6	1

*Move by California Angels from Dodger Stadium is not included because the Angels did not have an ownership interest in the stadium.

CONCLUSIONS

Economics is the study of costs and benefits generated by a decision in hopes of promoting more enlightened decisions. From the preceding evidence it is clear that the benefits of a professional sports facility are more likely to exceed the sacrifices when the facility is privately constructed and operated than when the stadium is constructed and/or operated by the public sector.

Few would argue against the economic and cultural contributions of a stadium or arena. By attracting out-of-town patrons who would not have visited the city otherwise, and by providing employment to administrators and event-day workers, the facility does much to broaden the economic and tax base of a community. Similarly the facility provides a site for culturally enriching events such as concerts, charitable benefits, trade shows, and conventions in addition to sporting events.

This survey has shown that these benefits can be achieved using fewer resources when the site is built and operated with private property incentives. The facilities constructed by private entities were done so at a cost significantly less than their public-sector counterparts. The provision of amenities, as measured by available parking spaces, was usually more appropriate in the case of private facilities.

Not only are the costs of the private facility less than the costs of a public facility, but these lower costs may yield greater benefits. Privately owned and operated indoor arenas are used more intensively than similar public facilities, therefore contributing more to the host city's cultural tapestry and economic growth. In addition, teams that own their facilities are more likely to remain in the city, and the city benefits fiscally by maintaining the site on the property tax rolls.

This survey looks at only a small fraction of human behavior and a minuscule segment of the economy, but it does provide support to those who argue for the presence and strength of private property incentives. Even when dealing with recreational facilities, people are motivated by their own interests to act in ways that will simultaneously produce a socially beneficial result.

NOTES

1. U.S. Department of Commerce, *Construction Review* (July-August 1983):56. For structures or renovations completed after 1982, see *Construction Review* (September-October 1984):54.

2. J. M. Hunnicut, "Parking Demand for a Large Public Stadium," *Traffic Engineering* 39, no. 10 (July 1969):48. See also J. Ashwood, "Transportation and the Planning Consideration for New Stadia," *Traffic Engineering* (July 1973):37.

3. Hunnicut, "Parking Demand," p. 48.

4. The most celebrated of these cases is Los Angeles Memorial Coliseum Commission vs. the National Football League, 726 F.2d1381, 1984, which claimed that the NFL's restriction on franchise movement was a restraint of trade. This permitted the Oakland Raiders to move from Oakland to Los Angeles without league approval.

5. "Extortion or Extinction?" *Los Angeles Times*, 25 February 1985, Sports, p. 10.

6. For a compilation and an analysis of the proposals to restrict franchise relocation, see A. T. Johnson, "Municipal Administration and Sports Relocation Issue," *Public Administration Review* 43, no. 6 (November-December 1983):522–525.

7. Ibid.

8. B. Shannon and G. Kalinsky, *The Ballparks* (New York: Hawthorne Books, 1975), pp. 259–265.

9. Information received through a 4 March 1986 telephone conversation with Ellis Smith of the New Orleans Assessor's Office and his assistant.

8

PRIVATIZING, DIVESTING, AND DEREGULATING THE POSTAL SERVICE

Douglas K. Adie

INTRODUCTION

The starting point of this chapter is the proposal made in 1982 before a subcommittee of the Congressional Joint Economic Committee.[1] Although some of the proposals at that time seemed radical, in less than four years the march of events has made many of the proposals more politically feasible.[2] The air traffic controllers' (PATCO) strike, break-up of the phone system (AT&T), and deregulation of airlines, bus transportation, and trucking industries and increased competition from abroad in the steel and auto industries allow a new agenda for reform in the Postal Service. Whatever failures exist in the Postal Service are not so much failures of individuals as they are of organizational structure. The beginning point for reform is not primarily one of finding the right leadership and employees but of creating the right organizational structure where the incentive and motivational system tends to encourage the desired results.

For this reason this chapter contains proposals addressing the larger questions of overall direction and organizational structure. Many critics are still mired in a personnel view of postal difficulties rather than the organizational view and blame postal employees for difficulties when they are not responsible.

PRIVATIZING AND DIVESTITURE—A LOOK AT AT&T

The changes that are taking place in the communications industry now have obvious implications for future directions in the Postal Service.

One proposal recommends denationalizing the Postal Service and abolishing the Postal Rate Commission.[3] This could be done by divesting the Postal Service into a number of smaller regional companies along the lines of AT&T[4]; deregulating it by repealing the Private Express Statutes[5] and abolishing other rules, regulations, and privileges[6]; and then selling shares in the postal companies to private investors.[7] This entire process is called privatizing.

When the present Postal Service was reorganized along the lines of the Kappel Commission Report in 1970, AT&T was used as a model. Still an appropriate model for the reorganization of the Postal Service, AT&T's structure now suggests divesture and deregulation. Observing the changes in the communications industry can be helpful in understanding the causes of problems, suggesting organizational reform, and anticipating possible future consequences of policy actions.

Policy changes in the communications industry did not take place easily or quickly. The Federal Communications Commission (FCC) has gradually been opening the telecommunications industry to competition beginning in 1968, when the Supreme Court's Carterfone decision permitted phone customers to connect non-AT&T equipment to the AT&T system.[8] It is not necessary, however, for similar policy changes in the postal industry to take this long. The FCC, with the help of the Justice Department, which was active in the break-up of AT&T, could assist in engineering divestiture, privatization, and deregulation of the Postal Service. An immediate but less consequential implication of the changes in the communication industries for the Postal Service is to allow homeowners and businesses to own their own receptacles and post office boxes and to use them in connection with any delivery system, in the same way as they can own their own telephone equipment.[9]

Consider another policy change in the communications industry and its implications for the Postal Service. In 1969 the FCC gave MCI the right to hook its long-distance network into local phone systems. The implication of this for the Postal System is that local geographical postal delivery systems need to receive presorted mail for delivery in their area at reduced rates, passing on some of the handling cost savings to their customers, who may themselves be in the mail-handling business. To some extent this is being done now for businesses, but the Private Express Statutes prohibit private entrepreneurs from making these savings available to smaller customers.[10]

It might be easier to ensure a successful transfer of ownership and control of the Postal Service from government to private hands if Postal Service privatization and divestiture came first and deregulation last. Privatization involves a change in ownership from the government to the private sector. Divestiture concerns the organizational division of the large and monolithic Postal Service into its component parts, which are the geographical regions, delivery, transport, and management systems. Deregulation involves repeal of the Private Express Statutes and abolition of the Postal Rate Commission and the many other rules and privileges that apply to the Postal Service.

Though privately owned, the Bell System acted like a private welfare system with the power to tax and use its proceeds for beneficial purposes. Its pricing scheme made the more profitable services to businesses, urban, and long-distance users subsidize the unprofitable ones to residences, particularly local and rural users. In addition, infrequent callers subsidized their talkative neighbors. While long-distance and local rates are still under some regulation, prices will move in the direction of reflecting the cost of providing service. The Postal Service, contrary to the terms of the Reorganization Act of 1970, is still a welfare system in which first class, urban, and some business mailers subsidize other classes of mail, namely rural mailers and homeowners.[11]

An important area of potential gain in reorganizing both the Postal Service and AT&T is the reduction of overall inefficiency of operations. Costs in both are higher than they need to be because of overstaffing, which is typical of monopolies. A glimpse of the potential for efficiency measures in AT&T surfaced in August 1983, when the 700,000 unionized workers who went on strike were hardly noticed except for the curtailment of equipment installation. As the 1986 strike proved, the Bell System is so highly automated that it can function well in the hands of its 300,000 management employees. In this respect it differs greatly from the Postal Service, which pays 85% of its total costs for wages, salaries, and benefits. This high percentage of costs going for wages, salaries, and benefits indicates that the potential gain from privatization is enormous. Because the telephone service affects 95% of the population, its divestiture will affect the entire population. When the benefits are perceived, this will contribute to the strong base of public support for changes in the Postal Service.

The Justice Department's antitrust settlement with American Telephone and Telegraph Company led to the divestiture of the seven regional holding companies, which owned twenty-two local phone companies. The divestiture of AT&T's local phone companies was the biggest step yet in the deregulation of the communications industry. The entrepreneurial spirit long suppressed by regulation and bureaucratic red tape is now free to soar. How desperately the Postal Service needs this same breath of fresh air! The diversification of AT&T and efficiency change that are taking place are painful, and the Postal Service can expect to go through similar adjustment difficulties. Users and producers need to cope for the first time with competition, which will drive down the price of some services, push up the cost of others, and lower the cost of equipment. Most economists believe that as a result of divestiture and deregulation, telecommunications will be more productive, more efficient, and less costly.

The divestiture of the Bell System requires reorienting managers. Undoubtedly a similar task awaits postmasters and postal executives when the Postal Service becomes free to compete. For instance, most of AT&T's managers were trained to excel in a regulated monopoly that was hierarchical and functional. In this regard AT&T's organization was similar to that of the Postal Service. The Bell System, like the Postal Service, attracted to its ranks those with a high sense of mission who desired the security of a structured environment. When AT&T was reorganized most of Bell's managers were not equipped for competition. Deregulation, divestiture, and growing competition now make this old organizational structure obsolete.

Altering the Bell culture from a monopoly to a competitive enterprise, from the telephone company to an information systems supplier, is difficult. AT&T executives need retraining. Managers should be redeployed and dispersed throughout the system. When necessary organizational changes were made to minimize personal insecurities, instead of being concentrated in single units, shortages and surpluses of people were spread among the companies. Jobs should have been redefined throughout the system. The majority of people who were placed in new organizations retained their same jobs at the same locations. To be efficient, decision-making power needs to be decentralized and redistributed.

An area vice president for AT&T Information System in New York named Ken Foster used to get laughs by telling people he was a salesman for the telephone company. Everyone knew the Bell System was a monopoly that provided telephone service its own way or not at all. Can the divested companies now learn to sell? Will they be able to keep pace with MCI and Sprint, which continue to capture long-distance business through rate cuts? Can AT&T compete with Westinghouse, Duke Power, Irving Trust, and Olympia and York, which are setting up their own communications networks? The divested regional companies that in the past bought AT&T equipment made by Western Electric will also be shopping for the best buys. These changes will bring a new way of life with uncertainty and excitement. Middle managers will face opportunities and be given freedom to compete. Teamwork and risk-taking have become new requirements for successful performance. Lessons learned from the AT&T experience can be helpful for the Postal Service in making its organizational transition.

DEREGULATION—A LOOK AT THE AIRLINES

For more than one hundred years regulation was justified by economists in industries that were "natural monopolies." The government required the business to submit to regulation in return for a government-granted monopoly. Economists have argued that government regulatory bodies eventually become captives of the industries they are supposed to regulate, subvert the workings of the market, and encourage inefficiencies whose costs outweigh whatever dubious benefits regulation might have created. More recently the very existence of natural monopolies has been questioned when conditions of technological innovation are present. Administratively, the price-setting function of regulation proved to be a perennial problem because no competitive market existed to give the regulators signals. Regulators soon found themselves relying on ad hoc methods to make crucial price decisions.[12]

Deregulation, which involves the return of business decision-making from government regulators to businesses operating under competitive pressures, is revitalizing three basic industries—finance, telecommunications, and transportation—by encouraging innovation, increasing productivity, and reducing prices. Deregulation is most developed in the airline industry. An examination of its consequences is instructive for assessing the effects of postal deregulation on mail service.

Dismantling the Civil Aeronautics Board (CAB) freed airlines to compete.[13] As a result of deregulation, long-distance airfares have declined by almost 50% in the last nine years. This was accompanied by increased efficiency as the entire industry provided 19% more output with fewer than 1% more employees. A number of airlines failed (Continental operated under Chapter 11; Eastern, Republic, and others struggled to survive), and fourteen new airlines entered the industry.

The move toward deregulation has not been a partisan policy but was born out of need and justified by experience. Trucking deregulation advocated by Senator Ted Kennedy was one of the first cases. In transportation more than 300 trucking companies have gone bankrupt and 10,000 small new operators have entered the industry. Efficiency gains were so great that when fuel costs were at their height, truckload rates were still 5% lower than they had been in 1980 before deregulation. Many trucking rates have fallen more than 30%, adjusted for inflation.

The financial markets are in the process of being deregulated through laws, rule changes, and innovation. The financial industry is offering the public a huge array of products and services. As an indication of the benefits to the public, the cost of buying stock has fallen by almost 60%. Deregulation in the telecommunications market, of which the Postal Service and AT&T are parts, is just developing.

The switch from a regulated market, where inefficient operators are protected, to price competition is difficult. Businesses in this transition need to learn to cater to their consumers, define their markets, price by product line instead of by cross-subsidy, and reduce costs to compete with new entrants. When under this pressure firms must have the ability to abandon unprofitable markets and cut their losses.

Changes in the airline industry provide a good example of working out the process and effects of deregulation. For forty years of regulation in the airlines industry the spirit was "all for one and one for all." Until 1978 most airlines had minimal competition on their routes, and where more than one airline operated on the same route, all offered the same fares and service. Airline managers were spoiled: government regulations protected them from competition and almost automatically approved fare increases when their costs went up. In a case in which a carrier experienced financial problems Washington supervised a merger with a stronger airline.

Under deregulation the proliferation of new low-cost airlines, motor carrier, and intercity bus competitors is doing to the transportation industry what foreign competition has done to the steel and auto industries. A two-tiered industry has come into existence: the large, heavily unionized carriers with high fixed labor costs, and the small nonunionized carriers. Vast wage differences exist between the old and new carriers. The large carriers did not worry about labor costs under regulation because they could always pass along higher union salaries in higher fares. The troubled airlines all have one problem in common—high labor costs. Wages grew steadily during forty years, as carriers shifted most of their costs to consumers. Labor costs amount to 33% to 37% of total operating costs for unionized carriers as compared to 19% to 27% for new nonunionized carriers. As a measure of relative inefficiency, this compares with 85% in the Postal Service.

Deregulation made it possible and profitable for new airlines to enter, and because they could set any price they chose, the nonunionized carriers offering inexpensive fares attracted business and expanded their share of the market. The new airlines charge less by holding down costs and paying lower wages. For instance, a pilot for a nonunion airline earns a maximum of $52,000 as compared with over $100,000 for a unionized carrier. Despite the lower pay, flight attendants on small airlines often work as reservation and ticket clerks, baggage loaders, and plane cleaners; pilots dispatch and sell tickets. Cut-rate carriers such as Southwest and People Express resemble flying bus lines, running infrequent flights with high-density seating over simple route systems. Both have low costs and highly motivated workers who own a sizable stake in their companies.

Larger carriers have been trying to compete by cutting wages and fares. Because labor costs are the largest controllable expense, workers bear the brunt of the pain. Labor costs in deregulated sectors are being slashed. "The only people calling for deregulation are those whose monopoly rents are being squeezed," says William A. Niskanen.[14] The wage and efficiency adjustments in the airline industry are indicative of the kind of adjustments that are needed in the Postal Service. If there is a sense of equity that assigns greater adjustments to workers who have earned greater amounts of economic rent over long periods of time, then postal workers will have to make substantial wage adjustments.

In intercity bus lines a number of strategy techniques surfaced to bring about decreases in wages. Greyhound Buslines confronted its workers with a choice of much less pay for much more work or no jobs at all. Some companies formed nonunion subsidiaries and offered equity participation in exchange for various labor concessions.

Continental Airlines and others used the bankruptcy law to abrogate labor contracts. In a dramatic attempt at reducing wage costs, Continental temporarily went out of business on 24 September 1983. Francisco Lorenzo, chairman of Continental, said the airline had filed for protection from creditors under Chapter 11 of the Bankruptcy Code of 1978 because they were unable to win $100 million in cost savings from its unions. He said they would shut down for two days and then begin flying a truncated schedule at sharply reduced fares with one-third of its former employees working at one-half their former wages. They closed down the airline and reopened a smaller carrier with lower costs. Within fifty-four hours of filing petitions for reorganization under bankruptcy Continental had reestablished service to one-third of the cities formerly serviced. It fired 12,000 employees and invited 4,000 back at half their former wages.

Within forty-eight hours of this, Frank Borman, chairman of Eastern Airlines, said that unless his workers accepted a 15% wage reduction, the carrier would be forced to shut down completely or follow Continental in filing Chapter 11 and reopen under new rules and wage scales. Failing companies filing for bankruptcy have the right to void collective bargaining agreements and repudiate union contracts. Airline deregulation removed protection and pressured all airlines to establish costs similar to those of the low-cost carriers.

Employees generally do not understand the function of profits and the need for lowering costs in order to remain competitive. They are, however, learning these lessons through their experiences in the airline industry. This understanding also is spreading among employees in other industries as a result of labor mobility and continued competitive pressures being applied to new industries. Postal employees will not be able to insulate themselves indefinitely from these changes. In the airline industry People's Express started the trend of reducing labor costs, which it claims is based more on productivity than on low salaries. Its labor costs, however, are only 20% of total costs.

There has been some resentment on the part of established carriers toward the new airlines. For instance, Allied Executive administrator Ralph I. Harkenrider said, "Every fly-by-night fast-buck operator who wants to start an airline can." "We've had a lot of cannonball entries into the airline market who just want to do the job as cheaply as they can and skim off the profits," said Daniel May, president of Republic. Although some worry that cost-cutting will jeopardize safety, CAB chairman Dan McKinnon says that is unlikely because maximum workload is still set by the FAA.

The hard-pressed airline unions long for a return to regulation, higher profits, and greater job security, but Congress shows little interest. The International Association of Machinists lost its strike at Continental because 600 union members crossed the picket line. It is doubtful whether such a walkout, or even another airline bankruptcy or two, would cause Congress to consider reregulation. Despite the pain it has caused, deregulation still gets a majority vote and the Reagan administration will almost certainly continue to support it. Alfred Kahn, former chairman of CAB in 1978 and patriarch of deregulation in the airline industry, said, "The purpose of deregulation was not to make life easy for the airlines. Survival is part of the discipline of the competition process."

The circumstances justifying deregulation in the airline industry are even more prevalent in the Postal Service. Moves to improve efficiency and service have been made and will continue to be made, but this is mere window-dressing compared to the changes that are made under the threat of competition when regulations are removed. Experience in the airline industry also indicates some of the kinds of changes that are made in labor relations and the overall organization of factors in these circumstances.

PATCO—A WATERSHED FOR LABOR RELATIONS

The confrontation with PATCO was a watershed event in labor relations which set the scene for labor relations in the airline industry, the federal government, and, indeed, for the entire country. Except for those representing the quasi-private postal workers, government unions are forbidden to bargain over pay and benefits. PATCO established its ability to negotiate these by power, not law. It was so cohesive that the FAA was reluctant to enforce its prohibition.

Fifteen thousand members of PATCO, the Professional Air Traffic Controllers Organization, illegally struck to cripple the nation's air transport system. The president replied with an ultimatum—get back to work or be fired—and resumed operating without them. The Federal Aviation Administration put together military controllers, supervisors, and 3,000 nonstrikers to staff the towers. For the president the stakes were the integrity of his economic program, the health of the airline industry, and his bargaining posture with other federal employees.

The FAA offered an 11.4% pay raise—more than double the administration's offer to other federal employees—which PATCO rejected.

When they struck, Reagan said, "The law says they cannot strike. If they strike, they quit their jobs." Moreover, he insisted, there would be no negotiation while the strike continued and no amnesty for strikers. The ultimatum was softened slightly with a forty-eight-hour grace period for strikers who changed their minds.

The rebuilding of the traffic controller system was done without PATCO. Helms quickly trained thousands of replacements for the strikers. The strike revealed that the system was overstaffed by 3,500 controllers. The FAA was flooded with applications for its controllers' school in Oklahoma City, where it could train 6,000 controllers a year.

The planes flew; the law of the land was upheld; the public rallied to the president; PATCO destroyed itself and became an object lesson to other government unions and the Postal Service. The PATCO strike set a precedent for labor relations in the public sector and was a turning point that had wide ramifications for postal workers. In collective bargaining, postal unions fear an "Inspector Callahan" who says with a wide grin in response to a strike threat, "Go ahead. Make my day."

REVERBERATIONS AT GREYHOUND

The effects of deregulation in the airline industry brought about immediate and direct repercussions in intercity bus transportation. Greyhound lost 45% of its New York-Buffalo business to People Express, which charged half Greyhound's fare. Southwest Airlines flies from Phoenix to Denver for $65 versus $99 by Greyhound. Who's going to ride the bus and pay more for the privilege?

After being hurt by the fare cuts of cut-rate airlines, intercity bus companies were given freedom to raise or lower fares. This triggered a price war between the two big carriers, Greyhound and Trailways. Greyhound also planned to cut the pay of its employees and thereby provoked a strike. The decision to resume operations during the strike prompted the worst outbreak of labor-related violence since the 1974 truckers' strike.

The company argued that it had to reduce high labor costs to compete effectively following deregulation of intercity busing. After five strike days, Greyhound had 53,000 job applicants, many of whom were truck drivers and airline employees. This compares to the 980,000 people who in 1982 applied for one of the 27,000 open positions in the Postal Service.[15] Greyhound restored partial service by hiring nonunion replacements. This also tended to weaken the union. In the face of this pressure, union leaders reluctantly agreed to submit a new company proposal for wage and benefit cuts to a rank-and-file vote and shortly thereafter settled the dispute. This discussion indicates how competitive pressures from deregulation in one industry—namely the airlines industry—brought about adjustments in another—namely bus transportation. Even without organizational changes, the Postal Service faces the possibility of being overtaken by developments in telecommunications even as the bus transportation industry was overtaken by the effects of deregulation in the airline industry.

A GENTLE ADMONITION—LET'S BE POSITIVE

As Thomas P. Costin, Jr., president of the National Association of Postmasters has said,

We must gear ourselves for action not reaction. We must not wait until it is too late to respond to threats. Rather, we will begin a positive campaign to be certain that we do not lose what we now have. . . . It's not going to be business as usual within our organization. . . . We have to make things happen. Postmasters can expect fresh innovative ideas from this administration.[16]

This positive attitude on the part of postmasters, executives, and postal workers is necessary to effect successfully the necessary policy changes. By doing this they can have a role in the changes rather than letting the changes overtake them. Studying proposals for change and indeed sponsoring them will help. Postal executives, managers, and workers need to keep an open mind to the larger issues of privatizing, divestiture, and deregulation while looking for ways to take care of the private interests of their constituents on the details. It is necessary to follow noble ideals in facilitating what is best for postal consumers and the economy.

There are different scenarios for privatizing and deregulating. There are many important questions that still need to be answered. There are many ways of doing things although, as time passes, some options close. The best way to take care of special interests is with a positive attitude, openness, and even vulnerability. By resisting the march of events, postmasters and workers might slow things down, but the cost will be that all the detailed decisions will tend to run in a direction that is unfavorable to the very constituency they seek to protect.

NOTES

1. See D. K. Adie, *The Future of Mail Delivery in the United States*. Testimonies in hearings before the Subcommittee on Economic Goals and Intergovernmental Policy of the Joint Economic Committee, 97th Congress, 2d sess. 18–21 June 1982, pp. 282–313, 323–324.

2. Senator Symms of Idaho, who was sympathetic to the proposals, doubted their political feasibility at that time.

3. *The Future of Mail Delivery in the United States*, p. 297.

4. For a description of the process of divesting AT&T from the inside, see W. B. Tunstall, "Disconnecting Parties," in *Managing the Bell System Break-up: An Inside View* (New York: McGraw-Hill, 1985).

5. A recent call for repealing the Private Express Statutes was made by the new chairman of the Office of Management and Budget, J. C. Miller III, in "End the Postal Monopoly," *The Cato Journal* 5, no. 1 (Spring/Summer 1985):149–155. See also my response, "Abolishing the Postal Monopoly: A Comment," *The Cato Journal* 5, no. 2 (Fall 1985):657–661.

6. *The Future of Mail Delivery in the United States*, pp. 295–297.

7. The process of privatization, which has been used successfully in Britain, Canada, and other countries, is documented by M. Pirie in *Dismantling the State: The Theory and Practice of Privatization* (Dallas: National Center for Policy Analysis, 1985). Also see J. C. Goodman, ed., *Privatization* (Dallas: National Center for Policy Analysis, 1985); and M. L. McMillan et al., *Privatization: Theory and Practice, Distributing Shares in Private and Public Enterprises* (Vancouver, B.C., Canada: The Frazer Institute, 1980).

8. For a good discussion of the legal battle leading to the divestiture of AT&T, see H. M. Shooshan III, ed., *Disconnecting Bell: The Compact of the AT&T Divestiture* (New York: Pergaman Press, 1984).

9. Thomas Moore, a member of the President's Council of Economic Advisors and head of the administration's interagency task force on privatization, favors allowing anyone to stuff material in private mailboxes and then gradually eliminating all the laws that gave the Postal Service a monopoly. See B. Neikirk, "Putting Government on the Auction Block," *Chicago Tribune*, 23 March 1986, Section 1, p. 18.

10. The Postal Service has a presort program, but it is not viable unless a mailer has large volume. The program involves a reallocation of postal operations from the Postal Service to a private operator (not necessarily the mailer itself but an independent business) who does the sorting that would otherwise be done by postal employees. The American Postal Workers Union understands this and opposes presort discount programs.

11. In the Reorganization Act Congress ruled out the redistribution of discriminatory pricing by instructing the Postal Service to charge for each class of mail according to costs. Congress charged the Postal Rate Commission with monitoring this behavior.

12. See W. C. Shepherd and C. Wilcox, *Public Policies Toward Business*, 6th ed. (Homewood, Ill.: Irwin, 1979), chap. 3.

13. For a discussion of the effects of deregulation of the airlines, see E. E. Bailey, D. P. Kaplan, and D. R. Graham, *Deregulating the Airlines* (Cambridge, Mass.: MIT Press, 1985). Also see J. R. Meyer and C. V. Oster, Jr., *Deregulation and the New Airline Entrepreneur* (Cambridge, Mass.: MIT Press, 1984).

14. W. A. Niskanen, *Bureaucracy and Representative Government* (Chicago: Aldine-Alberta, 1971), p. 73.

15. A large queue like this usually indicates that employees are overpaid. A large queue usually is accompanied by a low quit rate. For a study of Postal Service wages and salaries using this information, see D. K. Adie, *An Evaluation of Postal Service Wage Rate* (Washington, D.C.: American Enterprise Institute, 1977). Also see D. K. Adie, "How Have Postal Workers Fared since the 1970

Act?" in R. Roger Sherman, ed., *Perspective on Postal Service Issues* (Washington, D.C.: American Enterprise Institute, 1980), pp. 74–93.

16. T. P. Costin, Jr., "Thank You," *Postmasters Gazette* (National Association of Postmasters of the United States) (January 1984):4–8.

9

THE PRIVATIZATION OF MONEY: A
SURVEY OF THE ISSUES

Larry V. Ellis

INTRODUCTION

What is it about the money and banking industry that has prompted
even the most dedicated advocates of laissez-faire to exempt it from the
reform agenda of full deregulation? Although it has not escaped the
current wave of deregulation and, in fact, has provided one of the more
dramatic instances of such reform, it seldom has been considered one
of those industries that could be left entirely to the forces of the free
market. Only recently has there emerged any serious discussion of the
nature and feasibility of a completely private monetary system. Although
highly abstract in nature, this chapter may supply important insights
into some very practical issues such as the advisability of further deregulation of the financial system and the possible reform of monetary
policy and central banking activities.

The primary purposes of this paper are to isolate and examine the key
analytical issues involved in those arguments that focus on the privatization of money,[1] to develop a taxonomy to aid in delineating the
various schools of thought that have emerged, and to offer some policy
implications and conclusions.

A GUIDE TO THE LITERATURE

Recently a number of writers have tried to envision a monetary system
devoid of any substantive government intervention. In a pioneering
effort, Black[2] argues that a laissez-faire financial system is compatible
with the absence of money as we know it. This theme is further refined
by Fama,[3] who describes a competitive banking system that manages

portfolios against which depositors hold claims that pay a competitive return and also provides transactions services in a pure accounting system of exchange. This exchange or payments system is based on an arbitrary unit of account (e.g., tons of beef or barrels of oil) and employs no physical medium of exchange.

Hall[4] has argued that Fama's primary contribution to the argument is the insight he provides into how a pure fiduciary system such as our current one works. Fama points out that government need not control the stock of money in order to control the price level. It only seems that money stock control is necessary for price level control because society chooses to quote prices in the unit of the medium of exchange. Given that the unit of account is identical to the unit used to denominate the medium of exchange (i.e., the dollar), it is necessary to control the supply of exchange media in order to control its relative price and thus the price level. Historical forces could have just as easily led to the design of a system in which prices were quoted in barrels of oil and the medium of exchange did not exist or was measured in some other unit. The price level in such a system could be controlled by controlling the quantity of oil rather than the quantity of money.

In an excellent summary of the major contributions to the debate, Greenfield and Yeager[5] tie together these various arguments by creating the BFH (Black-Fama-Hall) system, a sophisticated form of barter in a laissez-faire economy that, they say, contains none of the textbook disadvantages of barter exchange. Its primary advantage is that it represents an efficient system of exchange that has none of the instability associated with modern fiduciary systems. The analytical centerpiece of the BFH system is taken from Fama's argument that the unit of account can, and probably should, be separated from the medium of exchange.

The Black-Fama-Hall literature is tied together by a single underlying theme: the emphasis on the difference between combining and separating the medium of exchange and unit of account functions of money. This common theme groups this set of authors under a label suggested for them by Hall.[6] He has referred to their line of argument as the "new monetary economics" (NME). As a school of thought, the NME attributes distinct advantages to a laissez-faire monetary system that involves the separation of the medium of exchange from the unit of account. The feasibility and implications of such a separation will be referred to hereafter as "separability."

A perspective slightly different from that of the NME has recently emerged and will be referred to here as the Austrian Free Banking (AFB) school. There are two versions of this approach to the privatization of money. The scheme developed by Hayek[7] would permit any private firm to issue its own banknotes or deposits, the value of which the firm would maintain relative to some specified bundle of goods. Each note issuer would maintain the relative price of his exchange media by adjusting the supply of it relative to changes in the demand. Such a system could potentially yield a different unit of account for each note issuer.

The other version of AFB has been offered by White.[8] Similar to Hayek's in that currency and deposits would be supplied only by private issuers, it differs in that there would be a single unit of account, the unit in which exchange media would be denominated, and that notes and deposits would be convertible into a designated amount of specie. In other words, White's version of AFB has the private sector determining the type and quantity of exchange media and also maintaining the relative price or value of the exchange media by means of a commodity or specie standard that allows convertibility and the free movement and coinage of the commodity. Private issuers of banknotes and deposits agree to redeem them for a specified amount of the commodity so that it is the value of the commodity that ultimately determines the value of the notes and deposits. Thus White achieves complete privatization of the system including the exchange media by combining "free banking" with a privately administered commodity standard that is based on free convertibility of the exchange media into specie.

Distinguishing White's approach from either Hayek's or that of the NME school is his insistence on the need for privately issued notes and deposits to be convertible or redeemable into an ultimate money originating outside the banking system. For a fully privatized monetary system to function properly, the inside money produced privately by the banking system must be redeemable in a basic or outside money. Government, however, must not be able to influence the quantity of inside or outside money.

A third approach to the analysis of a laissez-faire monetary system has become known as the "legal restrictions theory" (LRT) of money and is associated with Wallace.[9] Wallace argues that government's role in the monetary system is artificial in that it results largely from legal restrictions imposed on private financial intermediation and the types of assets that can be held by the private sector. He arrives at this conclusion, somewhat indirectly, by addressing the following question.

How can Federal Reserve notes coexist with default-free, interest-bearing securities such as Treasury bills? He concludes that this can occur only in the absence of laissez-faire or, in other words, in the presence of various kinds of legal restrictions. Wallace is able to show that if the large denomination restriction on the issuance of T-bills were removed and they were actually issued in small denominations, they would sell and circulate at par (i.e., not bear interest) with Federal Reserve Notes. The large denomination restriction is not sufficient, however, to explain the coexistence paradox. If it were the only relevant restriction, then financial intermediaries would arbitrage the market by buying large-denomination, default-free securities such as T-bills at a discount and issue bearer notes in small denominations that would circulate at par as exchange media. Thus the prohibition of private bank note issue is also an important part of the explanation for why Federal Reserve notes can coexist with default-free, interest-bearing securities. In other words, prohibiting private note issue creates a demand for government currency. The removal of this and all other restrictions would reduce the demand for government currency possibly to zero and create a natural transition to a largely or wholly privatized monetary system.[10]

A TAXONOMY OF MONETARY STANDARDS

Economists are well acquainted with the familiar dilemma associated with attempting to control both the price and quantity in any market. If only the supply is subject to influence from outside the market, then it is possible to fix or stabilize either the price or the quantity. Both variables cannot be controlled. When the focus is placed on stabilizing one of them, the other becomes demand-determined. This dilemma has also characterized the administration of monetary systems or standards. An important aspect of such systems is the interaction of the supply and demand for money and the adjustments that result from supply and demand disequilibrium. Assuming that only the supply of money can be manipulated from outside, there are only two options in designing a monetary system. The system can be characterized by either exogenous control of the *quantity* of money, which implies that the market will determine its value, or exogenous control of the *value* of money with the market determining its quantity.

Before going further it is important to clarify the price and quantity dimensions of money. Price refers to the real value of a unit of money in terms of goods and services, or its relative price. It is the reciprocal of the price level and is dependent on money prices or the unit of account for its meaning. Determination of the relative price of money is a manifestation of money's function as a unit of account. Quantity is dependent upon money's function as a medium of exchange. Determining the quantity of money requires measuring the unit of account value of all exchange media. The price dimension of money is a reflection of its role as a unit of account, whereas its quantity dimension is a function of money as a medium of exchange.

The price-quantity control dilemma can now be restated in slightly different terms. When only the supply and not the demand can be influenced from outside the market, it is possible to fix or control either the value of the unit of account or the quantity of exchange media but not both. This proposition will generally hold as long as the unit of

Figure 8-1
Monetary Standards—Current and Proposed

		Value of Money (Unit of Account)	
		Determined Exogenously	Determined
Quantity of Money (Exchange Media)	Determined Exogenously		Current System
	Determined by the Market	New Monetary Economics (NME)	Austrian Free Banking (AFB)—Hayek Austrian Free Banking (AFB)—White Legal Restrictions Theory (LRT)

account and medium of exchange are tied together in the sense that the unit of account is the characteristic unit of the monetary system's exchange media—in other words, as long as prices are quoted in the same unit that exchange media are measured.

The parallel that exists between the price-quantity dimensions of money and the unit of account and medium of exchange functions of money provides a convenient mechanism for classifying and delineating the issues that separate the NME, AFB, and LRT schools in the privatization literature. The taxonomy is summarized in the 2 x 2 matrix of Figure 8–1, where the rows of the matrix represent the options available in terms of the value of the unit of account.

The fiat money standards that characterize many of the developed Western nations including the United States can be found in the northeast cell of the matrix. The central bank has been assigned the task of determining the quantity of money, which means its value becomes demand-determined. Given that the market for money is only an analytical device and does not exist in reality, excess demands or supplies can be eliminated only through the adjustment of resource and commodity prices. Because these prices are sometimes sticky, the short-run adjustment often manifests itself in the form of output fluctuations to be followed later by gradual adjustments in the prices. A widely accepted criterion for judging the performance of a monetary standard is its ability to provide reasonably stable prices. By this test the current system has performed poorly and can be expected to do so in the future.

Traditionally the option, depicted in the southwestern cell of the matrix, of having government define and fix the value of the unit of account while the market determines the quantity of exchange media has been associated with monetary systems that employ a classic commodity or specie standard. "The new monetary economists," however, have something different in mind. Their system would yield a stable value for the unit and account, and thus a stable price level, by breaking the link between the unit in which prices are quoted and the characteristic unit of the exchange media. They could, of course, be the same unit (e.g., the dollar), but the size of the unit of account would no longer be a function of the number of units of exchange media. The former would be fixed exogenously by government by defining the value of the unit of account in terms of a specified bundle of commodities, whereas the latter would be determined entirely by the private sector in a "free-banking" environment. The bundle of commodities used to define the unit of account would be defined comprehensively enough so as to have a relatively stable value against goods and services in general. Checks and currency would be "indirectly redeemable" in the sense that financial intermediaries would "cash checks" by redeeming them with some widely agreed-upon commodity or type and amount of securities.

The southeastern cell of the matrix in Figure 8–1 depicts a pure laissez-faire approach in that both the quantity and value of money are determined in the private sector without any form of government intervention. Under Hayek's version of the AFB approach a stable value for the unit of account is assured by competitive market pressures that would force private producers of money to adjust the supply of their money issue in response to changes in its demand. This would maintain the value of what could be a variety of units of account against some agreed-upon baskets of goods. In contrast, White's version of the AFB approach would guarantee a stable value for the unit of account by means of direct covertibility into specie under a market controlled rather than government-controlled specie standard.

Neither version of the AFB approach advocates a separation of the unit of account from the units in which exchange media circulate. In fact, White[11] argues very strongly that such a separation is unlikely to be successful and would never evolve naturally. The LRT approach is categorized as a pure laissez-faire approach, although Wallace is not specific about the mechanics or operation of his system.[12] He does suggest, however, that such a system does not ensure a stable price level. Some of the implications and conclusions that can be drawn from these various approaches to monetary reform will be discussed in the following section.

POLICY IMPLICATIONS AND CONCLUSIONS

For years economists have debated the merits of a monetary standard based on a rule opposed to our current approach to policy that rests on the discretion of the monetary authority. Only recently has there been any serious attempt to pose the more basic question of whether the existence of a monetary authority or central bank can be logically justified.

The focus of monetary policy as conducted by modern central banks in most developed nations today is the control of the money stock in a manner designed to stabilize real output and the price level. Our experience of recent years makes it apparent, however, that control of the money stock for stabilization purposes is becoming either increasingly difficult or of low priority for the central bank. One of the arguments common to both the new monetary economics (NME) and the legal restrictions theory (LRT) is that the basic notion of controlling the quantity of money is flawed. As both Hall[13] and Wallace[14] have argued, what an economy employs as money depends, importantly, on the prevailing set of monetary regulations and institutions. Identifying and controlling a quantity of money whose definition changes as regulations and institutions change, either gradually or in discrete jumps, becomes haphazard at best.

Of course under a fully deregulated monetary standard there is no need to control an ambiguous and illusive quantity of money. The one element common to the various schools advocating the privatization of money is that no economic justification exists on grounds of efficiency or stabilization, for a central bank or monetary authority. White[15] has masterfully shown that the traditional litany of arguments used to demonstrate the need for a central bank cannot withstand the light of evidence. Arguing from both a theoretical model of free banking and the historical experience with Scottish free banking (1716–1844), White is able to sweep away traditional justifications for central banking based on arguments such as the need for a lender of last resort, required reserves, or the existence of a natural monopoly in the production of currency.

Greenfield and Yeager argue that a fully deregulated monetary system without a central bank would have important advantages from the point of view of macroeconomic stability. They claim the following advantages for their system which, it should be recalled, is based on "separability" in the sense that the value of the unit of account is not dependent on the quantity of exchange media.

The very concepts of quantity of money and of possibly divergent actual and demanded quantities become inapplicable. . . . Media of exchange would no longer have a fixed price in the unit of account. . . . No longer could the pressures of imbalance between money's supply and demand be tending to change the purchasing power of the unit—but only sluggishly, with adverse effects on quantities of goods and services traded and produced.[16]

Furthermore, Wallace has argued that removal of all legal restrictions and regulations from the monetary system would cause the central bank to "wither away" because monetary policy in the form of open-market operations could not affect the level of economic activity. An open-market operation would simply shift the location of currency production from the private sector to the public sector, in the case of an open-market sale.[17]

The arguments surveyed here combine to make an impressive case for the elimination of central banking and, more generally, for the privatization of our monetary system. As these same arguments demonstrate, however, there are subtle yet important issues that divide the schools surveyed here with respect to the workings of a private monetary system. Hayek's version of AFB, which involves competing monies and a multiplicity of units of account, could impose significant transactions costs on the economy, thus violating microeconomic efficiency criteria. On the other hand, White's version of AFB, which combines the "outside" money of a private commodity standard with free banking, would seem to violate macroeconomic stability criteria in that it could potentially reproduce our experience under the gold standard of the nineteenth and early twentieth centuries. Indeed, Wallace points out that there is no assurance of price stability under free banking. In terms of both efficiency and stability criteria, the Greenfield-Yeager version of the NME approach may offer the greatest promise. As noted earlier, it is essentially a barter exchange system without the traditional inefficiency associated with barter. If White[18] is wrong and "separability" of the unit of account and medium of exchange is both feasible and desirable, then the Greenfield-Yeager system also has very attractive macroeconomic stability properties.

NOTES

1. *Privatization* is used here to mean the elimination of all regulations restricting the nonfraudulent activities of financial intermediaries as well as the removal of the central bank and monetary policy, generally, from the monetary system. Depending on the privatization scheme adopted, there may still be a minimal role for government. This would probably take the form of defining the unit of account.

2. F. Black, "Banking and Interest Rates in a World without Money: The Effects of Uncontrolled Banking," *Journal of Bank Research* 1 (Autumn 1970):9–20.

3. E. Fama, "Banking in the Theory of Finance," *Journal of Monetary Economics* 6 (January 1980):39–57.

4. R. Hall, "Monetary Trends in the United States and the United Kingdom: A Review from the Perspective of New Developments in Monetary Economics," *Journal of Economic Literature* 20 (December 1982):1552–1556.

5. R. L. Greenfield and L. B. Yeager, "A Laissez-Faire Approach to Monetary Stability," *Journal of Money, Credit and Banking* 15 (August 1983):302–315.

6. Hall, "Monetary Trends."

7. F. A. Hayek, *Denationalisation of Money* (London: Institute of Economic Affairs, 1978).

8. L. H. White, *Free Banking in Britain: Theory, Experience and Debate, 1800–1945* (Cambridge: Cambridge University Press, 1984).

9. It could be argued that LRT is actually a part of the "new monetary economics" because some of the new monetary economists have used arguments similar to those of Wallace. Hall, for example, has argued that the money stock and its relationship to aggregate demand is dependent on the particular set of financial regulations in existence at the time. The LRT does not speak to "separability," which has been made the common theme of the NME, so it will be set apart here as an approach distinct from NME. N. Wallace, "A Legal Restrictions Theory of the Demand for 'Money' and the Role of Monetary Policy," *Federal Reserve Bank of Minneapolis Quarterly Review* 7 (Winter 1983):1–7.

10. It would also be true that under laissez-faire the monetary policy activities of a central bank would become obsolete because they would have no effects on the economy. An open-market purchase of securities with Federal Reserve notes, for example, would involve a one-for-one substitution of government currency for privately issued currency. This simply changes the location of currency production in the economy and affects nothing else.

11. L. H. White, "Competitive Payments Systems and the Unit of Account," *American Economic Review* 74 (September 1984):699–712.

12. Wallace is more concerned with understanding in a theoretical way how a pure laissez-faire monetary system contrasts with our own and less concerned with the mechanics of how it would work.

13. Hal, "Monetary Trends," pp. 1552–1556.

14. N. Wallace, "A Legal Restrictions Theory of the Demand for 'Money' and the Role of Monetary Policy," *Federal Reserve Bank of Minneapolis Quarterly Review* 7 (Winter 1983):1–7.

15. L. H. White, *Free Banking in Britain*.

16. Greenfield and Yeager, "A Laissez-Faire Approach," p. 310.

17. Wallace, "A Legal Restrictions Theory," pp. 1–7.

18. White, "Competitive Payments Systems," pp. 699–712.

ADDITIONAL REFERENCES

Fama, E. "Financial Intermediation and Price Level Control." *Journal of Monetary Economics* 12 (July 1983):1–29.

King, R. G. "On the Economics of Private Money." *Journal of Monetary Economics* 12 (July 1983):127–158.

Niehans (or Niehaus), J. *The Theory of Money.* Baltimore: Johns Hopkins University Press, 1978.

Rockoff, H. "The Free Banking Era—A reexamination." *Journal of Money, Credit and Banking* 6 (May 1974):141–167.

Rolnick, A. J. and W. E. Weber. "Free Banking, Wildcat Banking, and Shinplaster." *Federal Reserve Bank of Minneapolis Quarterly Review* 6 (Fall 1982):10–19.

Tobin, J. "The Overlapping Generations Model of Fiat Money: A Discussion." In J. H. Kureken and N. Wallace, eds., *Models of Monetary Economies* (Minneapolis: Federal Reserve Bank of Minneapolis, 1980).

Vaubel, R. "The Government's Money Monopoly: Externalities or Natural Monopoly?" *Kyklos* 37 (1984):27–57.

Wells, D. R. and L. S. Scruggs. "Deregulated Financial System Scenarios: Two Austrian Free-Banking Models." *Journal of Economics* 9 (1983):81–86.

10

PRIVATIZATION: THE ENTREPRENEURIAL RESPONSE

Calvin A. Kent and Sandra P. Wooten

Critics are skeptical that private entrepreneurs will be able to respond to the opportunities privatization presents. This concern overlooks the essential feature of the entrepreneurial process: niche-finding. Entrepreneurs are those who see what others have overlooked and act on the insight. In the case of privatization the niche is almost obvious and there appears to be an abundance of those willing to respond. Entrepreneurship involves one of five phenomena.

1. Bringing a new product or service onto the market
2. Developing a new technology
3. Finding a new source of supply of some resource or expanding an existing one
4. Opening a new market
5. Reorganizing an existing enterprise

The result of the successful entrepreneurial event is always to produce a product, service, or organization that better satisfies the consumer or lowers the costs of production. Sometimes the entrepreneurial event encompasses both.

The following case studies are examples of how entrepreneurs have responded to the opportunity of privatization. In many instances the entrepreneurs themselves were former public employees who seized upon the opportunity to compete with public agencies with which they were intimately familiar. In other cases, such as the postal system, privatization is ocurring without official government sanction. In this latter

case the public merely seeks out alternative suppliers for functions previously provided them by government either in inadequate quantity or
quality or at too high a price.

The one essential feature of entrepreneurship remains risk-taking.
Through privatization the government in essence transfers the risk of
service provision to the private sector, which is better equipped to deal
with the uncertainties of the marketplace than is government bureaucracy. Privatization will involve some failures. There is no reason to
mourn these failures; this is the way the private sector advances. Private
producers may desperately seek to insulate themselves from competition
when they contract with the public sector, but this should be resisted.
If it is not, a major incentive for privatization has been lost.

As has been indicated in previous chapters, hundreds of governmental
functions have been successfully privatized. Some cities and counties
have been particularly active in privatizing public services. Los Angeles
County has issued 407 separate contracts since 1979, saving the county
an estimated *$51 million*. The cost of providing the same services would
have been 55% higher if the county had not contracted out.[1] The city of
Phoenix saves $2.3 million a year on seventeen services provided by
private contractors. It saves an additional $3 million in costs that are
avoided because city departments are required to bid against private
contractors for the right to perform many municipal services.[2]

Several nationwide studies have been conducted of the cost savings
resulting from privatization. In 1984 Ecodata, Inc. conducted a carefully
controlled study of eight public services in twenty different cities. The
research documented dramatic savings for all but one of the eight services. Average savings were as follows:

Street cleaning	43%
Janitorial services	73%
Traffic signal maintenance	56%
Tree pruning	37%
Refuse collection	42%
Payroll administration	NS*
Repair to asphalt surfaces	96%
Lawn care	43%

*Not significant

The study found no significant differences in the quality of services
provided by municipal departments and private contractors, but it *did*
find that contractors had a lower ratio of supervisors to workers (1:12
versus 1:8 for municipal departments). More private contractors were
also found to perform their own vehicle maintenance.[3]

The following case studies of entrepreneurial effort in twelve areas of service products give insights as to how privatization has worked.

LANDSCAPING

The city of Pasadena, California, contracts with two for-profit firms for landscaping services.[4] The first contracts were issued in 1978, and the number of areas maintained by the contractors has increased as the city staff is reduced by attrition. The contracts specify the frequency of mowing, watering, fertilizing, litter clearance, and cleaning for each area.

The city divides all the areas that require landscaping into two districts and solicits separate bids for each. In this way the city is able to compare the performance of the two firms. The firms are allowed to bid for both areas, however, and the two districts will be merged if one firm is the successful bidder for both districts.

Contracting out landscaping has allowed Pasadena to eliminate fourteen staff positions since 1978. In 1982, when the contracts were last bid, the winning bids were an amazing 60% lower than the cost estimated by the city's project engineer. The city has been satisfied with the quality of the contractors' work.

MASS TRANSIT

In the city of Chicago private subscription buses carry nearly 5,000 passengers each day.[5] Offering monthly subscriptions at less than half the price of public rail services, these buses operate on routes parallel to those of the city's heavily subsidized Regional Transportation Authority (RTA) and are patronized almost entirely by former commuter railroad passengers. The private bus companies utilize a variety of cost-saving techniques, including putting labor on split shifts. Off-peak charter work is aggressively marketed and most vehicle maintenance is done internally. The result is remarkably inexpensive transportation: 4.7¢ per passenger mile versus 12¢ for the city's public rail service.

Chicago's subscription buses are an example of privatization that occurred spontaneously, without the aid of enabling legislation and, in fact, in spite of common carrier legislation that could be used to shut them down. They succeed even though their public-sector competitors are massively subsidized. They generally do not advertise their services for fear of legal complications.

The Department of Transportation now has an Office of Private Sector Initiatives (OPSI) designed to study ways to cut costs by private-sector competition and efficiency. Despite the success of mass transit privatization, efforts have been made to eliminate OPSI's ability to fund additional investigation.[6] Further discussion of privatizing mass transit appears in chapter 5.

FIRE SUPPRESSION

In 1983 seven fire protection firms banded together to form the Private Sector Fire Association, a trade group.[7] This is a rapidly growing area in the municipal services privatization. Cost control and the necessity of covering large rural areas have caused many cities and counties to look toward private firms for management of fire stations and sometimes ownership of facilities as well.

The oldest privatized fire protection service is in Scottsdale, Arizona, which has contracted the service since 1952. Rural/Metro Fire Corporation offers fire suppression service on a contract or subscription basis for communities in six states.[8] Contracts with Rural/Metro generally specify a guaranteed cost over a number of years, ongoing training of emergency personnel, work schedules, and a number of employees. Rural/Metro currently employs nearly 1,500 full- and part-time employees, operates over 300 vehicles, and responds to 9,000 calls every month. Residents pay just 48% of the national average for cities of its size. Rural/ Metro Chairman Lou Witzeman estimates that Scottsdale saves over $3 million a year by contracting out. A study conducted by the Arizona Tax Research Association found that tax rates in fire districts served by Rural/Metro were just 26% of the average for non-Rural/Metro service areas. A 1976 study by the Institute for Local Self-Government found that in comparison with nearby cities using government fire services, Scottsdale had a faster response time, comparable insurance rating and comparable average annual fire loss.[9]

The city of Grants Pass, Oregon, has had a private fire department since 1979. Although most of the 30,000 residents live on the north side of the Rogue River, which divides the town, 15% of the city's population lives on the south side. Grants Pass contracted with Phillip R. Turnbull's Valley Fire Company to build a station south of the river and provide the necessary equipment and labor. Residents in the covered area paid between $1.15 and $2.15 per $1,000 of property assessment in 1984.[10] The city paid $17,800 a year. City manager J. Michael Casey estimates the city would spend $125,000 a year to operate a station there. The city has continued to operate its north-side station.[11]

Elk Grove, Illinois, with a population of 12,000, has also contracted its fire service to a private firm. The Elk Grove fire district has built a station and pays Wheaton-based American Emergency Services (AES) to provide firefighters, paramedics and equipment.[12] In 1984 the city paid AES $549,000 to operate the station, saving an estimated $451,000 from the cost for the city to operate it.[13] AES was started in 1979 by 43-

year-old Gary Jensen. Jensen had had experience as a firefighter and a consultant to insurance companies. To start the company he borrowed $100,000 from banks and individuals to purchase fire trucks and an ambulance. The service operated out of a rented garage until the town built a station in 1984. AES is not charged any fee to use the premises.

TOWING VEHICLES

In October 1984 the city of Chicago announced plans to privatize the towing and impounding of illegally parked and abandoned autos.[14] In 1983 city departments towed over 85,000 vehicles to ten pounds operated by the Chicago Police Department. The net cost of this service (total cost minus $3.9 million in fees) was $6 million in 1984.

Under the new arrangement private firms will receive $25 for each vehicle towed and another $5 per day storage fee. The city will collect an additional $20 per vehicle to cover its record-keeping and administrative costs. The $45 fee paid by vehicle owners is the same as was previously charged.

Chicago Police Superintendent Fred Rice estimates that the city was losing $50 for each vehicle it towed. With the new plan, the city expects to make a total net profit of $175,000 a year. The Chicago Police Department expects to eliminate 54 positions and the City's Department of Streets and Sanitation an additional 168 positions.

DAY CARE CENTERS

Hennepin County, Minnesota, uses a voucher system for day care services.[15] Prior to 1982 the county contracted out the operation of nineteen day care centers and determined the amount of reimbursement according to annual budget estimates provided by the private firms. Under the new plan low-income parents receive vouchers that can be used only at county-licensed day care and family care facilities. Participating centers then bill the county at predetermined rates for services rendered.

Under the voucher plan the number of low-income parents using day care facilities rose from 919 to 1,087 in the first five months. The number of centers parents could choose from increased substantially and the type of service they preferred (family care rather than day care) cost substantially less ($9.25 per day per child versus $11–$17). The new system reduced the county's bookkeeping requirements, created incentives for day care centers to operate more efficiently and reduced a previously observed geographic concentration of low-income day care facilities.[16]

MAIL SERVICES

As chapter 8 reported, although first-class mail delivery is a legal monopoly held by the United State Postal Service, a number of firms have found ways to circumvent the restrictions and sell profitable mail services. In 1981 Californian Scott Adler opened a World Mail Center to provide stamps, postage, registered mail, and overnight delivery services. Prices are 5% to 20% cheaper than government prices. Adler can offer these lower prices for two major reasons. First, his employees are paid between $4.50 and $9.00 an hour, whereas USPS workers average $12.00 per hour. Second, the centers provide only those services that are profitable; the USPS must offer certain services regardless of profit. By May 1984 Adler had opened nine more centers.

Some better-known postal service competitors include the overnight delivery services: Federal Express, Emery Air Freight, and United Parcel Service. Emery Air Freight was founded by John C. Emery in 1946. John Emery, Jr., took over the company only after working as a truckdriver, salesman, and sales manager. Emery has guided the firm through a transition that has dramatically improved profitability since 1983.

Competition, especially from Federal Express, has been rising in the package delivery industry. Businesses are placing an increasing emphasis on speedy, reliable delivery of documents and packages. The 1970s deregulation of the airline industry reduced service to some locations, hampering Emery's efforts to provide fast service. Emery's response was to buy and operate its own aircraft, which now serve 130 U.S. cities, beginning in 1981. It also revived a product created earlier—the Emery Urgent Letter. Emery's overnight service is distinctive in that it has no weight restriction and is a flat $14 price anywhere in the continental United States. International deliveries are usually made within two days.[18] Federal Express, by contrast, charges $240 for overnight delivery of its maximum 150-pound package. The response of the United States Postal Service was to begin its own overnight "express mail" service.

AIR TRAFFIC CONTROL

During the PATCO strike in 1981 the FAA closed numerous control towers at small airports in order to concentrate controllers at busier ones. Since that time a number of private companies have begun providing air traffic controllers to municipal airports. The largest of these is Barton Air Traffic Control, Inc., based in Tennessee. Hugh Barton and Robert Lynch, both retired military controllers, organized the firm in 1968. Barton competes with International Technical Aviation Professionals (ITAP) and Midwest for the estimated 500 to 800 small airports with towers. Typically the city or airport authority leases the tower from the FAA and subcontracts the controlling to a private firm. Barton staffs towers with retired military controllers and former FAA controllers. Costs are lower for the firm than for the FAA because Barton pays lower wages and runs towers with smaller staffs.[19]

There have been suggestions that the FAA turn air traffic control over to the private sector. American Airlines' Thomas G. Plaskett advocates the creation of a corporation to perform some functions of the FAA, including collection of airport taxes and performance of air traffic control. Airline inspection and certification would still be handled by the FAA under the plan backed by the airline trade group, The Air Transport Association. The airlines are frustrated by the Reagan administration's refusal to spend $4 billion in accumulated airport taxes, which could be used to increase the number of controllers and upgrade control equipment.[20]

SATELLITES

An example of privatization at the federal government level is the 1985 transfer of the Landsat satellite system to Earth Observation Satellite Company, or EOSAT. EOSAT is a partnership formed in 1972 by Hughes Aircraft and RCA Corporation. The firm operates the satellites and ground control equipment, as well as selling photographs at nominal cost to oil exploration companies, crop forecasters, mining companies, and other firms.[21]

When the decision was made to turn the system over to a private company, firms were allowed to submit bids of the amount of subsidy each would require to operate it. EOSAT's request for $295 million was the lowest. The amount included $250 million to replace the two aging satellites as well as $45 million for their launch from a space shuttle.

The future of Landsat has recently become threatened due to three factors. In February 1986 the French government began operation of a similar system, Systeme Probatorie d'Observation de la Terre, or SPOT. Some observers do not believe a large enough market exists to support both systems. In addition, if one of the two Landsat satellites "dies" as expected in 1987, customers may be lost to SPOT in the interim before replacement.[22]

Financial viability is the second concern. The Reagan administration's budget cutting is endangering the federal subsidy. Although $125 million of the $295 million has already been appropriated, Reagan's budget for fiscal 1987 eliminates the other $170 million under the rationale that those who benefit from the system (photo purchasers) should bear the full cost of the product. Finally, the market for Landsat photos is uncertain. Dropping oil and mineral prices in 1986 means there is little incentive for exploration, from which the demand for satellite photos of geological formations is derived.[23]

REFUSE COLLECTION

Savas studied garbage collection costs in 1,400 communities and found that for cities with over 50,000 population, private collectors were 30% less costly than public ones.[24] Savas also found that private contractors used fewer workers to do the same amount of work (2.1 versus 3.2 workers per crew), had lower rates of absenteeism (7% versus 12%), and used superior equipment.[25]

Phoenix, Arizona, has privatized more than a dozen of its city services, including refuse collection. The city accepts bids from both private firms and the city collection department before awarding five-year contracts. Bids are made on the basis of service districts so that a contractor might cover some while the city department would be awarded others. Waste Management, Inc., currently operates in the city. Waste Management provides refuse collection for over 400 other cities. Although city workers are unionized, competition has enabled the city to win cost-saving concessions, according to Phoenix Public Works Director Ronald W. Jensen. In 1984 the city refuse collection department was able to cut costs enough to win a contract after bidding against private firms.[26]

Waste Management, Inc., was formed in 1969 when several Chicago refuse collection companies combined their businesses.[27] Waste Management executives exercise strong cost control by purchasing equipment according to efficiency criteria, careful scheduling of routes, and use of small crews. Use of new technology is also emphasized. Waste Management bought British equipment and modified it to develop an innovative disposal system that dries and deodorizes garbage—the first of its kind in the United States.[28] The firm competes with Browning-Ferris Industries of Houston and SCA Services of Boston. Although Browning-Ferris is larger, Waste Management is the most profitable of the three industry leaders.

WEATHER FORECASTING

In the 1970s the number of private firms selling weather forecast information grew dramatically. By 1985 it had grown to a $100 million industry, according to the *Washington Post*.[29] Purchasers of forecasts include the news media, trucking firms, shipping companies, offshore drillers, building contractors, vacation resort areas, commodities traders, school districts, cities that hire snow-clearing crews, and agricultural companies.[30] One advantage of private firms over the National Weather

Service is that they can provide specific forecasts for designated areas, thus giving more reliable information.

Accu-Weather, founded by Joel N. Myers in 1962, now has more than 50 meteorologists and sells forecasts to about 500 organizations. Myers began his forecasting business while in graduate school, advising a Pennsylvania ski resort when it should use snowmakers. Accu-Weather is one of about 100 private U.S. forecasting services.[31]

Ocean Routes, Inc., based in Palo Alto, California, specializes in forecasts for offshore drilling and steamship lines.[32] Earth Satellite Corporation generates crop forecasts based on its aerial photos. Some companies have their own forecasters, including Pacific Gas and Electric, E. F. Hutton, and Sears Roebuck. Cargill grain company follows worldwide weather conditions in estimating crop yields.

Most private forecasting firms buy raw data from the National Weather Service and then subject the information to a more specific analysis according to customer needs. Weather data bases created by the National Weather Service in 1983 are available with a one-time entry fee, annual maintenance fee, and user fee.

WASTEWATER TREATMENT

Envirotech Operating Services, based in San Mateo, California, has been managing municipal wastewater treatment facilities since 1972. Today it operates more than twenty plants across the United States, including facilities in California, Montana, Massachusetts, Ohio, New York, Arizona, Michigan, Texas, and Mississippi, with more contracts than any other firm in the field. Its major competitor is Metcalf and Eddy, a plant design firm that has expanded into operations management. EOS is able to manage facilities more efficiently than municipal governments due to economies of scale and specialized expertise. The resources of the headquarters staff are available to help plant managers nationwide with any problems. In addition, EOS has developed a computerized system called "CAMEO" (Computer Assisted Management for Environmental Operations). It coordinates both process control and maintenance management for maximum performance within a cost-effective program. EOS sells the management information system outside the company as well, customizing it to the facility for which it is purchased. A typical system includes a microcomputer, communication link, and software.

When EOS first began contracting to manage wastewater treatment facilities, its biggest challenge was one of educating and developing the market. Wastewater treatment does not usually receive much attention in a community unless there are operational difficulties. Those communities with such problems tended to be more receptive to proposals for private management. Difficulty in complying with new federal regulations governing effluent standards has also been a strong incentive for municipal governments to hire specialists from the private sector. Today there is more market awareness of the convenience and cost advantages of contracting for this service, and EOS is facing more competition.

One city that has been very satisfied with EOS management services is Vancouver, Washington. The city signed its first contract with EOS in 1978. In 1984 it signed a new, ten-year contract with EOS. The contract was distinctive in length and terms. The city's payments to EOS are based upon indices that gauge labor, materials, and energy costs. Any savings generated are divided between the city (75%) and the firm (25%). An escape clause gives the city the option to break the contract after five years if one year's notice is given and a $150,000 fee is paid. Although the city is responsible for any capital improvements, it is relieved of duties relating to personnel, accounting, operations management, and effluent regulation compliance. The increasing complexity of facility equipment is also a factor in contracting. Private firms can pay salaries to attract top engineers and technicians capable of operating and maintaining the sophisticated new plants.[33]

PRISONS

The largest private prison management firm in the United States is Corrections Corporation of America (CCA).It was started by attorney Tom Beasley from Nashville, Tennessee, in 1983. At present it has contracts to manage three Texas facilities that house illegal aliens; two Memphis, Tennessee, juvenile detention centers; and a workinghouse near Chattanooga, Tennessee.

Buckingham Security, Inc., has a contract with Butler County, Pennsylvania, to manage that county's 95-bed prison. The company both builds and operates security facilities.[34] Buckingham was started by Charles Fenton, who had been a corrections officer and federal prison warden. The firm intends to specialize in what Fenton terms the "special needs" inmate. Such inmates are in protective custody and thus cannot be housed with the general prison population. (An example is a drug dealer who agrees to give authorities information on other dealers in exchange for a lesser charge.)

Behavioral Systems Southwest, Inc., began in 1971 as a halfway house for heroin addicts. Former California parole officer Ted Nissen opened the nonprofit facility with a federal contract that paid $85,000 a year. In 1978 he borrowed $60,000 from a bank and incorporated. Behavioral Systems works under contract for the governments of California and Arizona, as well as the federal government. The firm is involved with "minimum security prisons, immigration control, half-way houses for addicts and drunk driving schools."[35]

In Minnesota a nonprofit group called the Volunteers of America has contracted with two counties and state and government entities to operate a jail in Ramsey County since 1984. In addition to housing the female inmates, the group offers the women courses in such subjects as job hunting, cooking, and budgeting.[36] Other nonprofit groups in other areas are providing similar services for humanitarian reasons.

CONCLUSION

This review of several case studies of where privatization of public functions has taken place leads to the following conclusions:

1. Entrepreneurs are both ready and capable of responding to the opportunities that privatization presents.
2. There is no standard model that privatization always or usually follows.
3. The results of privatization are lower costs with no diminution in the quality of service.
4. Public officials are generally pleased with the results of privatization, particularly at the local level.
5. Privatization works best in an environment of competition. Single suppliers with exclusive long-term contracts tend to blunt the entrepreneurial spirit and reduce, if not eliminate, the benefits of privatization.
6. Privatization achieves its successes principally through paying lower salaries, the adoption of more efficient technologies, and greater flexibility in service delivery.

The trend toward privatization not only produces benefits for governments in the form of lower expenditures but also opens the door for the creative genius of the entrepreneur to flourish.

NOTES

1. E. S. Savas, "Tax Plans Boost to Privatizing Services," *The Wall Street Journal*, 10 July 1985, p. 25.

2. P. A. Holmes, "Taking Public Services Private," *Nation's Business*, August 1985.

3. B. J. Stevens, ed., *Delivering Municipal Services Efficiently: A Comparison of Municipal and Private Service Delivery*, prepared by Ecodata, Inc., for the U.S. Department of Housing and Urban Development, June 1984.

4. C. F. Valente and L. D. Manchester, *Rethinking Local Services: Examining Alternative Delivery Approaches*, Management Information Service Special Report, (Chicago: International City Management Association, 1984), p. xv.

5. J. P. Schwieterman, *Private Sector Participation in Chicago Mass Transit* (Chicago: The Heartland Institute, 1984), p. 1.

6. S. Moore, "Saving Money and Saving OPSI," Executive Memorandum, Heritage Foundation, 23 June 1985.

7. K. Farrell, "Public Services in Private Hands," *Venture* (July 1984):36.

8. L. Witzeman, "The Fire Department Goes Private," in *This Way Up: The Local Official's Handbook for Privatization and Contracting Out*, (Chicago: Regnery Gateway, 1984).

9. R. W. Poole, Jr., "Municipal Services: The Privatization Option," *The Heritage Foundation Backgrounder* (11 January 1983), p. 7.

10. Farrell, "Public Services in Private Hands," p. 36.

11. S. Koepp, "Public Service, Private Profits," *Time*, 10 February 1986, p. 65.

12. Ibid.

13. Farrell, "Public Services in Private Hands," p. 35.

14. The *Chicago Sun-Times*, 22 October 1984; *Chicago Tribune*, 30 October 1984.

15. Valente and Manchester, *Rethinking Local Services*, pp. 231–235.

16. Additional case studies can be found in three excellent books: Poole, *Cutting Back City Hall*; Armington and Ellis, *This Way Up: The Local Officials Handbook for Privatization and Contracting Out*, (Chicago: Regnery Gateway, 1984); Valente and Manchester, *Rethinking Local Services*.

17. Farrell, "Public Services in Private Hands," p. 40.

18. H. Stieglitz, "Maneuvering in a Dog Fight," *Across the Board* (March 1985):16–23.

19. J. Veasy, Director of Personnel, Barton ATC, Inc., in a telephone interview 30 May 1986.

20. J. Main, "The Worsening Air Travel Mess," *Fortune*, 7 July 1986, p. 52.

21. A. Large, "High Hopes Riding on Privatized Landsat," *The Wall Street Journal*, 18 March 1986, p. 6.

22. Ibid.

23. Ibid.

24. E. S. Savas, "Policy Analysis for Local Government: Public vs. Private Refuse Collection," *Policy Analysis* (Winter 1977):49–74.

25. E. S. Savas, "Private and Public: The Record," *Government Union Review* (1982):31–42.

26. P. Holmes, "Taking Public Services Private," *Nation's Business* (August 1985):20.

27. C. Burck, "There's Big Business in All That Garbage," *Fortune*, 7 April 1980, p. 106.

28. Ibid., p. 111.

29. Quoted in "Weather Watching," *In Business* (December 1985):37.

30. J. Duscha, "Doing Something about the Weather," *Nation's Business* (July 1984):61R.

31. Ibid.

32. "Perverse Weather," *Business Week*, 27 February 1978, p. 60.

33. Information obtained from Rosanne M. Vidaver, Manager of Marketing Communications, Envirotech Operating Services, in a personal interview 2 June 1986.

34. Koepp, "Public Service, Private Profits," p. 65.

35. Farrell, "Public Services in Private Hands," p. 40.

36. D. Youngblood, "Private Firms Find New Ways to Deliver Public Service Needs," *Minneapolis Star and Tribune*, 23 February 1986, p. 1D.

III. PRIVATIZATION: INTERNATIONAL ISSUES

11

PRIVATIZATION IN EUROPE

Franke Burink

For while privatisation without liberalization will yield disappointing results, so will liberalization without privatisation.[1]

INTRODUCTION

An increasing number of countries in the world are beginning to realize
more and more that the government can and should play only a limited
role in regulating the economy and the daily life of its citizens. As a
result of the growing support these ideas are gaining among politicians
and economists and the translation of these ideas into policy, some
commentators are already characterizing the 1980s as the decade when
"the market mechanism returned to favor."

According to this "liberal economic theory" the government's influence on the economy is already much too great. All sorts of negative
economic developments—high real interest rates, declining investment
ratios, high unemployment, and so on—are attributed to pervasive government intervention. There is no one indicator that best measures the
"red-tapism" of the State, but for a global approach the rise in government expenditure over a longer period will suffice.

For the Organisation for Economic Co-operation and Development
(OECD) as a whole, these expenditures as a percentage of gross domestic
product (GDP) climbed from 28.4% to 41.7% between 1960 and 1983.

This chapter is based on an article, "Worldwide Developments in Privatisation," *ABN
Economic Review* (ABN Bank, April 1985). The author thanks Peter van Bergeijk and Kees
Eitjes of ABN Bank for their comments on an earlier draft.

By decreasing the role of the government, especially the central government, and allowing economic affairs to be determined more by the working of the market mechanism, the economy should become healthier again. Three key concepts can be distinguished in this respect: decentralization, deregulation, and privatization.

Decentralization reduces the central government's economic power by devolving responsibilities to local government; that is, by shifting power within the government sector from one level to another. *Deregulation* diminishes government interference in the functioning of the private sector by reducing the amount of obstructive legislation.

This chapter looks primarily at *privatization*—a concept that actually covers many ideas. In my use of the term *privatization*, however, tasks carried out by the government are made more independent by either decreasing or completely removing direct government influence. Attention is focused in particular on the partial or total transfer of ownership and control of government businesses to the private sector, a process that is also known as *denationalization*.[2]

The thesis that underlies this chapter, however, is that privatization will succeed in the long run only if it is combined with an endeavor to liberalize the economy (i.e., more competition, deregulation, decentralization, etc.). Therefore government's plans to sell state enterprises to make them more efficient must be judged in relation to measures to create an "enterprise culture" in society and to restore the role of market forces.[3]

To put the subject—privatization in Europe—in perspective, it is helpful first to review global developments in this area. Looking at privatization in Europe (a concept of place that is generally more real for non-Europeans) means looking at the various countries with their different economic-historical cultures. This will be done with a bird's-eye view.

Afterward I will examine in more detail the background and motivation for privatization in the Netherlands as an example of this process in a medium-sized European country. Finally, I will consider the concrete measures that have already been taken in the Netherlands in regard to privatization as well as those now on the books in the Netherlands. In the last paragraph I will try to make some general conclusions.

THE EXAMPLES: REAGANOMICS AND THATCHERISM

As was stated in the introduction, privatization has to be viewed within the context of the worldwide trend toward "less government, more market." The most characteristic example is probably President Reagan's supply-side approach in the United States, which started in 1981. The emphasis here was initially on deregulation and is now increasingly on regulatory reform that concentrates primarily on improving the quality of government intervention. This is being combined with proclamations about the virtues of voluntarism in the area of social services.

In Europe Mrs. Thatcher in the United Kingdom has attracted the most attention with her program "to roll back the frontiers of the State." In particular her attempts to privatize a large number of state industries have been reported in the world press. Because the privatization experience in Britain is the example for all European "privatizers," it is useful to look first at British motivations and measures.

One major motivation for privatization is provided by the fact that many state industries have acquired monopoly positions that could promote inefficiency, decrease the urge to innovate, and restrict the supremacy of the consumer. Conversely it could be argued that replacing a government monopoly with a private company monopoly would probably not improve the situation.

The British government has attempted to counter this criticism with a number of measures pertaining to market liberalization and the regulation of monopolies. On one hand, competition must be encouraged with state companies that are about to be privatized. Therefore, in the midst of its denationalization process, British Telecom—the big telecommunications service—was having to compete in one small market area with Mercury Communications. On the other hand, there must be regulations to prevent the private monopoly from abusing its powerful position in the market. In the case of British Telecom, the public Office of Telecommunications (Oftel), has to supervise in this regard and ensure that prices of telecommunication services not subject to effective competition do not rise faster than inflation.

The experience of the United States in regulating private monopolies is much more extensive and has always been carried out in the context of the antitrust policy. The breakup of Standard Oil in 1911 and more recently of AT&T are two well-known examples. (Growing foreign competition is, however, influencing antitrust legislation.) The United Kingdom, though, still lags behind in regard to its policy on competition, despite the presence of the Monopolies and Mergers Commission, the Restrictive Practices Court, and the Office of Fair Trading.[4] For government monopolies that are not being privatized (for the time being), thought is being given to improve efficiency by organizational decentralization, franchising, or completely stopping unprofitable activities. But with the privatization of British Gas and the privatization of Water Boards, a start is being made with the ending of so-called natural monopolies in the public realm. Regulatory bodies will be necessary here, too.

Other motives for denationalization that can be mentioned are the continuing political intervention in state businesses that makes profitability impossible, and the fact that labor unions can achieve higher wages here than in the private sector (with negative consequences for inflation).

Moreover the British government has argued that the sale of state assets contributes to a reduction in the Public Sector Borrowing Requirement. The total privatization program should bring in about £10.3 billion in eight years: equivalent to 3.4% of 1983 GDP (£4.75 billion per annum in 1986–1988). A point of strong criticism here has been that the temptation to maximize short-term proceeds from privatization can come into conflict with the policy of liberalizing the economy and encouraging competition. For the more privileges a company is allowed to retain after its privatization, the larger the proceeds from its sale.[5]

Finally, the British government also hoped that the privatization program would help spread share ownership among more people, thereby making it more difficult for a future government of a different political color to renationalize industry. To make the selling of the state assets a political and an economic success much attention has been paid to creating enthusiasm not only among the general public but also among the management and employees of state-owned concerns. So, for example, buyers of British Telecom shares were offered reductions on their telephone bills and employees were offered free shares. Every case has been considered unique with a separate approach to its situation. Pirie counts twenty-two techniques that have been used in the privatization programs to take full account of the political and social problems of the public sector, as well as of its economic shortcomings.[6]

The privatization of British Telecom signaled a start on the list of companies that belong to the group known as the "commanding heights" of the economy. Earlier, denationalizations involved companies that were in the public sector primarily because of historical accident (e.g., Cable and Wireless in Telecommunications) or companies that already competed with private companies (e.g., Britoil in energy). It seems that for Mrs. Thatcher, no sectors are considered "strategic" from a national point of view and therefore in need of protection from private ownership. The only concession to national interest is merely the presence of a "golden share" for the government in some companies, allowing it to veto actions such as foreign takeovers.[7] In the British context, of course, ideological differences between the main parties play a significant, perhaps the most important role. The history of nationalizations and denationalizations since 1945 clearly illustrates this. This is possibly the chief difference with what is going on in continental Europe.

PRIVATIZATION AROUND THE WORLD

Before turning to Europe it might be useful to show how the examples of the United States and the United Kingdom are being followed throughout the world. Not only in other industrialized countries but also in Third World countries, and even in the centrally planned economies, governments are undertaking schemes that could be labeled "privatization." However, a warning is in order here: privatization in one country is generally not comparable to that in another. Sometimes the results of a spectacular selling of state enterprises are more than canceled by increased regulation in other sectors, whereas the slowly developing economic liberalization in another country makes more sense in bringing back state intervention in the economy.

In Canada the government has resolved to sell off some C$10 billion (= 2.5% of GDP in 1983) worth of state assets in industrial companies including aircraft manufacturing, uranium production, and the communications sector. The fear of an assault by U.S. business has for the moment, however, hindered the development of a large-scale privatization program of its more than 180 Crown corporations.

Japan, which already has a small public sector, is starting to transfer its big telecommunications system and its tobacco monopoly to the private sector. Furthermore the government is planning to privatize Japan Airlines and Japan National Railways.

The private sector in Eastern Europe is still very small. Of the centrally planned economies, Poland has the most private enterprises in both industry (3% of output) and agriculture (78% of output). The relatively successful economic development of Hungary, which is being accomplished on the basis of expanding the scope for individual initiative, is attracting the attention of the other countries. Hungary is now especially keen on establishing joint ventures with Western companies to further technological development. A major breakthrough in Eastern Europe, however, seems dependent on an eventual major economic reform in the Soviet Union.

For developing countries, Glade sees at least four global factors that appear to support the adoption of privatization policies:[8] (1) the International Monetary Fund (IMF) has stabilization programs for countries with balance-of-payments problems that tend to favor the export sector and push resources in a private sector direction; (2) the World Bank is more explicitly orientated toward private-sector promotion than in the past;[9] (3) in general the views on development policies are changing (from inward-looking toward placing the emphasis on export expansion and diversification, priority for agricultural development above industrialization, and the more specific attention for small-scale enterprises); and (4) a more positive view on the role of multinational enterprises.

In Latin America, meanwhile, the years of growth in investment by the state in state enterprises ended with the debt problems of 1982–1983. Now the trend is being slowly reversed in countries such as Chile, Mexico, and Brazil. In Argentina the second phase of the Austral Plan to make the economy healthy includes plans to privatize state-owned enterprises in the steel and petrochemical sectors.

Even in Africa signs are growing that governments are planning a bigger role for the private sector (e.g., Togo in steel, milk, and plastics).

In Asia, privatization is quickly gaining ground. Not only in newly industrializing countries with large private sectors, such as Malaysia, Singapore, and South Korea, are state-owned airlines, banks, telephone companies, and so on being sold; programs for slimming the state sector are also being developed in countries such as Bangladesh and Sri Lanka.

The most remarkable example in this region is perhaps the communist People's Republic of China, which is trying to liberalize its economy very rapidly and has even begun issuing shares again.

The emphasis that the IMF and other supranational organizations now give to the working of the market is unmistakably inspired by the ideas and policies of the U.S. and U.K. governments. The same can probably be said of developments in western Europe.

PRIVATIZATION IN EUROPE

In 1983 a book was published on state enterprises in Europe in which the authors argued that the widespread nationalized companies of Europe were unfair competitors and urged American policymakers and business executives to rethink their trade policies so that they could reclaim the advantage.[10] How much has changed since then! A recent article even states that the United States lags behind Europe in privatization.[11]

The next paragraph sketches privatization in different European countries, but the reader should not expect a systematic up-to-date comparison of all deregulation and privatization activities in Europe.[12]

On the outskirts of Europe, Turkey drew great attention in 1984–1985 with a flying start to its privatization program when the bridge over the Bosporus and the Keban Hydrolectric Dam were sold to the public and plans were announced to privatize 263 other state-owned enterprises. These events were in contrast with the silence that followed. In the meantime, however, studies have been undertaken by consultant investment bankers. With the December 1985 opening of the Istanbul Stock Exchange to sell stock to the public, one obstruction has been eliminated on the road to success in new privatizations. Current plans focus on the sale of 15% of the equity of Turkish Airlines to its employees in 1986, and later in cement, textiles, and fertilizer industries.

In Spain, the socialist government has shown that it is no longer willing to write off big losses in state industries and has therefore carried out a highly pragmatic policy. The state holding company, INI, has

already divested itself of several companies, including textile and cel-
lulose industries. Seat, the car manufacturer, has been sold to Germany's
Volkswagen. Of the 245 real companies of the highly inflated Rumasa-
empire that was nationalized in February 1983 to prevent an economic
collapse of the group, most have been reorganized and are already privatized.

State influence is strongest in Austria. Among other things, by using
these enterprises the successive governments have managed to keep
almost full employment through the 1980s. But big losses by the state
holdings, in addition to growing budget deficits and public debts, now
demand strong measures. The socialist government is currently reorganizing the management and structure of the holdings. The opposition,
however, sees no long-term solution in this and wants an overall privatization program.

In the Federal Republic of Germany the federal government has a
share of more than 25% in about 1,000 companies, and 88 of the 500
largest companies are in the government's hands. The economic policy
of the Kohl government, which is designed in part to reinforce the market
sector, has more and more scope for partial or total sales of government
companies. In 1984 the state share in the big energy group VEBA was
diminished from 43.7% to 30%. In a privatization plan from 1985, thirteen
state enterprises were designed for sale, but implementation of the plan
has been very slow. During 1986–1987 the West German government
expects income of two billion deutschemarks ($888 million) from partial
privatization of state-owned companies, of which the VIAG aluminum,
chemicals, and energy group and the energy exploration company
Prakla-Seismos are at the top of the list. By not participating in a stock
offering, the state also reduced its share in Volkswagen, the car manufacturer, from 20% to 14%. Alternative study points out that privatization targets of 20 billion deutschemarks (1.1% of 1985 GDP) can be
reached.

The same story holds true for almost all Western European countries,
which set out to emulate the example of the United Kingdom. After a
first phase in which extensive privatization plans were designed with
enthusiasm, however, actual implementation has taken place on a much
smaller scale. The difference between the ongoing process of privatization in the United Kingdom and the somewhat hesitant approach of
the continental countries can be partly explained by the following factors.
As in the United Kingdom, the main thrust behind these programs in
most countries has been an alarming budget deficit, although most countries preferred to deal with the problem through a diminished growth
of government outlays. After several years of austerity, countries such
as Germany and the Netherlands did indeed succeed in diminishing

deficits by means of the latter method (along with help in 1985 from a growing economy). Quite apart from this remains an overall desire to lessen state influence in the economy.

An extra complication in countries such as Turkey and Spain is the small size of their capital markets. Their stock exchanges can absorb only a limited amount of new issues from privatized state enterprises,[13] and most governments are not prepared to sell the full 100% to foreign investors.

Probably the most important factor is the sociopolitical culture prevailing in the United Kingdom, which is quite different from that on the Continent. Privatization in the United Kingdom is only one of the manifestations of recent changes in the balance between different political ideologies in favor of Thatcherite-liberalism—or, in other words, "privatization is based on the ascendency of a particular set of values and beliefs in the long-term structural conflict between social classes in Britain."[14] It is not denied in this instance that significant problems with efficiency also exist in the British public sector,[15] but views on the subject are more polarized than on the Continent.

On the other hand, France initially appears to be the "odd man out" in this European trend of liberalization. Indeed, after the Socialist Party won the elections in May and June 1981, the new government nationalized many large industrial firms and almost the entire private banking sector in 1982. The dogmatic and interventionistic economic policy that was led by the French socialists can for the greater part be explained by their not being in power for twenty-five years after 1956. However, the French government learned fast. After severe economic problems emerged (big balance of payments deficits, three devaluations of the French franc), the trend of their policy was radically changed in March 1983. In macroeconomics an austerity course was pursued with favorable results for inflation and balance of payments. The industry was approached in a more liberal nonintervening way and then minister of industry (later premier) Fabius declared in April 1983, that "the State should not take over the role of the entrepreneur."[16]

Following the first series, no new nationalizations have occurred. Even important private concerns (e.g., steel concern Creusot Loire) with insurmountable financial problems have not been taken over by the French state for rescue. Liberalization after 1983 has probably gone farthest in the domain of financial markets and banking.[17]

The new prime minister, Jacques Chirac, has stated that privatization will be the backbone of his economic policy. The coalition of center-right parties in France that won the parliamentary elections of March 1986 has pushed through the French Legislature a bill to sell 65 state-owned companies including most of those naturalized by the socialists in 1982. However, the French state has always been characterized by *dirigisme*, or centralized authority, an attitude from which former and current governments could not and cannot escape. So it will take more than one government term to create an "entrepreneurial state," for, "between state capitalism and private capitalism, there is hardly a difference in France."[18]

To say the least, Europe is no longer striving to expand its public sectors. Serious attempts are being made to roll back the overall presence of the state in the economy, in part by selling state-owned companies to the private sectors. Big disparities, however, exist in the execution of privatization plans among the various European countries. These differences, caused by the diverse economic, historical, political, social, and institutional backgrounds, will continue to exercise their influence for some time. The next example, the Netherlands, will give a more detailed description of the context of a privatization program in one European country.

THE NETHERLANDS: REDUCING THE ROLE OF GOVERNMENT

For some time in the Netherlands thought has been given to the role of the government and its expenditure. As early as 1971 the Commission for the Development of Policy Analyses proposed limiting expenditure in the collective sector, but in practice hardly anything happened. The continuing growth of government expenditure and, with it, the growth of the financing deficit in the second half of the 1970s, however, necessitated real intervention. In the terminology being used in this nation of gardeners, "Pruning (the problem) is no longer sufficient; it has to be dug out by the roots."

A broad program of activities has gradually been instituted, aimed at getting control of the collective sector and making it function better. To this end the so-called reconstruction rounds have been set up. These rounds are chiefly characterized by official work groups that meet annually to scrutinize in great detail a number of existing policy areas within the collective sector and to make proposals on how to limit expenditure. The policy areas examined are those within the sphere of the national budget in the narrower sense as well as those pertaining to social security expenditures, health care, and the salaries and pensions of civil servants and the so-called trend followers (employees whose salaries and conditions are linked to those of civil servants). Examples of the resulting reconsideration reports include the government's rent and subsidy policy and the deficits in public transport that are now still being fully covered by the state.

The cabinet of Prime Minister Ruud Lubbers, which took office in November 1982, has traveled farther along this road under even greater duress from these financing deficits. Some seven "major operations" have been implemented or continued in order to attack the problem from different directions and to get the collective sector under permanent control. The emphasis is on well-based selective reductions in government expenditure. These major operations encompass the following:

—deregulation
—decentralization
—privatization
—reorganization of the government service; that is, improving the administrative organization
—rationalization of specific payments from the national government to local governments for which the purpose of the expenditure is stated beforehand
—the 2% personnel cut operation, with the goal of reducing the number of national government personnel by 2% annually (between 1975 and 1983 the number of civil servants that made laws and regulations grew 14.5 times as fast as the personnel working for private companies and subsidized organizations)
—reconsiderations, which means the government can select from among the reconsideration reports in stock at any time and use them as the basis for new cuts in public expenditure.

The present government's policy on privatization of *government services* is based on a report entitled "The Real Cost Principle and Privatization" that resulted from the Second Reconsideration Round in 1982. The report lists four motives for privatization in the Netherlands:

—*the budget motive*: In this way the government expenditure can be made structurally lower.
—*the administrative motive*: A slimmer government sector will lead to a more efficient government apparatus (smaller span of control) and reinforce the democratic element in the political decision-making process.
—*the innovation motive*: Companies will find more impetus for innovation, development, and exploration in the market sector.
—*the macroeconomic motive*: More scope for the operation of the market mechanism would stimulate economic recovery.

Three possibilities have been mentioned for reducing the government's influence: total abandonment of government services, subcontracting of services, or making government bodies independent.

In November 1982 an Interdepartmental Steering Committee for Privatization was established and was given the role of advising, stimulating, and coordinating efforts toward privatization. This commission selected fourteen subjects from twelve departments that could be considered for privatization in a first round (e.g., technical police services, forestry management, pilot service, and so on). Apart from the coordinated interdepartmental approach, each department was encouraged to investigate independently the possibilities for privatization.

From the government's answer to questions in the Lower Chamber of Parliament, it appears that in principle all government activities are suitable for privatization. The government considers privatization a difficult proposition, however, for matters such as maintaining public order, national defense, judicial powers, and policy formation. It is possible, though, that some concrete operations in these areas could indeed be considered for privatization; for instance, voluntary arbitration in civil court cases by private individuals in lieu of having official judges.

Only a few definite privatization decisions have meanwhile been taken. Services for weights and measures testing, assay, and the government car center will become companies with limited liability. On other services (e.g., pilot service and the state fishing company) positive decisions were taken as well, but the implementation is a long-term process. Discussions of the new legal position of the civil servants take the most time.

Overall, concrete results of privatization of government services in the first round have been especially meager, certainly in comparison with developments abroad. Complete privatization of the fourteen tasks named would involve only 10,000 of the 729,000 national government employees and 380,000 trend followers.

A second privatization round started in September 1985 with some thirty possible subjects for privatization, such as audit services, departmental supporting services, government printer, state building services, and so on. Having learned from experience, however, the accent in privatization is now no longer placed on abandonment or subcontracting, as in the first round, but rather on making services independent.

PRIVATIZATION OF GOVERNMENT COMPANIES

Government companies are one area that so far has remained almost untouched by privatization in the Netherlands, although it should be noted that state participation in companies here is not especially large. The state participates directly in 41 companies and indirectly in many others through organizations such as the National Investment Bank and the Industrial Guarantee Fund. The most important participations are listed in table 11–1. It should be remarked that most of the state-owned enterprises already possess a large degree of independence, which is in line with the government's goal of limiting its influence in companies.

As elsewhere in the world, privatizing an airline seems relatively the easiest task in the Netherlands. In 1984 a share issue and the sale of

Table 11–1

The Most Important Government Share Participations
(as of 31 December 1983, in millions to Dutch guilders)

Company Name	Most Important Sector	Value of Government Participation	In % of Capital Placed
Staatsbedrijf der PTT[1]	Telecommunications (tekst)	26,800	100
Rijkspostspaarbank[1]	Savingsbank (see tekst)	3,315	100
N.V. Dutch State Mines (DSM)	Chemicals (see tekst)	3,135	100
N.V. Nederlandse Spoorwegen	Railroad	2,750	100
De Nederlandsche Bank N.V. (DNB)	Central Bank	1,829	100
N.V. Bank voor Nederlandse Gemeenten	Local Government financing	780	50
Koninklijke Luchtvaart Maatschappij N.V. (KLM)	Airline (See tekst)	698	55
N.V. Luchthaven Schiphol	Airport	673	76
Maatschappij voor Industriële Projecten (MIP)	Equity fund	331	57
Nederlandsche Middenstandsbank N.V. (NMB)	Banking, commercial	199	22
Nationale Investeringsbank N.V.	Long-term loans	181	50
Koninklijke Ned. Hoogovens en Staalfabriek N.V.	Steel Manufacturing	174	29
Staatsdrukkerij en Uitgeversbedrijfl[1])	Government printer	118	100
Nederlandse Energie Ontwikkelings Mij B.V.	Energy	107	100
N.V. Nederlandse Gasunie	Energy	40	10[3]
Other national companies		217	—
Total		41,470[2]	

[1] Legally there is a distinction between the PTT, RPS, the State Printer, and other government companies. The first three are classified as state businesses according to company laws and have another relationship to the national budget.

[2] Valued on the basis of intrinsic worth as taken from the company's published balance sheet except when the state has a minority participation (Hoogovens, NMB)—in which case the stock market value is used. If the nominal value of the shares of the government companies is taken excluding the three government businesses given here, then the total government participation amounts to £ 2891 mln, £ 2934 per 31 December 1984. As per 31 December 1983: $1 = £ 3,06, and per 31 December 1984: $1 = £ 3,55.

[3] DSM (100% state-owned) holds 40% of the shares of the Nederlandse Gasunie.

Source: Budget 1985; Press Release Nr. Y 304, Ministry of Finance, 20 September 1984.

shares enabled the government to decrease its holding in KLM, the Royal Dutch Airlines, to 55.4% (against 78% previously). An issue marketed in 1986 brought the state share under 50%.

DSM range listing among the large government concerns in table 11–1 is Dutch State Mines. This competitive company, which now operates primarily in the chemical sector, has developed into a multinational with good profitability and in its daily business independent of government. In mid–1985 the Minister of Finance declared that there are no principal reasons why DSM should not become a private company. So far no concrete action has been taken.

A breakthrough was reached on 1 January 1986 when the Postbank (Post Office Bank) started its operations. As early as 1977 plans were presented to merge the Rijks-postspaarbank (State Postal Savings Bank; see table 11–1) and the Postal Cheque and Giro Services into the Postbank. Balance sheet totals indicate the Postbank will be the fifth general bank of the Netherlands. Shares will stay in government hands. The competition on the business market with the other banks for the time being will be restricted to current account credits.

Plans exist to create within two years two separate corporate entities from the PTT (Post Office, Telephone, and Telegraph Service): one Post PLC and one Telecommunications PLC. The PTT also will lose its monopoly on traditional telephone equipment and allow unfettered competition in regard to newly developed digital peripheral equipment. The PTT, however, is keeping its monopoly on public telegraph, telephone, telex, and data transmission services.

In September 1985 a report by an interdepartmental commission entitled "Selling of State Participations" was presented with the budget for 1985. The commission's conclusion was that state participation in enterprises should be allowed only for specific decisive reasons. If these reasons are missing, then state participation should be ended. The commission, however, is completely positive on the selling of participations in only 18 companies, which include Hoogovens (steel) and NMB (bank). According to the commission conditions for privatization are that stock prices should not be influenced too much; income from the share emission should be in a reasonable ratio to the revenues previously received by the governments; international agreements should be observed; and property and control of the companies should not fall into undesirable hands. An amount of £ 250 million income from privatization has already been entered in the budget for 1986.

Although it has not been mentioned previously, in the Netherlands, as in other countries, privatization often progresses much faster at the local government level. Within municipalities in particular subcontracting or the relinquishing of municipal services is occurring, as for example with trash collection and maintenance of public roads and gardens.

The presence of the Dutch government as an entrepreneur in the market by means of state companies is relatively limited and privatization apparently does not have any great priority. By contrast the volume of government services in Holland is generally deemed too great and much more attention has been lavishing on diminishing the role of the state in this area. Still actual privatization results so far have remained modest, completely in line with the careful and pragmatic policies in other fields (e.g., monetary policy) of successive Dutch governments. Budget reasons are the main impetus for the various privatization plans, but at the same time no far-reaching privatization program has been developed and executed for fear of increasing the already high unemployment.

CONCLUSION

The notion is growing throughout the world that "The State" is big enough now. Reaganomics and Thatcherism are two examples that have inspired Western European and other governments to tackle their own overgrown public sectors. All Western European countries have developed policies and taken initiatives for privatizing state enterprises, but the process has not yet become very dynamic. Whereas in North America, properly speaking, nobody questions the supremacy of the private sector,[19] and whereas in the United Kingdom the privatization process is the result of a special sociopolitical development, the Western European countries for more than thirty years have been pursuing the idea of welfare state for which governments seemed responsible. As discussion on privatization is part of the established debate on resource allocation between "marketeers" and "nonmarketeers,"[20] it is understandable that European governments take a middle-of-the-road position in the matter of privatization as well. Nevertheless it can be said that European mentality now is moving in the direction of "more market" and that growing privatization will be part of this process. Nevertheless the diverse sociopolitical, economic, and institutional backgrounds in the various European countries will ensure that each country inevitably makes its own choices.

NOTES

1. S. Brittan, *Financial Times*, 17 November 1983.
2. "Destatization." There are as many terms as there are methods, and even the word "privatiz/sation" is not spelled uniformly.
3. See also "Privatisation, Everybody's Doing It, Differently," *Economist*, 21 December 1985, p. 83.
4. J. A. Kay and Z. A. Silberstone (members of the CLARE group), "The

New Industrial Policy—Privatisation and Competition," *Midland Bank Review* (Spring 1985).

5. J. A. Schackleton, "Privatization: The Case Examined," *National Westminster Bank Quarterly Review* (May 1984). Critics argue, however, that to make the placements successful most share issue prices have been greatly undervaluated. See, for example, Dr. O. McDonald, "How the Taxpayer Has Lost Out," *Financial Times*, 26 February 1986.

6. M. Pirie, *Privatization in Theory and Practice*, (London: Adam Smith Institute, 1985), p. 21.

7. *Economist*, "Privatisation, Everybody's Doing It, Differently," p. 83.

8. W. Glade, "The Privatisation and Denationalisation of Public Enterprises," in G. R. Reddy, ed., *Government and Public Enterprise, Essays in Honour of Prof. V. V. Ramanadhan*, (Totowa, N.J.: F. Cess Co.) Glade, however, sees this impetus toward full privatization diminished by the growing capacity to manage complex public enterprises.

9. See also *World Bank News*, 6 March 1986.

10. R. J. Monsen and Kenneth D. Walters, *Nationalized Companies: A Threat To American Business* (N.Y.: McGraw-Hill, 1983).

11. P. Young and J. C. Goodman, "U.S. Lags Behind in Going Private," *Wall Street Journal*, 20 February 1986.

12. Recent overall views are offered in "Privatization around The Globe: Lessons for the Reagan Administration," N.C.P.A. Policy Report 120 (Adam Smith Institute, January 1986); "The Perils of Privatization," Euromoney (February 1986); and the previously mentioned *Economist* article (21 December 1985).

13. *Euromoney* even questions the combined capacity of all stock exchanges throughout the world to absorb at least $20 billion of new shares from privatized companies in 1986. *Euromoney* (February 1986).

14. A. Walker, "The Political Economy of Privatisation," in J. Le Grand and R. Robinson, eds., *Privatisation and the Welfare State* (London: Allen Unwin, 1984), p. 27.

15. For example, before privatization there was one employee at British Telecom for every 83 telephone subscribers; this relation was 1:125 in France, 1:127 in Japan, and 1:181 with U.S. Bell Atlantic.

16. *Le Monde*, 13 April 1983.

17. For a description, see J.-C. Naouri, "La reforme du financement de l'e-conomie," *La Revue Banque* (March 1986).

18. B. Dethomas, "La privatisation en marche," *Le Monde*, 1 October 1985.

19. *Economist*, 21 December 1985, p. 82.

20. J. Le Grand and R. Robinson, *Privatisation and the Welfare State* (London, 1984), intro. to pt. I, p. 15.

ADDITIONAL SOURCES

In addition to the literature listed in the footnotes, the following books and articles have been used:

Boorsma, P. B. "Saneringen in de Collectieve Sector." *Enschede*, June 1981.
Boorsma, P. B. and N. P. Mol. "Privatisering." *SMO Informatief*, 1983–1984.

Butler, W. "Les dénationalsations en Japon." *Chroniques d'actualité de la S.E.D.E.I.S.*, March 1986.

Clichy, E. U. "ParallelWirtschaft und Wirtschaftsreform. Das Unorthodoxe Experiment der Ungarischen Volksrepublik." *Ost Europa Wirtschaft*, December 1985.

Dangeard, F.-E. "Nationalisation et dénationalisations en Grande-Bretagne." *La Documentation Française* (Paris), 1983.

Heroverweging Kollektieve Uitgaven deel Rapport 32. "Privatisering." *Tweede Kamer*, zitting 1981–1982, 16625 nr. 40.

Leenders, P. and O. van de Vijver. "De Lange Adem van de Privatisering." *NRC Handelsblad*, 12 February 1986.

Pelkmans, J. and M. van Nie, eds. *Privatization and Deregulation: The European Debate*. Working paper. Maastricht: European Institute of Public Administration, 1985.

Pliatzky, L. "Can Government Be Efficient?" *Lloyds Bank Review*, January 1986.

Soeterbroek, F. and A. Walravens. "Privatization in Nederland, Analyse Kritiek en Alternatieven." February 1985.

Sofaës, C. "Objectifs économiques et critères de gestion du secteur public industriel." "Les nationalisations." *Revue Economique*, May 1983.

Tomlinson, J. D. "Regulating the Capitalist Enterprise: The Impossible Dream?" *Scottish Journal of Political Economy*, February 1983.

Wilson, D. "The Privatisation of Asia." *The Banker*, September 1984.

12

THE ECONOMICS OF CANADIAN MUNICIPAL WATER SUPPLY: APPLYING THE USER-PAY PRINCIPLE

Steven H. Hanke

INTRODUCTION

The purpose of this chapter is to examine the user-pay principle as it applies to the municipal water industry in Canada. The user-pay principle requires that users pay the full economic costs of the goods and services that they consume. Equity, efficiency, and water conservation are promoted by the application of the user-pay principle.

This chapter compares current Canadian practices with those required by the user-pay principle. Recommendations are made with regard to the changes in Canadian practices that are required to bring the Canadian municipal water industry up to the standards required by the user-pay principle. In addition, recommendations are directed to the most appropriate means to attain the user-pay principle in Canada.

INDUSTRY STRUCTURE

Most (93%) of the municipal water systems in Canada are publicly owned and operated. Local governmental entities own 92% of these public systems, with the remainder being owned by provincial governments. The private systems, which account for only 7% of the total, are typically small and virtually all are located in Quebec.

The delivery of municipal water, although it accounts for only 8% of Canada's water intakes, directly touches most Canadians. For example, a 1981 survey of 3,212 municipalities, which contained 86% of the country's population, revealed that 96% of the population surveyed received water from a municipal distribution system. The survey also found that domestic households were the dominant customer class, accounting for 51% of total system pumpage. Industrial users who are supplied by municipal systems accounted for 19% of total system pumpage, while the commercial/institutional and losses/unaccounted classes each accounted for 15% of the total pumpage.

Although the number and quality of Canadian studies that have attempted to determine demand characteristics for aggregate municipal water use and that for various types of municipal customers have been limited, they do reveal findings that are similar to those found in studies from other countries. System demands vary during the year, with maximum day demands occurring in the warmer, dry summer months and the typical maximum to average day water use ratios ranging from 1.5 to 2.0. Aggregate water use is relatively insensitive to changes in the per gallon price of water. In consequence, if the real price per gallon of water is increased, water use decreases but less than proportionately to the price increase.

One domestic water demand study of high quality was conducted in southern Sweden. Because the socioeconomic characteristics of the population and the climatic conditions are similar to those that exist in many parts of Canada, it is worth noting that the water use responsiveness to changes in real price was found to be even less than that reported in the Canadian studies. For example, in southern Sweden a real price increase of 10% would reduce water use by only about 1% for domestic users.[1]

Industry Cost Accounting Practices

With the exception of very small communities, separate accounts for costs and revenues are maintained for publicly owned municipal water systems. However, the cost accounts do not record economic costs. For example, with the exception of Nova Scotia and Prince Edward Island, capital costs are not amortized and depreciation costs are not directly accounted for. Moreover, to the extent that provincial or federal grants are used to finance new works, these grant amounts are not carried on the books as part of costs of the new investments. The portion of the new works that is financed by grants is therefore not treated as part of a system's cost.

Capital costs, at best, are accounted for only indirectly. This occurs when capital is financed by borrowing, and debt serving costs are entered in the cost accounts. However, these costs usually do not bear a close relationship to economic amortization costs.

In consequence, in general recorded costs for municipal water systems are below real economic costs. So even in cases in which sales (user-pay) revenues are equal to reported costs, these revenues fall short of covering the economic costs of municipal water supply.

Revenue Sources

Municipal water systems generate revenues from two major generic sources: sales (user-pay) and intergovernmental grants. Sales revenues are raised by two basic types of water rates: a flat rate that is unrelated to water use and a commodity rate that is levied on the amount of water used. Most small systems do not install water meters but derive their sales revenues through a flat rate. Larger systems typically install meters and generate sales revenue through a two-part tariff combining a flat rate and commodity charge, with the commodity charge schedule per thousand gallons of water used declining as use increases. For both large and small systems sales revenues provide the major source of revenue for annual operating budgets, exclusive of revenue required for financing new works. For example, the average percentage of operating revenues derived from sales for all Canada was 85% in 1981.

Intergovernmental grants, the second major source of municipal water systems revenue, provide slightly more than half of the funds for new works (51% in 1981). The new works generated by grants have increased by 152% since 1975, when they accounted for only 27% of the total. So as a revenue source grants have dramatically increased, in both absolute and relative terms.

Recorded Costs and Revenue Levels

Recorded costs (which typically do not include capital financed by grants or economic amortization) are not covered by sales revenues. The proportion of sales revenues to recorded costs has risen on the average from 59% in 1975 to 75% in 1981. However, the level of sales (user-pay) revenue was actually well below 75% in 1981 because recorded costs are below economics costs. Without knowing the exact relationship between recorded and economic costs, there is no way to know if the ratio of sales revenue to economic costs has been increasing or falling or is constant.

FEDERALISM AND INTERGOVERNMENTAL COST-SHARING

To apply the user-pay principle, intergovernmental cost-sharing considerations must be addressed. The user-pay principle requires that two cost-sharing rules, the least-cost technique and the association rules, be applied.

The Least-Cost Technique Rule

The least-cost technique rule requires that, if any cost-sharing is afforded municipal waterworks, it be offered in the same proportion to all alternative means of supply. So, for example, if 25% of the cost of surface water supplies is covered by federal cost-sharing, then 25% of the cost of groundwater supplies must also qualify. If the rule is not followed and groundwater projects do not qualify for grants, while surface water projects receive 25% federal cost-sharing, then locals would be biased away from groundwater projects for which they would be paying 100% toward surface water projects, for which they would pay only 75%. This could create economic waste. For example, if a groundwater project and surface water project produced the same output and the groundwater project cost $85 million and the surface water project cost $100 million, even though the groundwater project was economically superior, locals would prefer the surface water project because it would cost them only $75 million. The economic waste from this decision—one that resulted from not applying the least-cost rule—would be $15 million.

The least-cost technique rule requires that the governmental entity supplying water supply grants must do so on the same terms—finance the same proportion of project finance—for all alternative projects, so that cost-sharing remains neutral among project techniques. The simplest way to apply the rule is to supply grants for water that are restricted as to the means chosen to provide supply. By doing this, local decisions about the best means of accomplishing the local water supply objectives will not be biased by cost-sharing programs.

The Association Rule

The association rule requires that residents of various political jurisdictions share project costs in proportion to the direct project benefits received within the respective political jurisdictions. For example, if all the direct benefits from a project are received by local residents, as is the case with municipal water systems, then local residents should pay all of the project costs and there should be no intergovernmental (provincial or federal) cost-sharing.

If the rule is not followed, intergovernmental subsidies occur. In consequence distortions in the demand for both waterworks and economic waste result. For example, if 100% of a project's benefits are received locally but only 50% of the project's costs are paid for by locals, with the remainder being paid for by provincial and federal governments (as was the average case in Canada during 1981), then local beneficiaries (users, politicians, and bureaucrats) demand too many overdesigned "gold-plated" projects. The locals' demand for projects is excessive for the simple reason that they are required to pay only 50 cents (rather than a dollar) for each dollar invested in new projects, although they receive all the project benefits. If the provincial and federal governments put no constraints on the size of their grant programs, the locals will stop demanding project monies only when the benefits derived from the projects equal 50 cents for each dollar invested in new projects. In consequence, economic waste will plague the municipal water industry because system investment will be overextended until the real cost of another dollar invested yields only 50 cents in real benefits.

Policy Observations

Because the direct benefits of municipal water supply are received directly by local users, the user-pay principle (the association rule) requires that no intergovernmental cost-sharing programs should exist[2]. Hence, in Canada both provincial and federal cost-sharing programs should be phased out. Particular attention should be focused on phasing out the large and rapidly growing provincial cost-sharing programs.

If these programs are not eventually eliminated, the following wasteful consequences will result:

1. Local demands for new water supply systems will become exaggerated.
2. Municipal systems will become overdesigned and "gold-plated."
3. Provincial and federal officials, in an attempt to control local demands and design practices, will become more involved in specifying the standards and designs to be used, resulting in a lack of flexibility and innovation in system design.
4. To the extent that grant monies are limited, local governments will begin to defer water supply investments in anticipation that they will be able eventually to receive grant subsidies if they wait.

THE USER-PAY PRINCIPLE: LEVEL AND STRUCTURE OF WATER RATES

Level of Water Rates

The user-pay principle requires that users pay water rates at the level at which the total revenues generated by the rates equal the total economic cost imposed by the provision of water supply and its use. The economic costs that should be covered by rates include out-of-pocket operating costs, economic amortization charges for all capital employed, and the opportunity costs (if any) for the raw water used.

The logic of requiring rates to be set at this level is quite straightforward. If, in total, users are willing to pay a sum equal to the total economic cost of providing municipal water, then we can conclude that the value of delivered water to the users (direct beneficiaries) is as great, if not greater than, the value of the resources used to deliver the water.

Structure of Water Rates

In addition to the proper water rate level, the user-pay principle requires that rates be structured, so that users are required to pay commodity charges (prices) that are equal to the incremental costs imposed by users' consumption decisions.[3] For example, if users decide to use water, they should be required to pay a price per unit for that water that is equal to its incremental cost. This element of a water rate structure is a commodity charge and signals users as to the costs that their decisions impose on water systems. By requiring such a price, each time users decide to consume water they value its use as highly, if not more highly than, the resources required to deliver that water.

Another rate structure element, the flat fee, is not directly tied to users' incremental water use decisions. This element—which can be applied in annual connection charges, monthly minimum charges, and so on—should be set so that the amount of revenue derived from it is equal to the difference between the revenue required to cover total economic costs and the revenue collected from commodity charges. This element of the rate structure is a residual element that guarantees that the rate level requirement and the desirable consequences associated with it are obtained.

Policy Observations

When judged by standards of the user-pay principle, the level of municipal water rates is too low in Canada. The revenues collected from users fall short of the total economic costs imposed on the systems by them. Specifically, although out-of-pocket costs are typically covered directly by users, economic amortization costs are usually not calculated and are not covered by water rates. In addition, rates for the abstraction of raw water are either not levied or are set below the opportunity cost of the water diverted to municipal use.

Municipal water systems should be encouraged to increase the level of rates to their true economic level, which would put the systems on a self-sustaining basis that was the sole responsibility of those who impose the costs on the system and also receive its benefits. To accomplish this intergovernmental water supply grants should be phased out and economic amortization should be required. In addition, those public entities that own raw water resources should charge municipalities abstraction charges for its use. That is, in the cases in which water diversion to municipalities imposes an opportunity cost, an abstraction charge should be set at a level that is equal to raw water's opportunity cost.

In addition to increasing the level of water rates, their structure should be altered. The commodity charge element of the structure should be retained, but it should be set at the incremental cost of water use. This would require that commodity charges that decline with increasing use (within a given billing period) should be eliminated, as the incremental cost of using water is the same for a gallon of water used by a smaller user or a large user. Within a given billing period, the price of water per gallon should remain constant, be the same for all users, and be set equal to the incremental cost of water use during the billing period.[4]

ORGANIZATIONAL OPTIONS FOR IMPLEMENTATION OF THE USER-PAY PRINCIPLE

Various public and private organizational options are available for the supply of municipal water. Each has different implications with regard to the user-pay principle and the general efficiency and costs associated with the delivery of municipal water.

1. Public Ownership

Bureaucratic Socialism. Bureaucratic socialism represents a generic type of management of publicly owned resources. It characterizes the publicly owned municipal water systems in Canada. With bureaucratic socialism the day-to-day management of the public water systems is carried out by public bureaucrats who operate by detailed rules that are largely self-imposed. Although politicians do not operate the systems, they do exert considerable influence over them through legislative mandates as well as their ability to influence the course of bureaucrats' careers as well as public sector budgets. In short, bureaucratic socialism is accompanied by high degree of politicization. Bureaucratic socialism is insulated from the forces of market processes such as consumer demands and economic costs. Instead, bureaucratic and political processes are the mechanisms through which decisions concerning the provision of municipal water are made.

The insulation of bureaucratic socialism from economic forces centers on the fact that systems under this generic form are publicly owned and their assets are not transferable. The consequences of the future actions of publicly owned enterprises are not capitalized into the current transfer prices of the public enterprise assets because there are no transfer prices. The ultimate "owners" of public enterprises, the taxpayers, have little incentive to monitor the enterprises' activities because they cannot sell the assets that they "own." Given that unlike a private enterprise, where shareholders have an incentive to monitor a private enterprise's behavior to maximize the present value of an enterprise's assets, public bureaucrats tend to behave in ways that are quite different from private managers.

The incentives that accompany bureaucratic socialism lead to a number of hypotheses that have stood the test of empirical investigation.[5]

1. Public enterprises would have less incentive to set price (rates) at wealth-maximizing levels. Evidence from studies about this hypothesis indicates that both average and marginal prices are lower for public than private enterprise.

2. Private firms would adopt more complex rate structures than public firms, reflectng the demand and cost conditions that are related to various customer classes. Studies have found that firms do have more price schedules and that these private rate schedules more closely reflect cost and demand conditions than do public schedules.

3. Public enterprises would price their output in a way that is more sensitive to those with political power than private firms. Evidence indicates that public enterprises favor commercial and industrial users, who have considerable political power, relative to the same class of users who purchase from private companies. Public enterprises also tend to attempt to cross-subsidize users who are voters by "overcharging" users who live outside the public firm's political jurisdiction.

4. Managers of public firms would be less willing to change prices in response to changes in cost and demand conditions than would managers of private firms, as the effects of correct (or incorrect) decisions are not capitalized into the transfer price of public assets and errors of commission are easier to detect than errors of omission. Not surprisingly, prices are more rigid in public than in private enterprises.

5. Public enterprises should be expected to be more highly capitalized than private ones. Indeed, the ratio of peak demand to total capacity typically is lower for public than private firms.

6. The cost of capacity would be expected to be lower for private than public firms. Econometric work confirms this hypothesis, with private capacity costs being 10% to 50% lower than comparable public costs.

7. Total operating costs would also be expected to be lower for private firms. In the United States, for example, operating costs for private water companies are 25% lower than comparable public enterprises.

8. Private firms would adopt new innovations at a more rapid rate than public enterprises. Data from the United States confirm that private firms adopted cost-reducing technology more rapidly than public firms.

9. On the theory that monitoring is less severe for public than for private firms, managerial tenure would be longer for public than private enterprise. Strong evidence exists to support the hypothesis that tenure is longer for public firms.

These hypotheses and supporting evidence are consistent with what we know about the publicly owned municipal water systems in Canada. From the user-pay principle point of view it is important to emphasize that bureaucratic socialism is accompanied by high capital and operating costs, rate levels that are below economic costs, and rate structures that are not geared to demands and costs.

Market Socialism. Market socialism represents a second generic type of management of publicly owned resources. The theory of market socialism (it should be emphasized that market socialism is a theory because it is not generally practiced and has only been applied, in varying degrees, over rather short periods of time) proposes that the public sector should try to mimic the results of the private sector. It requires that all investments be evaluated against economic benefit-cost criteria and that the output from publicly owned enterprises be rationed by setting the prices for enterprises' outputs equal to their incremental economic cost. In short, market socialism calls for the application of the user-pay principle.

The facts reveal that market socialism—a technocratic solution to the economic problem—has never been embraced. The major reason for this is that alternative property rights arrangements are not neutral. Public property rights mean that decisions are arrived at through bureaucratic and political processes. These processes and the discretionary power they generate for bureaucrats and politicians are incompatible with market socialism. After all, why would any bureaucrat or politician give up discretionary power, so that technocrats, who apply benefit-cost analysis and incremental (marginal) cost pricing policies, could make the economic decisions?

In the municipal water field bureaucrats and politicians have protected themselves from suggestions that they should adopt market socialism by arguing that market socialism is indeed an excellent theoretical idea, but that no one knows how to apply it to the water field. This claim is false.[6]

POLICY OBSERVATIONS

Property rights arrangements are not neutral. The incentives created by public ownership explain why bureaucratic socialism dominates market socialism. They also explain why the user-pay principle is not applied to the output from publicly owned resources. The consequences of the user-pay principle cannot be attained by reforming bureaucratic socialism and transforming it into market socialism. If they are to be attained, the public property rights in municipal water systems must be transferred to private ownership.

2. Private Ownership

Property Rights Theory Revisited. Property rights arrangements provide the key to understanding the behavior of private and public employees and the performance of private and public enterprises. Private enterprises (assets) are owned by individuals who are free to use and transfer, within the confines of the law, their private property (assets). Consequently those who own private property have residual claims on private enterprises' assets.

When private enterprises produce goods and services that consumers demand, at costs that are lower than market prices, profits are generated. As a result property owners' wealth is increased. Alternatively, if losses are realized, the value of private assets declines and their owners' wealth is diminished. Hence the owners of private firms not only appropriate the gains but also bear the costs that result from the way in which private property is used. In short, private property owners must ultimately face the "bottom line."

The incentives created by private property rights—by the linkage between the consequence of the use of private assets and their owners' wealth—have profound consequences. Private owners face significant incentives that make it desirable to monitor the behavior of private enterprise managers and employees, so that they will supply what consumers demand and do so in a cost-effective way. Consequently private managers and employees find it difficult to engage in shirking behavior or behavior that is inconsistent with maximizing the present value of the private enterprise (the owners' wealth). Hence private property puts in place incentives that tend to generate efficient performances by private firms.

"Taxpayer-owners" could capture some benefits from increased efficiency of public enterprises through tax reductions. However, if realized, incremental benefits from improved efficiency would be spread over many taxpayers, so that individuals' benefits would be rather small. In addition, individuals' cost of obtaining these benefits-acquiring information, monitoring bureaucrats, and organizing an effective political force to modify the behavior of public managers and employees—would be very high.

The consequences of public ownership are predictable. Public managers and employees allocate resources (assets) that do not belong to them. They do not bear the costs of their decisions, nor do they receive the gains from efficient behavior. Because the nominal owners of public enterprises (the taxpayers) have little incentive to monitor public managers and employees, the cost of shirking to a public bureaucrat is low. Consequently public managers and employees would probably engage in shirking activity and the acquisition of various perquisites that increase production costs. After all, the costs of shirking and perquisites are borne by taxpayers who have little incentive to police these activities, while the gains from them (more leisure and an easy life) all accrue to the public bureaucrats.

Private enterprises make plans based on what they expect consumers to demand and what they anticipate costs to be. Private owners bear the costs and capture the benefits associated with implementing their plans. While public enterprises also plan, their plans are fundamentally different from private plans, because they are developed by bureaucrats who neither bear the costs of their mistakes nor legally capture the benefits generated by foresight. Hence from a theoretical point of view private and public managers and employees can be expected to behave in different ways, and, as a result, private firms will be more efficient than public firms.

Comparative Cost Evidence and Implications. Although economic theory, as well as common sense, strongly support the notion that private enterprises should be more efficient and productive than public enterprises, one question remains: Does the evidence support the theory in the municipal water field? Studies of public and private systems in the United States reveal that comparative cost data support the theory. Private operating costs are 25% lower for private than comparable public water systems. In addition, private investment costs are about 20% to 50% lower than those in the public sector for comparable systems.[7]

The implications of these findings are rather profound. The privatization of municipal water systems would result in the adoption of the user-pay principle. But more important, it would result in a dramatic lowering of the level of the entire structure of real economic costs. The gains from lowering costs in most cases would exceed the benfits generated by adopting the user-pay principle. So a switch from public to private supply would not only bring forth the adoption of the user-pay principle, but it would also lower the economic costs of water supply.

The Natural Monopoly "Problem" and a Suggested Approach to Privatization. An alleged theoretical problem that gives support to those who argue against privatization of municipal water systems is the natural monopoly problem. It is argued that a firm will become a natural monopoly if the average cost of producing a product constantly declines as output is increased. In this case, if there is more than one firm supplying the total market, each firm must be producing at an average cost level that is above the average cost level that would exist if only one firm supplied the entire market. Faced with this situation, each firm will be inclined to cut price in an attempt to increase its market share and reduce its average costs. Economic warfare will result and there will be only one survivor—a natural monopolist. Moreover redundant facilities will exist.

The argument states that the natural monopolist will raise prices and

restrict output once it has established itself and this will create economical waste. Many analysts conclude from this that when the conditions
that spawn natural monopolies exist, government should step in and
supply the market by employing a single public enterprise. It is argued
that this will not only solve the problem of monopoly exploitation per
se but also that it will reduce the higher unit costs and eliminate wasteful
duplicate facilities that would occur if unregulated competition prevailed.

The nineteenth-century economist and philosopher John Stuart Mill
was one of the first to argue that under natural monopoly conditions
private water companies would engage in wasteful competition.[8] This
would result in the duplication of highly specialized assets and ultimately private monopoly power. The solution, as he saw it, was to
supply infrastructure and services in these cases by employing public
enterprise. But Mill's analysis did not go unchallenged. In 1859 Edwin
Chadwick argued that although in natural monopoly situations competition for the right to serve individual customers would indeed be
wasteful, this did not rule out competition and the desirable results that
accompany it.[9] The essential point made by Chadwick was that competition should focus on this right to serve an entire service area rather
than individual consumers. In short, Chadwick argued than an exclusive
franchise or concession to supply an entire service area be established
and that private water companies compete for the right to serve the
franchise.

Demsetz rediscovered and extended Chadwick's notion that competitive results could be obtained, even in situations in which natural monopoly conditions prevailed.[10] A desirable outcome could be obtained,
he noted, simply by establishing a franchise and the requiring competition for the right to serve the franchise rather than individual consumers. By doing this, Demsetz argued, public enterprise and its
accompanying inefficiency could be avoided, and yet the wastes and
inefficiency associated with a private natural monopoly could be
avoided. Instead the benefits of unregulated competitive private enterprise could be obtained.

The key to Demsetz's system is the bidding procedure. To obtain the
desired result of free competition and the cost-effectiveness of private
supply, the franchise must be awarded to the firm that agrees to serve
the market with the lowest prices for the output specified in a contract.
The public authority or private association establishing the franchise
would act as a bargaining agent for customers in the franchise area. The
public authority would seek to award the franchise to the private firm,
agreeing to supply a given quality and quantity of service over the
franchise's life at the lowest price. The successful bidder would then
have the contract for all consumers in the franchise area. Thus the natural

monopoly problem would be solved without recourse to public enterprise. It should be noted that public utility regulation, an approach to the natural monopoly problem often used in the United States, would not be required if the competitive franchise system was adopted.

Dealing with the natural monopoly problem, four outcomes are desirable:

1. Prices should be based on the marginal or incremental cost of supply.
2. The products supplied should be of the appropriate quality and quantity.
3. Production should be accomplished so that costs are minimized.
4. Profits should be just sufficient to attract capital into the particular line of production under construction.

Demsetz claims that his private competitive franchise arrangement would generate results that satisfy these desirable features. Moreover he questions whether these features can be obtained either by public enterprise or by regulated private enterprises.

There are two phases in a franchising system, however, where some argue that problems can arise: the bidding phase and the operating phase. During the bidding phase effective competition is alleged to be a problem. At the end of an existing franchise, for instance, the current franchisee, it is alleged, often has his franchise renegotiated without visible competition from other bidders. Many have suggested that this indicates conduct that leads to the exercise of monopoly power and poor performance, as competitive forces are not at work to regulate the franchise.

The critics of franchising speculate about the reasons why firms that win original franchises tend to retain them and why a visible competitive threat allegedly fails to appear. They suggest that an existing franchisee has an advantage over potential entrants, as an existing franchise has more and better information about the demand and cost conditions associated with the franchise, has an established working relationship with the franchiser, and is possibly able to mislead potential bidders. Potential bidders might shy away from bidding because of the transitional or start-up costs that it would have to incur, which an existing franchisee would not. It is argued that these factors eliminate potential competition from the franchise system.

In defense of the franchise system, we should mention the French water and wastewater industries, where franchising has been successfully used for over a century.[11] In these industries effective and vigorous competition exists as franchises are renewed. Similar strong competition has been reported in other sectors in France that use franchises.

The effectiveness of the franchise system for water and wastewater in France is attested to by the fact that the socialist government that came to power in 1981 did not nationalize these so-called public utilities—even though they did nationalize many firms engaged in commercial activity. The mayors, who act as agents for water and wastewater customers regardless of their political party affiliation, argued against nationalizing water and wastewater firms. They claimed that nationalization would lead to increased costs for these services.

Even in cases in which there are few visible bidders for a franchise, competitive results can be obtained if the market is periodically open to competitive bidding. Recent research in a new theoretical field known as *contestable markets* indicates that competitive results can be obtained even when there are only two bidders. This research indicates that if markets (in this case franchises) are contestable, potential entry or competition for the market disciplines behavior almost as effectively under natural monopoly-franchise conditions as if normal competitive markets had existed. So if a franchise can be contested, it will tend to perform in a competitive fashion.

Critics alleged that pricing problems could also arise during the bidding phase. For example, if service to the franchise involved decreasing costs with volume, it would be possible to have competitive bidding in which a winning bid generated accounting losses and yet the bidder's price for the output was equal to the marginal cost of the output. Demsetz has responded to this concern, noting that by allowing either two part tariffs or price discrimination in the bidding, both zero profits and prices at marginal costs could be obtained. However, this complication would require more specialized knowledge on the part of the franchiser who was evaluating the bids.

In addition to alleged problems during the bidding phase of a franchise, several concerns have been expressed about problems that might be encountered during the operating phase of a franchise.

Franchises typically last for a considerable length of time. In France, where franchises are common and where the capital infrastructure is both owned and operated by the franchisee, the franchise can last for as long as thirty years. In situations in which private firms have concessions only to operate and maintain capital that is owned by a public entity, the maximum length of the franchise in that country is twelve years. During this period, significant changes in demands, costs, and technologies will probably occur, requiring complex pricing formulas. These will require considerable expertise on the part of the franchiser, so that the original bids can be properly evaluated and the franchise monitored during its life. In addition to complex price formulas, contracts usually contain clauses that allow for renegotiation, if pricing formulas break down due to unanticipated shocks. If renegotiation takes place frequently, franchise bidding is said to be robbed of its most desirable characteristic—namely its reliance on price determination through competitive market processes.

The reason why pricing formulas complexity and contract renegotiations accompany long-term franchises is made clear with several examples. Early franchises were not bid on the basis of low price but usually on the basis of the maximum price that could be charged over the life of the franchise. These terms worked against the consumers during deflationary periods and against the franchisee during periods of inflation.

As a result of dissatisfaction with this simple type of pricing agreement, particularly during inflationary and deflationary periods, many franchises were simply abandoned or taken over by governmental entities, although in some cases they were retained and made more complex to deal with changing general price levels. For example, the franchise to supply gas for Paris specified a maximum price and also fixed a minimum profit for the firm. This arrangement created considerable problems for the city, however, because the price of coal used to manufacture gas increased rapidly during World War I. Consequently the average cost for gas was twice the maximum price allowed under the franchise. To maintain the franchise's minimum profit guarantees, the city had to subsidize the franchise from tax revenues.

To overcome the problems associated with early franchises, more and more complexity was built into pricing formulas and renegotiation provisions were included, so that the prices charged by the franchise could more closely reflect real cost and demand conditions. Although the complexity of franchise pricing formulas and evaluation and monitoring costs increase as the length of a franchise's life increases, the competitive price determination features of franchises are not lost if the franchise is contestable at the time of renegotiation.

A second potential problem associated with the operating phase of franchise occurs toward the end of a franchise's life, when it is argued that incentives exist that make firms underinvest in fixed assets and reduce maintenance.

These investment and maintenance problems can be overcome, however, by allowing the firm to amortize its investments fully during the franchise and also by requiring the franchisee to be bonded for performance. This latter requirement reduces the monitoring required by the franchiser because the bonding firm will, in effect, take over responsibility in this area and guarantee that the bonded franchisee meets the terms of the contract. However, there will still be considerable monitoring responsibility placed on the franchiser who is acting as the customers' agent.

CONCLUDING OBSERVATIONS AND RECOMMENDATIONS

The application of the user-pay principle requires that users pay the full economic costs of providing the water that the users consume. In consequence equity, efficiency, and water conservation objectives are attained.

- *Equity*: Only those who receive the direct benefits from municipal water systems are responsible for financing the systems that provide these benefits. All the economic costs incurred in the provision of municipal water are covered by those who impose these costs.
- *Efficiency and conservation*: Users, in aggregate, contribute revenues that are equal to the total economic costs (out-of-pocket operating, fully amortized capital, and the opportunity costs of raw water) of the water systems. In consequence, the users reveal that they value the water provided and the water services made available as much, if not more, than the value of the resources foregone by providing water and water services. Moreover users must pay water prices per unit of water used that are equal to the incremental cost of the water supplied. In consequence the users reveal that they value each unit of water used as much if not more than the value of the resources foregone by providing each unit of water consumed.

The municipal water industry in Canada does not achieve the results that would be obtained by applying the user-pay principle.

- The level of revenues obtained from users is well below the total economic costs of providing water.
- The structure of water rates is also inappropriate. Commodity charges (per unit water prices) bear little association with the incremental costs of supplying water and are generally too low.

When judged by the user-pay principle, the Canadian municipal water industry fails to achieve equity, efficiency, or water conservation standards. To remedy this, the following recommendations should be adopted.

- Intergovernmental grants for water supply should be phased out.
- Full economic costs—which include out-of-pocket operating costs, fully amortized capital, and the opportunity costs of raw water—should be computed. Water rate levels should be set at levels to recover all of these costs.
- The incremental costs of water should be calculated on a per unit basis. Water rate structures should be redesigned and commodity charges (prices) should be set equal to these incremental costs. If the revenues collected by these

commodity charges fall short of the total economic system costs, the shortfall should be made up by a flat rate charge.

The adoption of these user-pay recommendations will be facilitated if the following fundamental recommendation is adopted.

• The publicly owned water systems in Canada should be privatized. After privatization, these water systems should be regulated by competitive forces. This can be accomplished through a system of contestable markets and franchises, similar to the system that has served the water industry in France so well for over a century.

In addition to achieving the desirable consequences that accompany the user-pay principle, privatization would lower the costs of providing municipal water. These cost savings would not be trivial. In fact, they would exceed the user-pay benefits.

NOTES

1. S. H. Hanke, "Une analyse econometrique de la demande en eau domestique," *Techniques et Sciences Municipales* (Avril 1985) 203–205.

2. Note that the least-cost technique rule applies only if cost-sharing is justified, so that the least-cost technique rule is not applicable in municipal water supply.

3. This statement may not apply in all cases because it may cost more to meter and levy a commodity charge than the value of the price signaling benefits derived from such a charge.

4. In most situations it is probably economic to set inter-billing period commodity charges at the same level. However, in cases in which the incremental costs may vary greatly during the year, it might be economic to adopt commodity charges that vary on a seasonal basis.

5. L. DeAlessi, "On the Nature and Consequences of Private and Public Enterprises," *Minnesota Law Review* 67 (October 1982):191–209.

6. S. H. Hanke, *Economic Aspects of Urban Water Supply: Some Reflections on Water Conservation Policies* (Laxenburg, Austria: International Institute for Applied Systems Analysis, December 1982), pp. 1–90.

7. S. H. Hanke, "Privatization: Theory, Evidence and Implementation," in C. L. Harris, ed., *Control of Federal Spending* (New York: The Academy of Political Science, 1985), pp. 101–113.

8. Pedro Schwartz, "John Stuart Mill and Laissez-Faire: London Water," *Economica* 23, no. 129 (February 1966:71–83.

9. E. Chadwick, "Results of Different Principles of Legislation and Administration in Europe; of Competition for the Field, as Compared with Competition within the Field, of Service," *Journal of the Statistical Society of London* 22 (1859):381–420.

10. H. Demsetz, "Why Regulate Utilities?" *The Journal of Law and Economics* 11 (April 1968):55–65.

11. J. Monod, *The Private Sector and the Management of Public Drinking Supply* (Paris: Societe Lyonnaise des Eaux, January 1982), pp. 1–40.

13

ROLES OF THE PRIVATE SECTOR IN THE SUPPLY OF PUBLIC SERVICES IN LESS DEVELOPED COUNTRIES

Gabriel Roth

The purpose of this chapter is to present actual examples of private provision of public services—in education, electricity, health, telecommunications, urban transport, and water—in less developed countries (LDCs), and to draw conclusions that may assist concerned governments and aid agencies. The examples are taken from a book prepared in the World Bank. The World Bank supports the vigorous encouragement of indigenous private-sector enterprises in many countries because of their roles in mobilizing private savings, harnessing entrepreneurship, diffusing economic power, widening consumer choice, and stimulating competition.[1]

There are long-established traditions of the private provision of education and health services, and many examples in LDCs can be found today (e.g., Chinese schools in East Asia; traditional medical practitioners everywhere) despite attempts to follow Western fashions of "free" services provided by governments. But electricity and telecommunications do not follow this tradition and are only rarely supplied by the private sector in LDCs. There are no technical reasons why they should not be, as indeed they are in Brazil (electricity) and in the Dominican Republic (telephones).

Urban transport is provided by the private sector in hundreds of LDC cities efficiently, cheaply, and without subsidy. It is one of the earliest services for the private sector to supply, presumably because the main capital assets are mobile. Piped water, on the other hand, requires considerable fixed investment, which has not been forthcoming from the private sector. However, experience in West Africa shows that even this problem can be overcome by contracting with the private sector to manage capital facilities provided by the government.

EDUCATION

The tradition of private education exists in all known civilizations. When Confucius said that he would teach anybody who brought him a meal, he meant that he did not mind how much he was paid as long as the principle of payment was accepted. The idea that education should be free and supplied by the state is of fairly recent origin. It became established in Europe and North America in the nineteenth century and was subsequently embraced with enthusiasm in the twentieth by governments in Africa, Asia, and Latin America, with results that did not always meet expectations. Private education still survives in those countries because the public sector is short of funds and because the private sector can offer a better product, particularly for specialized purposes and for minorities.

The viability of private education for children of all age groups and income classes may be illustrated by the education provided by Chinese expatriate communities in Southeast Asia in the first half of this century. Chinese immigrants, some of them very poor, established new schools all over Southeast Asia to offer modern, Chinese-style education to all Chinese boys and girls. In some countries (e.g., Singapore) these Chinese schools received government help, but in others, such as the Philippines, they were privately financed. Children attending school in the Philippines received a very demanding education, as the Chinese schools were allowed to operate there only on the condition that they teach the normal Filipino curriculum in addition to the Chinese one. The usual way in which the Chinese schools met this requirement was by offering the Filipino curriculum in the morning and the Chinese in the afternoon. Students undertook the double primary curriculum in the normal six years, but whereas the normal Filipino secondary curriculum takes only four years, students studying the Chinese curriculum required six years to complete their secondary schooling. The quality of this education may be gauged from the fact that those who completed it were eligible to enter Taiwanese universities.

The number of children being educated in Chinese schools in the Philippines increased rapidly after the war, from 20,000 students in 1948 to 56,000 in 1956 to 64,000 in 1963 to 75,000 in 1971. During all this time there was some local hostility toward the Chinese schools, but they were allowed to operate by virtue of the 1947 Treaty of Amit between the governments of Nationalist China (Taiwan) and the Philippines. In 1975 the Philippines government ended diplomatic relations with Nationalist China and removed the main diplomatic reason for allowing the Chinese schools to continue. By 1976 there were only 138 Chinese schools operating in the Philippines, down from the 1971 total of 152. In April 1976 the government announced that all Chinese schools were to be banned in the future from offering Chinese subjects, other than the Chinese language, and that the Chinese classes were to be limited to two per day. The schools were also to be opened to Filippino students, and knowledge of Chinese was no longer to be a requirement for admission. In light of these restrictions, the future of the Chinese schools in the Philippines is uncertain, but the existence of these schools has shown very clearly that private education at both the primary and secondary level can be financially and academically viable.[2]

The financing of education raises serious problems, but the provision of free services by government employees is not necessarily the best way to deal with them. Education can be provided by private enterprise even if the financing is in the form of government grants or loans. Loan funds are particularly well developed in Latin America, where about twenty institutions cooperate internationally through the Pan-American Association of Educational Credit Associations (APICE). If it is felt that grants are more appropriate than loans, it is possible to use education "vouchers," which give the user the right to purchase education (up to a specified value) from approved institutions. This scheme was used very successfully in the United States for demobilized soldiers after World War II. A similar scheme is now in use in Chile; local authorities pay approved non-fee-paying schools a specified amount for each day that a child attends, with the schools being allowed to compete for enrollments. The value of this payment is of the order of U.S.$100 a year, which may be a fifth or sixth of the fees charged by equivalent schools in Chile. Nevertheless the amount is sufficient to enable groups of teachers—and of parents—to establish some new public schools. The Chilean voucher cannot be used to supplement fees in private schools. The system was introduced in the 1940s as part of a reorganization that devolved responsibility for the schools from central government to the counties. It was revised in the 1970s. No comprehensive evaluation of the Chilean voucher system appears to have been published.

ELECTRICITY

Electricity, unlike education, is of fairly recent origin, with its use for power and light little more than one hundred years old. But like education, it was established privately. Power stations were established in New York in 1880, in London and Shanghai in 1881, in Valencia (Venezuela) in 1888, in India in 1895, and in Manchuria in 1902.

A major obstacle to the improvement of electricity supply in developing countries is probably the belief that the industry should be treated as a "natural monopoly" and that electric power therefore has to be supplied by the public sector—or, at least, regulated by it. It can reasonably be argued that electricity transmission and distribution exhibit such scale economies that they can be regarded as natural monopolies, but the generation of electricity can be carried out, as in North Yemen, at widely scattered points, either for use by the generating firm or for sale. There is also the possibility of cogeneration (i.e., an industrial process that results in heat and electricity being produced simultaneously), with electric power being sold for use by the public.

In theory one can envisage a publicly owned and operated "grid" buying electricity from competing suppliers at prices that reflect supply and demand. This does not appear to be happening anywhere in the Third World; but in the United States legislation passed in 1978 requires electric utilities to buy power from certain classes of producers if offered at favorable rates. This legislation encouraged the emergence of hundreds of small companies that generate electricity from wind or water power.

Brazil and Korea are among the few LDCs that have passed laws designed to encourage the generation of electricity by the private sector. One firm that has taken advantage of this in the north of Brazil is SATHEL, which manufactures (under license) a Swedish type of wood-fired steam turbine. In the early 1980s it contracted with the city of Ariquemes (population 25,000) to sell bulk power at an agreed rate per kilowatt-hour. The contract is for a ten-year period, after which the city has the option of renewing it or buying the equipment from SATHEL at a price agreed to in the contract. SATHEL uses forest timber to power its turbines and has gone into forest management to ensure that the timber used in its operations is more than replaced. It currently has three electricity contracts in the Amazon state; two in Rondonia state; and three in Acre state. The contracts provide for a minimum quantity of power to be sold each year but do not give SATHEL a monopoly.

Most governments, unlike those of Brazil, Korea, and the United States, do not allow privately generated electricity to be sold for public use. This is a pity because electricity, generated privately in large or small quantities, if sold to the public network can supplement or replace public-sector generation at substantial overall savings.

One possible source of electricity, available to scores of developing countries, is from the burning of bagasse, which might be described as what is left of the sugar cane after the syrup is squeezed out of it. In its dried form bagasse is frequently used to provide the necessary fuel for the manufacture of sugar. With suitable upgrading of equipment it is, however, possible to generate from it more power than is required to make sugar, and this power can be made available to the public grid. In Mauritius, for example, it was calculated that 8% or 9% of total electricity used in the island could be met by burning bagasse instead of importing fuel.

TELECOMMUNICATIONS

In most Third World countries, demand for telecommunications services far exceeds the supply, as evidenced by the high prices at which telephone lines change hands in cities where such transactions are allowed (about $1,500 in Lima and Rangoon; double that in Bangkok). A recent World Bank publication[3] posed the question:

Who or what group has decided that telecommunications investment should be constrained relative to demand by closely regulating and controlling inputs to the sector, its organizational structure, and the internal procedures of telecommunications operating entities, and by imposing numerous restrictions under which operating entities must operate?

It then answered this question as follows:

From the evidence reviewed it is clear that it is not the subscribers to or users of telecommunications services. In developing countries telephones and other telecommunications services tend to be used for productive purposes that benefit users who, in turn, tend to pay relatively high prices for the services, sometimes in flourishing black markets. . . . If it is not the users or beneficiaries of telecommunications services who are signaling that sector expansion should be constrained, then, it must be the owners, suppliers and regulators of the services—which in most developing countries are governments.

In the past, LDC governments have generally made the judgment that food, transport, power, health, and so on were the most pressing needs and should receive appropriate emphasis. So long as telephones were viewed as nonessential and largely luxury consumption, investment in the telecommunications sector received low priority.

In the last few years this perception of the role of telecommunications has been changing, largely because of the explosion of telecommunications activity occasioned by this technological revolution. Modern telecommunications are becoming essential to business activity—initially to compete in the international marketplace but increasingly for domestic business activity as well. This revolution, not only in total demand but in the role of telecommunications in the conduct of business, is generating pressure for change in the traditional organization of telecommunications activity and in the priority it receives in the investment schemes. A good deal of discussion and investigation of reform is going on, with many different mechanisms being examined, to make telecommunications entities more flexible, commercial, and efficient. Proposals for full-scale privatization are extremely rare, even among the most active reformers, because most governments believe that even if ultimately deemed to be desirable, full privatization is too large a step to be taken all at once. Instead, some governments are seeking gradual reform in which the consequences of each change can be evaluated before the next step is taken. These reforms include (a) internal reorganization of tele- communications entities (e.g., changes in procurement, pricing, man- agement systems); (b) creation of autonomous or semiautonomous government entities to replace government ministries; (c) joint ventures and management contracts; and (d) permission to major competitors and users to create alternative systems and interconnect them to the public network.

One example of partial privatization involves a private facility access- ing the international telecommunications network and providing serv- ices to a limited number of special customers. This is the "Teleport" planned for start-up in 1987 in the Montego Bay Export Free Zone in Jamaica, with management and financing provided by a U.S./Japanese joint venture.

The purpose of a teleport (of which there were at least twenty in the United States in 1985) is to provide high-speed, high-quality voice and data lines for companies engaged in telecommunications. The Jamaica Teleport is designed to serve information-intensive enterprises in the Montego Bay Export Free Zone, such as telephone marketing operations, reservation centers, and data entry firms. The information between the United States and the Teleport will flow on voice and data lines via an American Satellite Corporation satellite and a specially constructed ground station in Jamaica. The price of private leased voice and data circuits will be comparable to U.S. domestic operations, which are com- petitively determined and therefore substantially lower than those nor- mally payable for international services. These low rates are expected to make the free zone's facilities especially attractive to U.S. firms. And many of the users accessing the operators at the Teleport will not realize that their phone calls, placed through the 800 network, will be earning valuable foreign exchange for Jamaica.[4]

Experience with private-sector operation of telecommunications in LDCs has been mixed. In a number of countries (e.g., Botswana) gov- ernment-owned companies have been managed by foreign private firms with reasonable success. Private companies owned by foreign interests were once common in Latin America; they operated for several decades, but most were nationalized in the 1960s, for reasons which cannot be pursued here. The Dominican Republic still has a public service supplied by GTE, but even this relationship appears to be getting difficult after many years of relative harmony. The Philippines have a fully private telephone system that is, and has long been, unsatisfactory for reasons that warrant further study.

The U.S. telephone network was built up from thousands of independent companies, many of them "Mom and Pop" operations, with "mother" operating the switchboard and "father" stringing the lines. Technology has changed since those days, but there are no technical reasons that require, say, Indian villages to do without telecommunications until a government agency provides service for them. It is mainly governmental restrictions that prevent the expansion of telecommunications in LDCs.

HEALTH

The health sector, like education, has a long history of private provision. Traditional medicine is widespread in Asia, Africa, and Latin America, and practitioners almost invariably operate on a fee basis. Major problems in the health sector are (a) organization of health insurance and (b) integration of the traditional and modern sectors.

Health insurance, like education loan plans, is highly developed in Latin America. In some cases the insurance covers groups of employees; in others insurance companies cover individuals. However, health insurance can also be found in more primitive societies; in many Indian villages it is traditional for farmers to bring the local practitioner a gift at harvest time, which serves as an "insurance premium" for care for the following year. Similar customs are found in Indonesia. An example of health insurance between these two extremes is provided by the schemes in the Lalitpur district of Nepal.[5] The annual premium for membership in two health posts was set at the equivalent of U.S.$1 per household per year. This figure was chosen because a cigarette in Nepal costs a twelfth of a dollar, and it was believed that households could forego one cigarette per month in order to purchase health insurance, which covered the costs of these health posts over and above a subsidy received from the government. At a third health post, which was not in receipt of a government subsidy, the premium was set at U.S.$2 per household per year, which was intended to cover all of the costs. People who took the insurance had the option of paying in installments or of contributing labor equal to the price of the insurance premium. Membership in the insurance schemes entitles beneficiaries to free medical services and drugs at the posts; to outpatient services costing up to U.S.$4 per visit at a local hospital; and inpatient services of up to U.S.$8 per stay.

The integration of traditional with modern medicine is found in many countries. In India it is supported in government medical schools. In

Ghana, there are government programs to give modern training to traditional birth attendants, who are allowed to charge higher fees to reflect their new skills. Traditional medicine in India and China is more advanced than in Africa, possibly because treatments and remedies are recorded and published and thus made available to the profession for testing and comment. In Africa, on the other hand, traditional remedies are handed down from one practitioner to another under conditions of secrecy, so the lessons learned get around much more slowly.

As in the case of education, there need be no conflict between governmental financing of services and private production. Under the National Health Service of the United Kingdom, individuals are encouraged to choose their doctors, who are then paid from public funds an agreed amount for each person on their lists.

URBAN TRANSPORT

It is generally believed that urban public transport cannot be provided at a profit, that it has to be supplied by publicly owned or franchised monopolies, and that services have to be slow and costly. This belief is based on conditions in the large cities of Europe and North America. However, in many developing countries pubic transport is provided competitively and profitably, demonstrating that with appropriate organization and incentives, urban public transport can be supplied without subsidy to meet the needs of travelers at prices that most can afford.[6]

Bus riders in Calcutta, for example, have the choice of traveling either on the buses of the state-owned Calcutta State Transport Corporation (CSTC) or on buses owned by private operators. Travelers may not notice much difference between the privately owned and the publicly owned buses, as they are all overcrowded and all charge the same fare. But the officials concerned with public finance in Calcutta appreciate an important difference: the public buses, which generally have the best routes, run at a deficit of some U.S.$1 million per month (not high by U.S. standards, but significant for a city that is desperately short of money) while the private buses run without subsidy. The success of the private bus operators has been attributed to leaner payrolls, more effective fare collection, and the ability to repair vehicles quickly so as to keep most of them running at most times.

A key factor in the operation of the private buses in Calcutta is the Route Association. These associations, generally one for each route, are formed voluntarily and spontaneously by the private owners and can be described as a cross between a trade association and a friendly society. Each owner retains control over the operation and maintenance of his vehicle and receives the fares collected on it. But the route is owned in common, and the associations have rules to govern relationships among members. For example, vehicles have to run on time, otherwise late buses receive more than their fair share of revenues. Buses that are late have to pay fines, either to the association or to the following bus.

Similar associations exist all over the world and enable individual owners to combine and provide scheduled public bus services. One of the most successful is in Buenos Aires, where, in 1951, a national enterprise known as Transportes de Buenos Aires took over all bus and rail transport operations. However, the services operated by the Transportes de Buenos Aires deteriorated rapidly both in quality and financially. By 1959 it was losing the equivalent of U.S.$40 million per year. In 1962 the situation became intolerable and Transportes de Buenos Aires was dissolved. All the transport services, except the underground railway, were turned over to the private companies that had been operating before 1951. Many of these companies were Empresas (route associations) of owner drivers empowered to serve just one route. The Empresas governed routes, fares, and schedules, subject to the rules determined by the regulating authorities. The vehicles used were typically 23-seat buses, which provided a high frequency of service. Competition was provided by the establishment of new Empresas, which duplicated the routes of existing ones. The microbuses still operate profitably and provide a level of service that is widely praised.

WATER SUPPLY

Of all the public services, the provision of piped water is the one with which the private sector is the least involved. It may be no coincidence that water is also the sector that, in less developed countries, seems to have the greatest problems. As a consequence of poor maintenance of water facilities and rapid population growth, about 100 million more people drank unsafe water in 1980 than in 1975, and about 400 million more relied on unsafe sanitation facilities in 1983 than in 1977. More people than previously are expected to lose their health and their lives due to water-related problems unless the most strenuous efforts are made to improve the situation. It is therefore a matter of concern that so little is being done to encourage the private sector to meet the demand for safe piped water.

There are, of course, numerous examples of water vending—the sale of water by carriers—which has been common ever since cities existed. But private enterprise outside Europe and North America has done little to supply water through pipes. This may well be due to fear of expropriation. Water vendors do not have to invest much in fixed capital and can move their business should government decide that they do not have to be paid. But a distribution system for water cannot so easily be taken up and installed in another city.

One way of dealing with this situation might be to make more use of the French *affermage* system, under which a public authority invests in a distribution system and invites an operator to operate it and to be compensated by revenues from the sale of water. Part of the revenues have to be paid to the city to amortize the investment in infrastructure, and the rest remains with the operator to cover his costs and, if he calculated rightly, give him a profit. Operators can be selected by a bidding process.

There are different ways of bidding. For example, the company might secure a contract by undertaking to provide a package of services at the lowest rate of charge to customers, or it might offer the lowest sum for the right to supply these services at prices determined by government. This system is fairly common in France and is also used in Africa, where the best-known example is probably the one operated by the Societe des Eaux du Cote d'Ivoire (SODECI) in the Ivory Coast, which supplies piped water and sewerage in Abidjan and 122 other urban areas.

For rural areas the development of private tube wells has been particularly successful in the Indus Valley in Pakistan. In the 1940s the government of Pakistan installed over 14,000 tube wells, mainly for drainage, although it was believed that improved irrigation would be a useful by-product. However, the Indus basin farmers preferred to have their own wells, and the 14,000 public tube wells were matched by 186,000 small capacity tube wells, which were installed by the private sector, 90% with no subsidy. Assessments by World Bank staff concluded that the private tube wells had been managed efficiently, imposed a relatively insignificant burden on public resources, produced returns that were economically justified, and did not lead to excessive exploitation of the aquifer.[7] Furthermore, private initiatives produced a remarkable range of ingenious inventions for the use of cheap local materials. For example, a bamboo tube well was developed in Bangladesh that is so cheap that several can be inserted in the same plot. Used in conjunction with an engine and pump made mobile by being mounted on a bullock cart, all of the farm area can be irrigated economically. It is not even necessary for every farmer to own a pump; pump contractors emerged to serve pumpless tube wells.

Agricultural production is often constrained due to lack of water, whereas surpluses exist in neighboring areas. Is there scope for the movement of large quantities of irrigation waters from areas of plenty to areas of shortage? One of the main constraints to activity of this kind is an absence of clear property rights in water. If such rights were clarified, it is conceivable that the movement of water over long distances could do as much to stimulate agriculture—for example, in India—as it already does in California. A transfer of water on the basis of property rights implies payment to the sellers at freely negotiated prices. This would be consistent with a recommendation made by World Bank staff that "a goal of full cost recovery" should be the cornerstone of any Bank involvement in this sector.[8]

A move toward the privatization of domestic water supply by the granting of property rights is reported to have taken place in Kenya.[9] In some regions villagers had not been paying the small monthly tax that was to be used to help operate and maintain their local water supply systems. Furthermore frequent acts of vandalism on faucets, drainage facilities, protective fences, and so on made it financially very costly and physically almost impossible to maintain many of the public standposts. To overcome this public standposts in a few areas were converted to water vendor operations; a licensed vendor pays a subsidized rate for the metered standpost water and sells it to users by the container (*debe*) at a slightly higher fee. The results of the switch to kiosks are that vandalism has been greatly reduced, thus saving government funds for repair and replacement costs; a small amount of revenue has been generated; and the rate at which people apply for house connections has increased. Some people presumably felt that if they were going to have to pay for water, it might as well be convenient water.

CONCLUSIONS

Without suggesting that every public service in every country should be run by private contractors, there is clearly enormous scope for the private sector to provide public services, not only in the West but also in less developed countries.

Of the services examined, telecommunications and electricity generation probably offer the greatest potential for private involvement because of the intense demand, the comparative ease of collecting payment, and the existing poor levels of service in most countries. Transport is also a fertile field, but one that is already being tilled. Education, health, and water are more difficult because payment by governments may be required. But even when services are paid for by the public sector, they can still be contracted out to private enterprise.

There are many examples of public services in developing countries being provided by the private sector, but very few cases have been documented of services being transferred from the public to the private sector, in the sense of ownership being vested in private hands. The reasons for this are not clear, but it may be hazarded that, as in the United States, the pressures to retain activities in the "public interest," without being subjected to the bothersome disciplines of markets, are well-nigh irresistible. In the cases in which ownership was transferred to the private sector (as in the example of Buenos Aires buses), the divestiture involved the return to private ownership of a concern that originally had been private and was not successfully run after being taken into the public sector. The Jamaica Teleport, with its low international transmission rates, illustrates a spillover into the international arena of the consequences of U.S. deregulation.

It may be that the most painless way of bringing about the private provision of public services in developing countries is to *deregulate* rather than to *divest*; to allow the private operation of competitive services while leaving in the public sector the operations under its control in the hope that competition would improve them also or make it easier for them to be wound up.

One may also conclude that a shortage of cash encourages divestiture—not to mention economy in the use of scarce resources—and that governments seeking economic growth should strive to abolish subsidies to failing public services. Subsidies can be designed, as in the case of the schools in Chile, to go to consumers without depriving them of the choice of supplier.

NOTES

1. A. W. Clausen, "Promoting the Private Sector in Developing Countries: A Multilateral Approach" (Speech delivered in London, February 1985, Washington, D.C.: World Bank, 1985).

2. C. Inglis, "Chinese Education in Southeast Asia," in K. Orr, ed., *Appetite for Education in Contemporary Asia* (Canberra: Australian National University, 1977).

3. R. J. Saunders, J. J. Warford, and B. Wellenius, *Telecommunications and Economic Development* (Baltimore: World Bank Publication, Johns Hopkins University Press, 1983).

4. "Teleport Study Looks to Montego Bay Zone," *FZA Review* 1, no. 1 (Arlington, Virginia: Free Zone Authority, Ltd., 1985).

5. D. S. Donaldson, *An Analysis of Health Insurance Schemes in the Lalitpur District, Nepal* (Washington, D.C.: Report to the USAID, 1982).

6. G. Roth and G. Wynne, *Free Enterprise Urban Transportation* (Washington, D.C.: Council for International Urban Liaison, Academy for State and Local Government, 1982).

7. World Bank, *Public and Private Tubewell Performance: Emerging Issues and Options* (Pakistan Subsector Report, South Asia Project Department, Irrigation I Division, 1983).

8. World Bank, *Rural Water Supply and Sanitation: A Framework for Improving Investments* (Washington, D.C.: Draft Sector Paper, 1985).

9. B. Kia, *Internal Financing of Water Supply and Sanitation in Developing Countries* (New York: UNDP, Division of Information, 1981).

INDEX

ABOUT THE EDITOR AND CONTRIBUTORS

DOUGLAS K. ADIE is Professor of Economics at Ohio University, Athens, Ohio, and works as a consultant to the U.S. Postal Service and is a research associate at the American Enterprise Institute.

CLIFF ATHERTON is Assistant Professor of Administrative Science and Research Associate, Rice University's Joint Center for Urban Mobility Research in Houston, Texas.

JOHN BADEN is currently Executive/Director of the McGuire Oil and Gas Institute at the Cox School of Business at Southern Methodist University in Dallas, Texas. He was formerly founder and director of the Political Economy Research Center at Bozeman, Montana.

DEAN BAIM is Assistant Professor of Economics at Pepperdine University, Malibu, California.

TOM BLOOD is a former Research Associate at the Political Economy Research Center and currently is a graduate student at the University of Washington.

FRANKE BURINK is a member of the Economic Research Department of ABN Bank in Amsterdam, Netherlands. He specializes in country studies and in international economic subjects.

LARRY V. ELLIS is Director of the Center for the Study of Private Enterprise at the College of Business, Appalachian State University, Boone, North Carolina.

JOHN C. GOODMAN is President of the National Center for Policy Analysis in Dallas, Texas. The center is a think tank applying economic analysis to current public policy issues. He was formerly Professor of Economics at the University of Dallas.

STEVEN H. HANKE is Professor of Applied Economics at the Johns Hopkins University in Baltimore, Maryland, and Chief Economist for Friedberg Commodity Management, Inc. in Toronto, Canada. He has done extensive work as a consultant to government entities in the United States, Canada, and in Europe.

CALVIN A. KENT holds the Herman W. Lay Chair in Private Enterprise at Baylor University's Hankamer School of Business in Waco, Texas. He directs the Center for Private Enterprise and the National Center for Entrepreneurship in Economic Education. He is former Chief Economist for the State of South Dakota and has served as a consultant to several state, local, and foreign governments in the area of privatization. He is mayor of Woodway, Texas.

LAWRENCE W. LOVIK currently holds the Adams-Bibby Chair of Free Enterprise in the Surrell College of Business at Troy State University, Troy, Alabama.

GABRIEL ROTH was formerly with the Economic Development Institute of the World Bank in Washington, D.C., and is currently a private consultant with the Services Group, Inc., Arlington, Virginia, specializing in privatization programs for underdeveloped countries.

ALAN RUFUS WATERS is currently Professor of International Business at California State University-Fresno and was formerly Professor of Management at the Babcock School of Business at Wake Forest University.

DUANE WINDSOR is Associate Professor of Administrative Science at the Jones Graduate School at Rice University in Houston, Texas, and a Research Fellow at Rice's Joint Center for Urban Mobility Research. He has been a visiting scholar at the LBJ School of Public Affairs at the University of Texas and at the Hoover Institution.

SANDRA P. WOOTEN was formerly a Research Associate in the Center for Private Enterprise at Baylor University and is currently a Financial Analyst for RepublicBank Dallas, Texas.